POLICY ENTREPRENEURS AND SCHOOL CHOICE

Policy Entrepreneurs and School Choice

MICHAEL MINTROM

GEORGETOWN UNIVERSITY PRESS
WASHINGTON, DC

Georgetown University Press, Washington, D.C.

Printed in the United States of America
10 9 8 7 6 5 4 3 2 1 2000

This volume is printed on acid-free offset book paper.

Library of Congress Cataloging-in-Publication Data

Mintrom, Michael, 1963–
Policy entrepreneurs and school choice / Michael Mintrom.
p. cm. — (American governance and public policy series)
Includes bibliographical references (p.) and index.
ISBN 0-87840-770-7 (cloth : alk. paper). —
ISBN 0-87840-771-5 (pbk. : alk. paper)
1. School choice—United States. 2. Education and state—United States. 3. Policy sciences. I. Title.
II. Series: American governance and public policy.
LB1027.9.M57 2000
379.1'11'0973—dc21 99-36842
CIP

For my parents,

Sybil and Allen

Contents

Preface

After several decades of focused scholarship, social scientists have made significant advances in their understanding of the policymaking process and the instances under which policy change occurs. Yet there is much about the process of policy change that remains mysterious. As the political economies of established democracies continue to undergo transformations in which the boundaries between politics and markets become increasingly porous, our established ways of understanding policy change may well become obsolete. In this book I argue that we can gain novel insights into the nature of policy change by considering the behavior of an identifiable class of actors, *policy entrepreneurs*. Although they have often been mentioned in the literature on policymaking, policy entrepreneurs remain ghost-like figures, in need of clearer definition. My purpose is to show why the concept of the policy entrepreneur holds considerable promise for those interested in explaining contemporary policy change across a range of settings. As well as giving the concept a sound theoretical grounding, I show how it can be used in the empirical analysis of policy change. Throughout this work I use the rise of school choice in the United States as my area of substantive policy interest. While constituting an important political phenomenon deserving close attention in its own right, the rise of school choice provides rich opportunities for theory building and empirical study.

Aside from making a contribution to the literature on the policymaking process, I believe this book contains a vital and encouraging message.

Stepping back from its theoretical and methodological preoccupations, this book tells a story about how individuals with convictions, energy, and creative minds can transform the nature of the political game and make important contributions to public policy. Such individuals need not hold traditional positions of power; even when outside government they can change how we think about policy problems and how we address them. Ultimately what they achieve matters far more than where they start from. In a period of rapid change in the broader political economy, and when more and more citizens appear cynical and disillusioned with government, a message that reminds us of our potential to make a difference is important. Reflecting on our political efficacy now and then strikes me as an important and positive thing to do. If more of us—particularly academics and other opinion leaders—were to do this, perhaps some of that cynicism and disillusionment would end. Although my approach to thinking about the policymaking process differs greatly from that of Steven Kelman (1987), in the end I find myself, like him, coming to a hopeful view of government.

Many people contributed to the development of this book. The empirical work hinged entirely upon the willingness of members of the education policy community in almost every state in the United States to complete surveys for me. In addition, many of these people agreed to share documents with me and have conversations about policy entrepreneurship and the rise of school choice in their states. I wish to thank them and the many policy entrepreneurs who agreed to assist me with my work. In determining the nature and scope of this study, I greatly benefited from conversations I had with John Kingdon, Elinor Ostrom, Vincent Ostrom, Mark Schneider, and John Witte. I also gained many insights from Joel Kaji and Douglas Lamdin, with whom I wrote papers and articles on related topics. Special thanks are due to Sandra Vergari, with whom I wrote several papers and articles on school choice, charter schools, and policy entrepreneurship. That collaboration and our ongoing conversations have been very helpful as I have worked on this book.

I wish to thank my colleagues in the Political Science Department at Michigan State University for their encouragement and advice. Malcolm Goggin and Carol Weissert provided extensive comments on various chapters. Thanks are also due to Stephan Kuhnert, who commented on draft chapters while visiting Michigan State University in 1998. For their research assistance I wish to thank Gina Lambright and Dee Syms. Several chapters in this book have been developed from previously published articles. For granting their permission to reprint material from those articles, I wish to thank the editors of the *American Journal of Political Science*, *The Journal of Politics*, and *Publius: The Journal of Federalism*.

I completed work on this manuscript during the period in which I was a National Academy of Education postdoctoral fellow. I wish to thank the National Academy of Education and the Spencer Foundation for their generous financial support and the many opportunities they provided for intellectual engagement with other scholars working in the education field.

Georgetown University Press director John Samples and editor Barry Rabe have given this project much support. I am also grateful to three anonymous reviewers for their enthusiasm for the manuscript and their many useful comments.

Finally, I wish to express my appreciation to Jacqui True for her numerous suggestions as the book developed and for encouraging me to break free from my training as a technician and to start thinking like a theorist.

Michael Mintrom
Michigan State University

ONE

Policy Entrepreneurs and School Choice

Public education issues often stimulate major political debates, especially in established democracies. In such nations, education has long been recognized as crucial for advancing economic development and citizen participation in government decisionmaking. Throughout the history of the United States public education issues have been debated at all levels of government, but most policymaking has taken place at the level of local communities and neighborhoods, where the bulk of the taxes used to support public schools are collected. Over the past two decades an important venue change has occurred, however. Education issues have steadily risen on the state and national political agendas in the United States. At the same time, the state and national governments have become far more active in the making of education policy than previously. Other important changes have accompanied this shift in the loci of educational debate and policymaking. In this book I explore one such change: the increasing attention that has been given to the school choice idea at the state level. Recently, a range of ideas for school choice has received sustained attention in legislatures across the United States. These include allowing parents and students greater choice to select among traditional public schools, the establishment of charter schools, and the provision of education vouchers.

Several plausible explanations could be developed to account for this growing interest in school choice. One popular explanation already current is that, increasingly, public intellectuals and policy analysts have employed economic reasoning and market analogies to discuss the appropriate role of government in society. The ideas of Milton Friedman and his colleagues that began to emerge from the University of Chicago in the 1950s have upheld the free market as the appropriate benchmark against which to evaluate the performance of various public policies. These ideas have had a significant bearing upon the thinking of public policymakers around the world and the nature of the policy changes that they have adopted. As it has gathered momentum, this general shift in public policy has been accompanied by a shift in normative views on the appropriate role and form of the state. Thus, reliance on government entities for both the funding and delivery of many basic social services has come under scrutiny and has been challenged from a variety of quarters.[1] When seen among these broader changes, the emergence of calls for the reform of education through school choice appears unremarkable. But even though this broader explanation holds appeal, it remains insufficient. Its major weakness is that it cannot account for the process by which a general set of ideas has been transformed into specific proposals for policy change. My interest lies in developing such an account.

Here I argue that the prominence of school choice in contemporary education policy discourse in the United States is not the result of some inexorable process. Rather, the prominence now given to this idea owes much to the efforts of a group of political actors whom I term *policy entrepreneurs*. Across the United States various individuals, driven by a range of motives, have been instrumental in articulating the school choice idea and getting it onto state legislative agendas. In so doing, they have contributed to the broader trend in contemporary American politics of using simple ideas about market processes to inform policy design. More specifically, they have oriented debates over public education away from questions of resources and their equitable distribution and toward questions of government management and accountability. The immediate result has been the casting of citizens in the role of consumers. On the one hand, this change opens the possibility for public schools to become more responsive to the needs of parents and students. This could promote greater innovation in schools, as teachers and administrators attempt to create methods of pedagogy and school management that produce improved education outcomes. On the other hand, if unchecked, the longer term consequence of this movement could be the erosion of the public space, perhaps even the further loss of opportunities for all citizens to participate in discussions over what constitutes an appropriate education for young people.

I do not seek to judge the overall merits of school choice. Actually, I do not believe it is possible to reach such a judgment at this time. School choice is not a well-understood, demonstrably workable means for improving public education; efforts to introduce it are still in their infancy. Thus, school choice remains primarily a *policy idea*. Because of this, social scientists lack sufficient good-quality evidence to support arguments concerning the workability and applicability of school choice as a policy instrument.[2] But this has not inhibited a range of advocates, critics, and commentators from making strong claims for why school choice represents a panacea for current problems in public education, or why it might simply serve to intensify those problems. This is a curious state of affairs. Even more puzzling, despite the dearth of good-quality evidence about its merits, school choice has clearly held considerable appeal for policymakers in many states. When thinking about the rise of school choice in the United States, this is the aspect that I find most fascinating. This puzzle—the power of an idea to prompt policy change, even in the absence of sound supporting evidence—has led me to consider more broadly the nature of policymaking and policy change. In so doing, I have gravitated toward the concept of policy entrepreneurship and how it might help us understand policy change.

This book presents a theory of policy entrepreneurship and some empirical testing of that theory. Throughout, the rise of school choice is used as a case study. So, while the merits of school choice and its local-level effects represent matters of considerable interest in their own right, my effort to explain the emergence of this idea across the states is intended first and foremost to support a more *conceptually oriented* project. I believe that the concept of the policy entrepreneur and an enhanced understanding of the actions of policy entrepreneurs in the policymaking process can improve our ability to explain many instances of policy change, not just the rise of school choice. For example, greater understanding of the nature of policy entrepreneurship could help illuminate changes in health care policy, environmental policy, and criminal justice, to name only three policy areas that have recently undergone significant changes. Further, when working with the concept of the policy entrepreneur, there is no reason why we should restrict ourselves to policy reforms that extend the reach of the market or just to instances of policy change in the United States.[3] That is why the greatest emphasis in this book is placed on theoretical rather than empirical substance. Even though the popularity of school choice in the United States prompts many questions crying out for urgent and serious consideration, the need is even more pressing for us to understand the *processes* that bring such ideas to prominence.

Understanding how policy ideas catch on—even when their workability remains in doubt—is a crucial task for social scientists and policy scholars. Of course, some progress has been made toward this end, but significant gaps remain in our knowledge. This theoretical and empirical study of policy entrepreneurship and policy change may not fill all those gaps. However, I seek to fill at least some of them and, in the process, alert others to how individuals with well-developed social skills are able to engineer major changes in how policy communities come to think about issues.

The Entrepreneur

Political scientists have often talked about actors in the policymaking process as being "entrepreneurial." Typically, the meaning and relevance of the description have been assumed to be obvious. Thus, while the term "policy entrepreneur" will be familiar to most political scientists and policy scholars, until now no effort has been made to construct a theory of policy entrepreneurship. In the absence of such an effort, it remains unclear just how helpful this concept might be for improving our understanding of the nature of policymaking.

In the marketplace entrepreneurs are significant figures because they attempt to introduce innovative products. Entrepreneurs begin with nothing more than imagination and insight. They perceive opportunities for gain through combining their own processes of creative thinking with careful observation of the world around them. Having perceived opportunities and assessed the likelihood of gaining from exploiting them, entrepreneurs attempt to bring new products to market. But such a process requires large amounts of social engagement. Entrepreneurs must introduce their ideas to others in ways that are persuasive, in ways that lead others to conclude that it is worth their while to work with the entrepreneur to transform an idea into a fully developed product.

The most important thing to note about entrepreneurs in the marketplace is that they are people who are prepared to act solely on the strength of ideas. When successful, their actions can be transformative, making people think and act in ways that represent a break with the past. Given this, it would appear that thinking carefully about what entrepreneurs do in markets might generate significant insights for those who seek to explain the emergence to prominence of ideas in the policymaking process. This is the rationale underlying the bulk of the theoretical work in this book. Although I am working with a familiar term—policy entrepreneur—my efforts constitute a significant departure from how scholars in the past have made use of it. I intend to revitalize this term, placing it on a solid theoretical foundation and then exploring how it helps us to better understand aspects of the policymaking process and policy change.

Politics and Markets

I have suggested that just as we find entrepreneurs working to create change in the market process, so we might find policy entrepreneurs who seek to change current policy settings. But the world of politics and policymaking is very different from the world of the market. And importing a concept from one world to another is never straightforward. In this case it is possible that without making the necessary translations, we might end up more mystified by aspects of policymaking than we were before we started. At the level of everyday speech it seems easy to draw distinctions between the worlds of politics and markets as operating environments. Yet when we begin to draw hard-and-fast distinctions between the functioning of markets and the functioning of political processes, many of the apparent distinctions appear chimerical. The reason is simple. In many ways markets and politics are inseparable. Markets can function only when the appropriate institutions are in place, such as property rights, trade routes, and a system of exchange. These institutions must be devised and maintained by some form of government. Thus, markets cannot function in the absence of political processes. Further, for all their efficiency in terms of allocating resources in society, market processes affect people in ways that often create the impetus for political action. Regulation of business, social insurance programs, and public funding of education and infrastructure can all be viewed as government activities emerging from concern or fear over the consequences of unfettered market activity. Government action typically does not suppress market processes, but it does serve to alter market outcomes in ways that accord with desires expressed through politics.

Despite the many interrelations between market processes and political processes, for analytical purposes, there is merit in attempting to distinguish between them. One way to begin drawing distinctions is to look at outputs. This approach necessarily serves to place limits on what we mean when we talk about politics and when we talk about markets. Yet, even with these limits imposed, we can say some interesting and provocative things about the nature of politics and the distinctions to be drawn between what takes place in the world of markets and the world of politics. Eventually, we will want to come back to thinking about the similarities between the actions of people pursuing their interests through politics and through markets. But this in no way negates the worth of initially drawing distinctions, even if some of those distinctions are, in fact, somewhat artificial.

In markets attention is focused on producing goods or services for trade. We measure success and failure by whether or not a trade occurs: an entrepreneur who devises an innovative product and who eventually manages to sell it for a profit can be judged a success. The relevant output is the sale of the product. By contrast, in politics our interest centers on the making of public policies. Individuals—let us say, policy entrepreneurs—can be judged as successful when they come up with a corpus of ideas for policy innovation and then take the steps necessary to secure their desired policy change. For the policy entrepreneur policy innovation is the relevant output.

Obvious distinctions can be drawn between products traded in markets and policies adopted and implemented by governments. Perhaps the most important difference is that products traded in markets represent private property. The individual who purchases a given product essentially purchases a set of rights to its use. To the extent that the product and its attributes represent private property, once purchased, a product can be used as the owner wishes. The purchase is made voluntarily. Individuals who dislike a particular product, or who believe they have no use for it, need not buy it. Through the institution of private property, then, individuals are free to choose the products they purchase and, in this way, come to have a large amount of control over the private environments they create for themselves.

A policy innovation adopted and implemented by a government is quite different from an innovative product traded in a market. Public policies, by definition, are public property. Policies consist of rules of behavior that apply universally to the target population. Policies are not "purchased" in any meaningful sense; they are adopted on behalf of all members of a given jurisdiction by representatives of the group. Once a policy is adopted, individuals in the jurisdiction can be sanctioned if they do not behave in ways consistent with it. Those who disapprove of the policy might voice their opposition, or they might even take action designed to eventually change the policy, but they cannot simply pretend the policy does not exist and act as they wish, regardless of its provisions. Public policies affect our environment, and there is little or nothing we can do to escape them, at least in the short term.

Given the significant differences between the outputs of markets and the outputs of politics, it is hardly surprising that important distinctions can also be drawn between the processes leading to their emergence. These distinctions revolve around the dual axes of, first, privateness and publicness and, second, volition and compulsion. For the most part, market processes are characterized by a series of private and voluntary exchanges, whereas political processes are characterized by those that are public. That is to say, the exchanges in politics typically have implications for more people than those immediately involved. Further, in politics exchanges are often compulsory: one or more participants in an interaction might do things that, if acting on their own preferences, they would not ordinarily do. Matters are not always this stark, hence my suggestion that we think in terms of axes or continuums rather than absolutes.

The process leading to the trading of a product can be characterized in large part as a series of private and voluntary transactions. Even when aspects of the production process involve some type of team or collective action, the membership of the team is predicated on a one-to-one contract between the relevant individual and the team organizer. As a result, a team organizer can dismiss a team member, or a team member can voluntarily resign without affecting—at least in any formal way—the relationships of the other team members with the organizer. The voluntary nature of interactions in the production process requires that each party to a given transaction find that transaction of value. So long as value exists, individuals face incentives to engage in trade. Often the nature of this value will be immediately apparent, but at other times the value of a trade will not be obvious to one party, requiring effort by the other to show that the trade is worthwhile. Persuasion, then, can be a vital aspect of market transactions. This suggests that while market processes involve the exchange of tangible goods or services between individuals, the processes can also involve the exchange of more intangible things. So, although we typically observe that market processes are based on individuals pursuing their private ends or their self-interest, we should also note that what is in our self-interest is not always clear. Sometimes we can benefit from others guiding us or persuading us to see where our interests lie.

The political process that leads to the adoption and implementation of a public policy is characterized by public deliberation and, ultimately, by some degree of compulsion by those who hold public power. As in markets, individuals in politics can be expected to act, at least to some extent, in their self-interest. They can also be expected to engage in efforts to persuade others to take particular actions. But in politics it is rarely the case that we observe the sort of neat close of transactions that we see in markets. This is because political actions typically have consequences for diverse groups of people, not for isolated individuals. When we observe an output from the market (i.e., the trade of a product) it is possible for us to trace back from this and map a chain of interactions among individuals that logically lead to that trade. In politics tracing back from a public policy is less likely to reveal such a logical chain. The political process involves a series of more unpredictable links. This arises because of the more public nature of the decisionmaking and the potential for differences to be resolved through the striking of compromises. In the world of politics, designated individuals are given the power to make choices that affect everyone in the relevant jurisdiction. Since the choices of decisionmakers in politics have public implications, and these can significantly affect our interests, individuals face incentives to select decisionmakers they believe will act in the individuals' interests. Once the decisionmakers are in their positions of power, individuals face incentives to persuade them to act in ways that accord with the latter's interests. We cannot assume that individuals seeking to influence political decisions will share similar or mutually consistent views about the relationship between their own interests and the "public interest." Definition of the public interest is itself open to debate, and might well change as a policy idea works its way through the policymaking process. Given this, in tracing back from the adoption of a given public policy, we should find several points at which the choices made could readily have resulted in quite different policies being adopted than the one observed.

When we think in terms of outputs and the processes leading to them, it becomes clear that what happens in markets and what happens in politics are distinctive in many ways. Further, we see that the politics associated with policymaking are potentially much more complex—because of the diverse interests at stake and the nature of the decisionmaking—than the set of interactions that support products being brought to market. In light of this, we might wonder why it is that people thinking about politics often try to draw analogies between what happens there and what happens in markets.

The approach that I use in this book represents yet another effort to generate insights into some features of government and politics through application of concepts derived from the analysis of markets. Why is it that political scientists so often subscribe to the view that we can achieve a deeper understanding of politics by working with concepts and modeling approaches developed by economists? For my part, I believe that working with the concept of the entrepreneur and reflecting on the role played by entrepreneurs in the market process can greatly improve our understanding of the processes that support policy innovation and change. In so doing, the concept of the policy entrepreneur can help us to better explain the rise of school choice as a policy idea. But is it reasonable to believe this? Why do we so often apply market metaphors to the analysis of politics?

Metaphors in Political Analysis

The primary reason that we use metaphors, both at the level of everyday speech and when describing complex systems or processes, is that they provide explanatory shortcuts. Metaphors give us insights into how complex things work, by simplification and the drawing of analogies and comparisons. Through the use of metaphors we are able to represent (i.e., re-present) complex things in ways that ignore all manner of details so that we can focus on those deemed of most interest. Road maps, the usefulness of which few would deny, use grids and colors as metaphors of complex systems, such as the organization of cities. The utility of road maps is based entirely upon the functioning of metaphors. When someone unfolds a map with "Chicago" written on it and says, "This is Chicago," and then proceeds to point to a colored line and says, "This is State Street," or point to the blue part, and says, "This is Lake Michigan," the action could be construed as quite bizarre. Of course the mess of lines is not Chicago. Of course the blue is not a lake. And where are the buildings, the people? Yet, if we suspend our disbelief we might well learn a lot by taking out a map, pointing to various parts of it, and talking. Inevitably, our "sense of place" in a city is developed as much through establishing simple, metaphorical mind-maps as by observing what is around us.

Like cartographers and many other analysts, political scientists frequently work with metaphors. We use a range of approaches to represent and discuss political phenomena. No matter what metaphors we work with, in doing so our aim is to cut through the complexities of the world of politics and focus on only those aspects of it that we believe are the most crucial to understand. Through the use of metaphors we hope to achieve new insights into the nature of political processes. Over the past few decades, when looking for metaphors to work with, political scientists have increasingly turned to the efforts of economists for guidance. Thus, political scientists have often attempted to analyze political phenomena through the application of market metaphors and the use of models initially developed to analyze aspects of the market process. The impetus for this style of analysis owes much to the efforts of a relatively small group of economists who, beginning in the 1950s, have considered the implications of assuming that actors in politics behave no differently than actors in market settings. That is to say, it is assumed that in both the world of politics and the world of markets individuals engage in rational action, seeking to achieve given ends in the most efficient manner. Note that in many ways this is a strange assumption, and one that is easy to critique.[4] Anthony B. Atkinson (1996, 708) states:

> The applicability of the approach clearly depends on the subject-matter. A model which is appropriate for the choice between wine and beer may not apply equally to the choice between Bush and Clinton. A decision made once every four years, under circumstances which are likely to be different each time, is not the same as one made every evening in similar circumstances. For many people, voting is an act of personal and social significance, which a visit to the liquor store is not.

If, in fact, we risk absurdity by using market metaphors in the analysis of political phenomena, why persist? One answer is that any effort to represent politics—or any real world phenomena—using metaphors is, in some sense, strange. Paul Krugman (1993, 28) has argued that most assumptions made by economists are silly, but some come to seem natural and, therefore, reasonable because they have received a great deal of use. "The reason for making these assumptions is not that they are reasonable but that they seem to help us produce models that are helpful metaphors for things that we think happen in the real world." The same could be said for why we use maps, and why we often use market metaphors in the analysis of politics. Anthony Downs (1957) deduced a series of predictions about the behavior of voters and political parties based on the assumption that voters, like consumers in markets, seek to maximize their own utility and that political party leaders, like the owners of firms, seek to maximize profits (i.e., maximize their vote count in elections). Downs assumed, as most economists do, that actors seek primarily to achieve given ends in the most efficient manner. Downs's effort involved a deliberate use of extreme simplification for the purpose of gaining new insights into political behavior:

> Thus we do not take into consideration the whole personality of each individual when we discuss what behavior is rational for him. We do not allow for the rich diversity of ends served by each of his acts. . . . Rather, we borrow from traditional economic theory the idea of the rational consumer. Corresponding to the infamous ***homo economicus*** . . . our ***homo politicus*** is the "average man" in the electorate, the "rational citizen" of our model democracy. (1957, 7)

Downs cautioned that such use of a deliberately stripped-down image of political actors would serve to limit the comparability of behavioral expectations deduced from his models and behavior in the real world. Nonetheless, he suggested that the assumption of rational action provides a fairly good approximation to real world behavior, both in markets and in politics.

In general, we might expect that some aspects of political behavior are more amenable than others to analysis using market metaphors. Thus, where market metaphors are used, this should not be seen as the only game in town. It is true that taking this approach holds the advantage that political scientists who use it can often also make use of the various techniques of mathematical modeling that economists have devised for analyzing the behavior of consumers and firms in market settings. This opens the possibility for us to derive hypotheses about political action that are consistent with our facilitating assumptions. However, if the use of a market metaphor is misplaced to begin with, or if its use serves to distort rather than illuminate our understanding of certain political phenomena, then no amount of mathematical manipulation will improve matters. Again, the point of using metaphors is to gain insights into complex processes and systems through simplification and the drawing of analogies. Using metaphors allows us to assign meaning to subjects that would otherwise remain opaque.

Most political scientists would acknowledge that the increasing use of market metaphors and the rational choice perspective in the analysis of politics have been fruitful for the discipline. Even for those who are disturbed by the simplifications embodied in these efforts or by the implications emerging from them, debates provoked through the use of market metaphors can often lead both proponents and opponents of the approach to come to new insights into the nature of politics. Of course, whenever we elevate one form of inquiry over others there is the danger that some adherents of the approach will come to value form over substance. Therefore, it is not surprising that some efforts to apply market metaphors and rational choice models in politics have been criticized for using sophisticated mathematical techniques to explore arid subjects, adding little to human knowledge.

The best efforts to take concepts and techniques developed by economists and use them in the analysis of politics involve thinking carefully about the similarities and differences between what happens in markets and what happens in politics. What is important to recognize here is that such efforts must precede the development of sophisticated mathematical models. Terry M. Moe's (1984, 1990) discussions of the potential utility of economic models in political analysis serve to remind us of this point. Moe's work also demonstrates that it is possible to gain many fresh insights into aspects of politics through the critical assessment of the plausibility of working with a particular metaphor. Thus, by considering the relevance to politics of the principal-agent models developed by economists to analyze contractual arrangements, Moe notes that bureaucrats are typically controlled both by the executive and by members of the legislature, and that these multiple principals often have incompatible preferences concerning bureaucratic actions. Through his critique of simplistic application of the principal-agent model to politics, Moe delineates the salient features of what he calls "the politics of structural choice." From there he develops an explanation of why government bureaucracies sometimes appear as administrative nightmares when compared with counterpart bureaucracies in firms. The lesson is that even through the careful exploration of the relevance of a given metaphor—not necessarily through its *application*—the potential exists for making important contributions to knowledge.

In the present work I seek to use the metaphor of the entrepreneur to extend our substantive knowledge of the processes that support policy innovation and change. Given, on the one hand, the present paucity of knowledge about how innovations are developed in the policymaking process and, on the other, the relative richness of knowledge regarding innovation in markets, there appears to be an opportunity for working with the metaphor of the entrepreneur to gain new insights into this area of politics. My thought experiment thus involves thinking about what an entrepreneur with an idea for an innovation would do if he or she were transplanted from the marketplace into the world of policymaking.

My interest here, and the way I proceed, does not involve the development and testing of mathematical models of aspects of policy entrepreneurship. For subscribers to the rational choice perspective in political science, such an approach to theory development might be disconcerting, even disappointing. But my approach is readily justified on several grounds. First, in the economics and business literature on entrepreneurship few exercises in formal modeling can be found. Nonetheless, that literature abounds with important discussions and insights regarding the actions of entrepreneurs in the market process. This suggests that we can learn a lot about policy entrepreneurship by proceeding in a similar fashion. Second, this is the first effort that has been made to develop a theory of policy entrepreneurship. As such, it constitutes exploratory work, and proceeding through verbal argument is well suited to the task. In contrast, the scholarly record suggests that formal modeling is largely pointless until the accumulation of theory, evidence, and scholarly debates reveal patterns of behavior worthy of more precise calibration. Finally, my preference here is to establish a fairly broad theoretical framework. Because they are best applied to the study of tightly circumscribed problems, exercises in formal modeling would not contribute to that task.

Having made these comments concerning the theoretical approach to be employed, I will now introduce the substantive policy area that serves as the site for my empirical explorations of policy entrepreneurship.

A Preoccupation with Education

Constitutional responsibility for public schooling in the United States resides at the state level. However, this responsibility has always been delegated to local school districts, where schooling takes place and where elected district officials have the authority to levy property taxes to fund the schools. This local control of schools has been jealously guarded. One supporting argument for it is that officials in relatively small school districts have a large amount of information about the needs and preferences of their communities regarding questions of education policy. Another supporting argument is that small local districts with elected officials serve to promote democratic values. Interested parties, the argument goes, can readily have their voices heard and influence school district decisionmaking when control of public schools is locally based. But reliance on local control and local funding of public schools can also cause problems. In particular, differences in the value of local tax bases means that large differences emerge across school districts with respect to access to resources. Inevitably these differences also end up having a strong socioeconomic dimension. With suburbanization, people in the United States have tended to live in communities where those around them share similar levels of personal wealth and income. Since wealth and income are often associated with a range of other demographic characteristics, not least of which is race, this geographic sorting raises questions about the ability of the public school system to deliver equal educational opportunities to all children. As well as this, local control can sometimes lead to narrow-mindedness, where school policy is developed with little reference to broader regional or national concerns.

Over the past two decades, many doubts have been expressed about the quality of public education in the United States. These doubts have emanated from various commentators and scholars as well as politicians at all levels of government, from presidents in Washington, D.C., to state governors, city mayors, and local school district officials. Given the local control of public schools, we might well expect local school district officials and some city mayors to routinely think hard about education policy issues. But the increased attention given to education policy by state- and national-level politicians is surprising and requires explanation.

For state-level politicians, a major impetus for increased interest in education policy has been the growing financial commitments that states have been making to public schooling. These commitments have increased steadily as a result of efforts to equalize funding across school districts. That is, state funds have been used increasingly to compensate for the inadequacies of local tax bases to support quality education. Thus, as they have routinely considered their budget priorities, state governors and legislators have often asked whether the public schools in their states are delivering value for money. Meanwhile, beginning in the Reagan years, the nation's presidents have expressed considerable concern over perceived problems with the quality of the education provided in public schools. For presidents and others who think in terms of "national interests," the nagging question has been whether the nation's schools are doing an adequate job of imparting the knowledge and skills required to ensure sustained economic growth. In a time of increasing integration of markets around the globe and the intensified competition that comes with it, the maintenance of an economic advantage for the United States will depend crucially on the quality of the workforce. Since this workforce requires more and more people to engage in interpersonal communication, problem solving, and conceptual thinking, the nature of the education and training that occurs in the public schools becomes all the more important.[5] Against this backdrop the school choice idea has risen to prominence on state government agendas.

The Rise of the School Choice Movement

In essence, school choice involves giving families the ability to break out of the traditional system that assigns children to specific public schools strictly on the basis of their residential location. While an apparently innocuous policy change, any move in this direction explicitly changes the relationship between families and schools. School choice means that parents and children can do more than voice their concerns about school policy. If, having expressed their concerns, they remain dissatisfied with the policies of a school and its administrators, they can move away: school choice confers market power on parents and children, transforming them from citizens into consumers. With school choice, parents and children can express their consumer choice with respect to schooling just as they express it in the purchase of goods and services in private markets. In many ways school choice is a policy that provides an escape hatch for parents and children where the family income, spending priorities, or other considerations make attendance at private schools or relocation too costly to consider. These are the people who, faced with a public school that they find inadequate or unresponsive, can do little to change the situation. In contrast, people of higher means can, if need be, leave a particular school by shifting to a new residence in another location or by placing their children in private schools.

Whether school choice and the competition it brings to the delivery of schooling actually raises educational quality remains an open and hotly contested question. Many other reform strategies appear to have much to offer as well. Clearly school choice is not the only solution worth considering, yet it has caught the imagination of policymakers and other interested individuals and groups. As I suggested above, this interest seems to have been spurred, at least in part, by a general trend in policy circles that, since the late 1970s, has favored the exploration of market-like approaches to the delivery of government services. However, the story of the rise of school choice is more complicated than is suggested by the claim that it reflects a broader interest in privatization and incentives-based reform. Advocates of such approaches have certainly weighed in on school choice debates, but so have many other people who have argued in favor of school choice approaches for quite different reasons.[6]

Theoretical Beginnings

Although the practice of school choice is relatively new in the United States, the theory is not. Milton Friedman (1955, 1962) provided the first sustained theoretical discussion of the idea. According to Friedman, while government financing and provision of education are typically combined, they could and should be separated. The financial function could be achieved by giving subsidies to families through education vouchers. Families would then be free to shop around for schooling at government-approved organizations, including for-profit and nonprofit institutions. Rather than elaborate on the details of this approach, he argued that the major criticisms of it could also be leveled at the present system of public schooling. For example, while it is possible that vouchers could exacerbate social stratification, Friedman noted that much stratification exists now, even when schooling is produced primarily in the public sector. Although his proposal is typically associated with political conservatism, subsequent developments of his voucher idea were initially undertaken by people of liberal political persuasions.

The liberal tradition started with sociologist Christopher Jencks (1966), who suggested that private schools could help remedy educational problems in the inner city. In developing his argument Jencks suggested government-financed education vouchers, or "tuition grants," combined with private school provision, would have two major benefits. First, private control would make it possible to attack management problems, and second, the use of tuition grants would put an end to neighborhood schools. Jencks believed that education involves interacting with others from a variety of socioeconomic backgrounds. However, the neighborhood schools with their specified attendance zones prevent this sort of mixing. Jencks admitted that these actions would destroy the public school system. In response to this, he said ". . . we must not allow the memory of past achievements to blind us to present failures" (1966, 27).

Mario Fantini (1973) provided another liberal contribution to the literature on school choice. In his discussion Fantini called for an "internal voucher" to be used within the public school system. According to Fantini, a voucher system would promote innovations in public schools and create options for children with different learning styles. Fantini opposed the use of vouchers for the private provision of education. This, he believed, could lead to "a slew of fly-by-night institutions" emerging. This model was designed to give parents, students, and teachers choice among alternative types of schools. In contrast, "minischools," that is, alternative educational programs organized within existing schools, could be used to ensure that students did not get "lost in the crowd." Fantini also anticipated that more intimate classroom settings would allow for greater parental involvement in schools. According to Mary Anne Raywid (1992, 107), Fantini's discussion of alternative schools ". . . remains the essential core of the education-inspired case for choice. . . ." Although his work received a wide amount of interest at the time it was published, Fantini is rarely cited in contemporary debates. But his ideas influenced individuals whose voices became important in the school choice debate.

Also working in the liberal tradition, education academics John E. Coons and Stephen D. Sugarman argued for the use of vouchers to address interdistrict equity concerns. This made their plan for a choice scheme complicated. Because they assumed that ". . . society's objective is to give families of all incomes as nearly equal access to participating schools as possible" (1978, 190), under their proposal vouchers would necessarily differ in size according to the tuition charges of each school being attended, each family's income, and each family's willingness to invest in education. Unlike previous theoretical work on school choice approaches, the proposal by Coons and Sugarman extensively considered the need for high-quality information to facilitate the making of meaningful choices, arguing that important equity concerns are bound up with the provision of information.

Local Experiments

The history of tentative, geographically limited steps toward school choice in the United States began in the 1970s with the voucher demonstration at Alum Rock, a suburb of San Jose, California. This demonstration had its origins in the theoretical work undertaken by Christopher Jencks. It was designed to demonstrate that inner city parents could cope with the use of vouchers and would adapt to the changing informational requirements such a system imposed.[7] During the demonstration, parents in voucher school attendance areas were allowed to choose among several "minischools" within schools, and during the five years of the experiment the number of programs increased from twenty-two in six schools to fifty-one in fourteen schools. These parents were allowed to choose among programs in any voucher school; parents and students in nonvoucher school areas were treated as controls. For voucher participants, free transportation was provided to nonneighborhood schools, transfers were permitted during the year, students who had attended in the past or who had siblings enrolled in a given school were granted preferential access, and a lottery was used to assign admissions to oversubscribed programs. Although closely monitored, the results of the Alum Rock experiment were mixed in terms of student performance and provided no basis for supporting or criticizing voucher initiatives. Other evidence regarding student behavior was more positive. Unexcused absence rates dropped slightly for voucher school students during the demonstration, and student attitudes toward school also appeared to improve (Bridge and Blackman 1978; Capell 1978; Cohen and Farrar 1977; Weiler 1978).

Following the Alum Rock experiment, many other school districts experimented with choice plans, frequently relying on a small number of alternative schools to break the usual procedures for matching students with schools. Among alternative schools the magnet schools approach has been quite popular. Magnet schools have been designed to offer innovative school programs that appeal to a cross-section of students and, most important, reduce racial segregation within school districts. Magnet schools have been especially popular among school district officials working in urban settings.[8] But it would be wrong to deduce that school choice is at all prevalent. Access to these specialty programs and magnet schools is often highly restrictive, and there is competition for the limited number of spaces. An important exception is District 4, located in one of the poorest communities in New York City.

The factors shaping the District 4 of today can be traced back to the late 1960s, when the administration of New York City's public school system was decentralized to allow for greater local control. In East Harlem the public schools were encountering a lot of problems with student behavior and performance, and rolls were declining as a result. To change this, small, alternative schools—often schools within schools—were developed. The district superintendent Anthony Alvarado wanted to have new schools spring up "that would look excitingly different, that would have a loyal, if small, following among families and strong professional leadership" (Meier 1995, 94). These schools were given greater flexibility in staffing, use of resources, organization of time, and forms of assessment. Attendance at the schools was based on parental and student choice, not compulsion. In 1972 the district consisted of twenty-two schools in the same number of buildings, but during the late 1970s and the 1980s about thirty alternative schools were developed along the lines proposed by Fantini, so that over fifty schools now exist. After 1982 all families of incoming seventh-graders had to choose a school (Fleigel 1990; Fleigel and MacGuire 1993).

District 4 has received much critical acclaim from outside observers. For instance, John E. Chubb and Terry M. Moe have suggested that "if there is a single school district in the country that deserves to be held up as a model for all others, it is East Harlem" (1990, 214). Those who tell the most rosy story of District 4 emphasize increased teacher enthusiasm and the considerable improvements that have been reported in aggregate student test scores. In the early 1970s the district was ranked the lowest in the city for math and reading scores; today, student performance in the district appears to be significantly improved over performance in the district before changes started being made in the mid-1970s (see Schneider et al. 1998). Schools in District 4 also seem to enjoy greater levels of parental involvement than schools in districts with less well-developed choice programs (Schneider et al. 1997). However, skeptics note that the apparent improvements in school performance in the district could be attributed to a variety of factors other than the introduction of school choice, including the exceptional leadership provided by Anthony Alvarado, the considerable infusion of federal funding the district has enjoyed, and the significant political support it has received from outsiders. (For a review of these points, see Henig 1994.)

Other local examples of public school choice have been in existence in Montclair, New Jersey, since 1976 and in Cambridge, Massachusetts, since 1981. In both cases districtwide choice was first introduced using magnet schools as a way to integrate schools that had become highly segregated along racial lines. These experiments represent cases where the magnet school concept has been extended to make each school unique and promote a sorting of students by academic interests rather than by race.

States and Open-Enrollment Laws

The emergence of local experiments with school choice has typically resulted from the actions of officials at the school district level who have sought innovative solutions to pressing problems. To make choice among public schools a practical option for many families, not just those who happen to be located in school districts headed by officials with a desire for experimentation, state legislative changes have been necessary. The first state legislative approval of open enrollment occurred in Minnesota in 1987. Under this plan, children are free to move from school district to school district, no matter where their residential location happens to be. Under the statewide plans that are in place, schools continue to receive their funding from centralized sources, although the funding is much more closely related to student numbers than in the traditional funding system. The achievement of the Minnesota school choice law required a significant amount of political effort. However, once the law was adopted in Minnesota, many other state legislatures also considered the idea. In subsequent years, legislatures in eighteen other states adopted some variation on the open-enrollment idea. The states with open-enrollment plans in place are listed in table 1-1.

State open-enrollment laws open the range of public schools that students can attend. However, school choice is limited under open enrollment because it involves choosing among existing public schools. If the majority of parents and children in a school or school district are content with present policy settings, there remains little incentive for schools to change to accommodate the needs of a minority of students or parents.

Table 1-1. ***States with Open-enrollment Plans***

State	*Year*	*State*	*Year*
Minnesota	1987	Massachusetts	1991
Arkansas	1989	Michigan	1991
Iowa	1989	Oregon	1991
Nebraska	1989	California	1992
Colorado	1990	Utah	1992
Idaho	1990	Indiana	1993
Illinois	1990	Utah	1993
Ohio	1990	Arizona	1994
Washington	1990	Missouri	1994
Alabama	1991		

Therefore, open-enrollment laws provide parents and children with an exit option from their present school but provide no guarantee that an alternative school will be much different.

A limited amount of research has been conducted on the effects of open-enrollment plans, and some early studies of the Minnesota experience have produced useful findings. Considering the actions of parents, several analysts have reported that the decision to move a child from one school to another has been based on the expectation that the child's needs will be better met and that the child will receive more personal attention from teachers in the transfer school (Delany 1995; Lau 1994; Tenbusch 1993; Ysseldyke and Thurlow 1994). With respect to the actions of schools and districts, analysts have found that open enrollment has stimulated changes in curricula and support services in schools, and has promoted more parental and teacher involvement in school planning and decisionmaking (Tenbusch and Garet 1993). From interviews with school administrators in districts that have lost the most students through open enrollment and with administrators in a control group of schools, other analysts have concluded that the districts losing students have been more likely to take steps specifically designed to attract students into the district and to discourage others from leaving (Funkhouser and Colopy 1994).

Charter Schools

While open enrollment provides greater choice among existing schools, charter schools are intended to increase the variety of schools available for parents and students to choose among. In this way, the concept of charter schools is similar to the alternative schools model of the 1970s in that it is aimed at promoting choice and innovation within the system of public education. Charter schools are conceived as autonomous educational entities operating within the public school system under contracts ("charters"). The charters are negotiated between organizers and sponsors: the organizers manage the schools, and the sponsors oversee the provisions of the charters. The organizers may be teachers, parents, or others from the public or private sectors; the sponsors may be local school boards, state education boards, or other public authorities. The charters contain provisions regarding issues such as curriculum, performance measures, and management and financial plans. Charter schools can be established in a variety of ways. An existing school might convert to a charter school. Alternatively, a charter school can be developed as part of an existing school, comprising a "school within a school." Finally, a charter school might emerge as a brand-new entity.

Since its development, the charter schools concept has gained support from various proponents with diverse agendas for educational policy. Some see charter schools as providing a degree of school choice while maintaining the public school system, whereas others see them as a useful step toward creating voucher programs of the sort advocated by Milton Friedman. Minnesota was the first state to adopt charter schools legislation in 1991. Subsequently, thirty-five additional states and Washington, D.C., have adopted charter school laws. By spring 1999, over 1,200 charter schools were operating across the United States, with a total enrollment of over 300,000.[9] Although charter schools still make up just a small component of the publicly funded schools in the country, they provide genuine public school options for parents and children. As well as this, they raise the possibility for innovative teaching practices and organizational arrangements to be developed at the school level. Finally, they provide a degree of competition for the traditional public schools because funding follows students who leave traditional schools and enter charter schools. The states that had charter school laws in place by spring 1999 are listed in table 1-2.

Public Voucher Plans

Public voucher programs have been designed to provide opportunities for children in public schools to attend private schools, with tuition fees

Table 1-2. ***States with Charter School Laws***

State	*Year*	*State*	*Year*
Minnesota	1991	Illinois	1996
California	1992	New Jersey	1996
Colorado	1993	North Carolina	1996
Georgia	1993	South Carolina	1996
Massachusetts	1993	Rhode Island	1996
Michigan	1993	Washington, D.C.	1996
New Mexico	1993	Wyoming	1996
Wisconsin	1993	Mississippi	1997
Arizona	1994	Nevada	1997
Hawaii	1994	Ohio	1997
Kansas	1994	Pennsylvania	1997
Alaska	1995	Idaho	1998
Arkansas	1995	Missouri	1998
Delaware	1995	Virginia	1998
Louisiana	1995	Utah	1998
New Hampshire	1995	New York	1998
Texas	1995	Oklahoma	1999
Connecticut	1996	Oregon	1999
Florida	1996		

being covered by the state. Advocates for children from poor, inner city, minority families have proposed voucher programs as a desperately needed measure to increase educational options. Meanwhile, Republican legislators, business leaders, conservative foundations, and church groups have advocated voucher programs for a variety of reasons, which range from the charitable desire to help poor children receive high-quality education, to the strategic goal of introducing greater competition in the delivery of publicly funded education.[10] Of the three key education reform initiatives that fall under the rubric of school choice—open enrollment, charter schools, and vouchers—voucher programs represent the greatest divergence from the traditional education system. Hence the voucher concept is highly controversial. Efforts to introduce voucher programs have been vigorously resisted by representatives of the education establishment, and civil liberties groups have engaged in court battles to prevent the use of public dollars for education at religious and other private schools (Heise 1993).

At present two public voucher programs exist in the United States. Both are quite small in scope. The introduction of a public voucher program in Milwaukee in 1990 and another in Cleveland in 1996 occurred only after pitched battles in the state legislatures in which the state governors became actively involved. While potentially able to instigate sweeping changes in the delivery of public education within their jurisdictions, state policymakers have had to fight hard to secure what, in the final analysis, represent small changes in the overall delivery of education in Wisconsin and Ohio.[11]

The Milwaukee voucher program is designed for use by children from low-income families. Initially, no more than 1 percent (approximately 1,000) of the students enrolled in the Milwaukee Public Schools (MPS) could enter the program, and the vouchers (equivalent to the state per student aid to MPS) could be used only at secular private schools. However, in 1995 the program was expanded to include up to 15 percent of MPS students. At the same time the restriction on voucher students attending religious private schools was dropped. This expansion to religious private schools was initially struck down by a state court, but it was sustained on appeal. Furthermore, the expansion of the program was given considerable support in November 1998 when the U.S. Supreme Court declined to review the Wisconsin ruling. (For a complete review of the Milwaukee voucher experiment, see Witte 1998.)

In Cleveland, up to 1,500 students from low-income families can use vouchers for tuition at any participating private or religious schools or at suburban public schools. Thus, the Cleveland public voucher program is especially significant for its inclusion of religious schools from the outset. The program has been upheld by the Ohio courts, but in August 1999 a Federal District Court judge in Cleveland stated that there was probable cause to believe that the program violated the constitutional separation of church and state.

Private Voucher Plans

Private voucher plans represent a quite distinctive effort to promote school choice. The first of these plans was established in 1991 by an insurance company executive, J. Patrick Rooney. Frustrated by the lack of action occurring in the Indiana state legislature to promote school choice, Rooney decided to establish his own charitable voucher plan. Under this plan children from poor families are provided with subsidies to attend private schools of their choice, including religious schools.

Table 1-3. ***The Location of Private Voucher Plans***

City (State)	*Year*	*City (State)*	*Year*
Indianapolis (Indiana)	1991	Jackson (Mississippi)	1995
Atlanta (Georgia)	1992	Knoxville (Tennessee)	1995
Battle Creek (Michigan)	1992	Orlando (Florida)	1995
Milwaukee (Wisconsin)	1992	Elizabeth (New Jersey)	1996
San Antonio (Texas)	1992	Jersey City (New Jersey)	1996
Albany (New York)	1993	Philadelphia (Pennsylvania)	1996
Austin (Texas)	1993	Pittsburgh (Pennsylvania)	1996
Denver (Colorado)	1993	New York City (New York)	1997
Detroit/Grand Rapids (Michigan)	1993	Chicago (Illinois)	1997
Little Rock (Arkansas)	1993	St. Louis (Missouri)	1997
Phoenix (Arizona)	1993	Birmingham (Alabama)	1998
Washington, D.C.	1993	Dayton (Ohio)	1998
Dallas (Texas)	1994	Louisville (Kentucky)	1998
Houston (Texas)	1994	Miami (Florida)	1998
Los Angeles (California)	1994	San Francisco (California)	1998
Midland (Texas)	1994	Chattanooga (Tennessee)	1998
Oakland (California)	1994	Hartford (Connecticut)	1998
Bridgeport (Connecticut)	1995	Memphis (Tennessee)	1998
Buffalo (New York)	1995	Minneapolis (Minnesota)	1998
Fort Worth (Texas)	1995		

Rooney saw this as a strategy that would provide immediate relief to poor families seeking to place their children in better schools. However, he also saw it as a way to alter the nature of the school choice debate in his state and to develop evidence of the workability of a voucher plan. Rooney's plan has now been successfully emulated by private charities in many cities across the United States. By spring 1999 thirty-nine plans were in operation in twenty-two states plus Washington, D.C., with total enrollments exceeding 16,000. An additional fifteen plans were slated to begin later in 1999.[12] The relevant cities and states are listed in table 1-3.

The Emerging Scene

Despite the range of approaches now in existence, school choice as presently available in the United States is only a pale shadow of the plans that various school choice advocates have proposed over the years. Nonetheless, it is important to recognize that these limited steps seem to be making a difference in the local setting. In combination, various school choice approaches have brought an element of competition and greater scope for innovation into the delivery of public schooling. This development of competition and innovation appears set to continue. School choice approaches have also created a great deal of discussion among interested parties and forced individuals and groups who were content with the traditional organization of public schools to consider embracing aspects of the choice idea. Although still in its infancy, school choice is changing the nature of the education sector and how people think about it. The older ways of organizing public schooling have become the target of hard questions, and significant policy changes are emerging as a result. For this reason it is not surprising that debate about school choice has been trenchant. A lot of power is at stake here.

Reflecting broader policy debates, recent discussion among academics of the school choice idea has run the gamut from strong support to deep opposition. Among political scientists, John E. Chubb and Terry M. Moe (1990) have supported a broad system of school choice. According to these authors, many of the present problems in public schools result from democratic control and the plethora of bureaucratic rules and regulations that, in their view, necessarily accompany public production of services. Chubb and Moe favor full privatization of the delivery of schooling, with public financing provided through a system of vouchers. Paul E. Peterson and his associates have likewise expressed considerable support for the use of school vouchers (see, e.g., Peterson and Noyes 1997; Peterson and Hassel 1998). Peterson has conducted studies of voucher approaches in several cities in the United States and has concluded from them that school choice approaches appear to improve educational outcomes. John F. Witte, with whom Peterson has frequently crossed swords, tends to take a more cautious view. While suggesting that problems in the current system justify experimentation with school choice, Witte has urged that it not be seen as a panacea for solving the complex problems that affect overall achievement and the variance in achievement across school districts (Witte 1990). According to him, the results of the Milwaukee voucher experiment are mixed at best and provide no clear prescription for future policy directions (see Witte 1998).

Other political scientists have expressed open hostility to school choice. Jeffrey R. Henig (1994) has argued that putting education in the marketplace will lead to an erosion of civic capacity and the role that public schools and school politics currently play in nurturing deliberative approaches to solving collective action problems. Kevin B. Smith and

Kenneth J. Meier (1995) have presented evidence that calls into question the validity of the quantitative work presented by Chubb and Moe (1990), and have strongly criticized school choice as a policy approach.

Through a variety of formal and informal relationships, colleges of education have traditionally been closely associated with the public school system. This may well explain why, among education scholars, views on school choice tend to be either somewhat negative or, at best, conditionally favorable. Forceful champions are few and far between. Mary Anne Raywid has long advocated school choice as a mechanism for achieving a greater balance of power between families and schools with respect to educational decisionmaking (see Raywid 1989, 1992). Diane Ravitch has also been associated with strong supporters of school choice approaches as ways to improve urban schools (Ravitch 1996; Ravitch and Viteritti 1996). However, the most common stance found among educationalists seems a lot like that taken by John E. Coons and Steven D. Sugarman (1978). That is to say, support for school choice is accompanied by a series of caveats intended to ensure that the anticipated positive effects of the policy are not swamped by unintended negative effects. Prominent scholars exhibiting this stance include Peter W. Cookson (1994), Richard F. Elmore (1991; see also Elmore and Fuller 1996), Herbert Gintis (1995), and Henry M. Levin (1998). Indicative of education scholars occupying this middle ground, Herbert Gintis (1995) argues that school choice has the potential to empower parents in positive ways, but he notes that implementation must be handled extremely carefully. Much thought must be given to the nature of the regulatory regime within which school choice occurs. Done right, Gintis believes that school choice represents a way that the market could be used as an instrument of democracy rather than as an alternative to it. Several educationalists have been prominent opponents of school choice. Keenest opposition comes from those who believe that school choice will exacerbate social stratification. Scholars who have argued this view most forcefully include Amy Stuart Wells (1993; 1996) and Valerie E. Lee (Lee and Bryk 1993; Lee, Croninger, and Smith 1996).

School Choice and Policy Entrepreneurship

Several case studies of the political debates that have accompanied the rise of school choice onto state legislative agendas have revealed the important role that particular individuals have played in bringing the idea of school choice to prominence. Paula King's (1988) doctoral dissertation presents a detailed study of the background to Minnesota's adoption of open enrollment in 1987. In her study, King argues that several policy entrepreneurs worked together for several years in Minnesota to generate support for school choice. Likewise, discussions of the background to the introduction of public school vouchers in Milwaukee typically note the important role that Polly Williams, a Democratic Party assemblywoman from Milwaukee, played in developing a winning coalition to secure the initiative (see Witte and Rigdon 1993). My own case study of Michigan, written with Sandra Vergari, also reveals the role played by a concerned citizen, Paul DeWeese, in generating support for school choice in that state (Mintrom and Vergari 1996).

Of course, it is difficult to make a compelling case about the importance of policy entrepreneurs in supporting the rise of school choice by using evidence from isolated cases. Many challenges could be launched, three of which I note here. First, one could argue that other factors led legislators in these states to become interested in school choice issues. Perhaps the policy entrepreneurs just happened to be at the right place at the right time, and so they were readily credited with bringing the issue to attention. Second, the argument could be made that these studies are flawed because they start with the dependent variable, a policy innovation, and then trace back to find the independent variable, the policy entrepreneur. In other words, selection based on the dependent variable ensures that the predetermined conclusion is reached, that policy entrepreneurs make a difference in the policymaking process. Finally, it is possible to argue that policy entrepreneurship is too vague a concept. If all it boils down to is the introduction of a new legislative bill, then every issue will have a policy entrepreneur at some point. The observation that policy entrepreneurs have helped raise interest in the school choice idea is therefore trivial.

Each of these challenges deserves serious consideration. By taking them seriously, it is possible to develop a research design that increases our confidence that policy entrepreneurs do, in fact, make significant differences in the policymaking process. The first challenge can be addressed by testing for the impact of policy entrepreneurs on legislative attention to an idea, while controlling for rival explanations. The second challenge can be addressed by extending the number of cases to be studied. In particular, to avoid the criticism of selecting based on the dependent variable, it is important to look for instances of policy entrepreneurship both in jurisdictions that have considered or adopted the policy innovation of interest and in those that have not. Finally, the third challenge can be addressed by ensuring that the definition of policy entrepreneurship is specific enough that we can readily determine who should and who should not be given this title. As will become apparent in the subsequent chapters of this book, my empirical research on policy entrepreneurs and the rise of school choice did indeed incorporate the important design features mentioned here. The results of my statistical research suggest that policy entrepreneurs have made a significant difference in promoting the idea of school choice. Given this, we can have more faith in the findings that have been obtained in previous investigations that relied on case study methods.

The rise of school choice represents an excellent case through which to examine the role played by policy entrepreneurs in the policymaking process. This is a policy innovation that in its various guises has diffused rapidly. As a result, it is possible to compare the processes that led to the consideration and adoption of this innovation across a broad range of jurisdictions. Because of the recency with which school choice legislation has been considered, it is also possible to obtain detailed information about these processes. Aside from these considerations, school choice is a good policy innovation to study because it can have significant effects. At the local level the introduction of school choice sets off chain reactions, altering the organization of social relationships and forcing people to break with their old ways of doing things. Studying the rise of school choice in the United States represents a worthwhile activity in its own right because of the many political questions that it raises. However, for my purposes, the rise of school choice offers a rich body of evidence regarding the policymaking process and the role that policy entrepreneurs can play in promoting policy innovations.

The Structure of the Book

In the chapters to follow, I argue that we should revise both the way we conceive of the process of policy change and the empirical strategies we use to investigate it. The previous literature on the policymaking process has done much to describe the patterns of stability and change in American politics. But explanations of the emergence of policy innovations remain quite rudimentary. Even when scholars have mentioned the role played by policy entrepreneurs as actors in the policymaking process, little effort has gone into explaining what precisely these actors do and how they manage the process through which change emerges. To develop my conception of how policy entrepreneurs promote policy change, I first explore the role of entrepreneurs in the market process and explain what it is that marks out entrepreneurs as unique actors. This discussion lays the foundation for carefully developing the notion of policy entrepreneurship. Having done that, I present my empirical explorations. The purpose of this empirical work is to test elements of my theory of policy entrepreneurship and to further clarify how policy entrepreneurs work to secure policy change.

In chapter 2 I review several explanations of policy change that have been presented by political scientists over the past few decades. Most of these explanations suggest that there is room in the policymaking process for determined individuals to contribute in significant ways to debates and, thus, to the outcomes of those debates. Having reviewed these explanations, I discuss the conception of the policy entrepreneur that is found in the extant literature. I then document the role that three policy entrepreneurs appear to have played in the rise of school choice in their respective states. This discussion sets the stage for the development of my theory of policy entrepreneurship.

In chapter 3 I discuss the development of the concept of the entrepreneur and how it has been treated in the neoclassical and Austrian school economic paradigms. I show that much of economics is concerned with predicting equilibrium conditions and that the analytical tools of neoclassical economics are not well suited to investigating change in markets. Hence the entrepreneur has been squeezed from much mainstream economic analysis. However, to explain dynamic market change, the concept of the entrepreneur is essential.

In chapter 4 I explain how entrepreneurs come to perceive opportunities for gain, how they develop innovations, how they develop strategies and work the system, and how they serve to coordinate others to ensure the introduction of innovative processes and products. With this as background I am able to present a clear summary statement about the role of entrepreneurs in the market process. This becomes the basis upon which to launch a theoretical discussion of the role of policy entrepreneurs in the policymaking process.

In chapter 5 I present my theory of policy entrepreneurship. My purpose here is to develop a concept that could be more widely used by social scientists seeking to isolate the sources of policy change. Toward this end, I systematically compare and contrast opportunities for entrepreneurship in the market process with those in the policymaking process. I end the chapter with an overview of my conception of the policy entrepreneur, highlighting the elements of entrepreneurship that seem most appropriate for application to thinking about the behavior of actors in the policymaking process.

In chapter 6 I introduce the research strategy used to generate the empirical evidence with which I work in the remainder of the book. Although many scholars have noted the role policy entrepreneurs play in promoting policy change, previous empirical work has tended to focus on isolated cases. I seek to demonstrate that beyond improving the way we conceive of policy entrepreneurship, we can also improve the way we study it in practice. After an initial discussion of the choices faced by researchers interested in policy entrepreneurship, I review how I have used survey techniques to locate school choice policy entrepreneurs in the states. I then present portraits of five of the policy entrepreneurs identified in the survey work.

In chapter 7 I directly confront the question of whether policy entrepreneurs promote policy change. To test the impact of policy entrepreneurs, I use event history analysis models on data from the forty-eight contiguous states for the years 1987 through 1992. Here I model the nature of the policymaking process in a way that pays more attention to the details of that process than previous quantitative work. My results suggest that the presence and actions of policy entrepreneurs can significantly raise the likelihood of legislative consideration and approval of school choice, even while controlling for a variety of other possible explanations for such legislative activity.

In chapter 8 I look more closely at the ways that policy entrepreneurs use social and professional networks as resources when attempting to influence policy agendas and promote policy change. I again use event history analysis techniques, this time to assess the importance of network involvement for improving the success of policy entrepreneurs. My results suggest that greater involvement in policy networks significantly increases the likelihood of policy entrepreneurs achieving their goals of policy change. These results also serve to increase our understanding of policy innovation diffusion processes.

In chapter 9 I explore how policy entrepreneurs work with others to build support for their policy goals. It is clear that entrepreneurship, be it in the marketplace or in the policymaking process, is a highly social act. Not surprisingly, then, to ensure that their ideas receive careful attention from decisionmakers, policy entrepreneurs must find ways to work with others and have others see the value of their ideas. In this chapter I discuss the notion of coalition building and the ways that policy entrepreneurs use arguments to build support. The discussion in this chapter is informed by descriptive statistics derived from my survey work. Also in this chapter I present three cases of how policy entrepreneurs sought to win support for their school choice ideas.

In chapter 10 I examine how policy entrepreneurs can benefit from shifting the venue of policy innovation and using local-level actions to promote state-level policy change. Following a discussion of how policy entrepreneurs use evidence in their arguments, I document how school choice policy entrepreneurs have recently developed local-level private voucher schemes as demonstration projects. These activities appear to have prompted state-level policy change. Thus it can be said that a state-local nexus exists in the diffusion of school choice. Based on an analysis of this nexus, I suggest that there is value in conceptualizing policy innovation diffusion in a federal system as both a horizontal (that is, state-to-state) and a vertical (that is, state-and-local) phenomenon. Policy entrepreneurs play a significant role in facilitating this diffusion.

In the final chapter of this book, chapter 11, I return to the general argument that policy entrepreneurs serve to promote policy innovations that can herald significant policy change. However, now I reflect upon this argument in light of the empirical work presented in the preceding chapters. I argue that the evidence presented here suggests that we can gain a richer understanding of the processes of both policy change and policy innovation diffusion by paying careful attention to identifying policy entrepreneurs and analyzing their actions. I then go on to discuss the ways that my theory of policy entrepreneurship relates to other theories of policy change, as discussed in chapter 2.

A common problem among policy scholars engaged in theory construction has been the tendency for new theories to be presented without discussion of how they relate to alternative approaches. Although I believe my theory of policy entrepreneurship is important for what it tells us about the nature of the policymaking process, I certainly do not think that it renders other approaches irrelevant. My aim in this final chapter is to show the points of convergence and divergence between the theory of policy entrepreneurship and alternative approaches. Such an exercise can be useful for further delineating the scope and limits of a theoretical perspective.

I conclude the book by drawing lessons about policy entrepreneurship that should be of interest to analysts, advocates, and interested observers of contemporary politics. I suggest that the approach developed and applied in this study holds promise for increasing our knowledge of the ways that individuals can promote important policy changes that, in turn, serve to transform political institutions and public organizations.

Notes

1. Several recent works document this transnational phenomenon. See, especially, Feigenbaum, Henig, and Hamnett (1999), Osborne and Plastrik (1997), and Yergin and Stanislaw (1998).

2. For further discussion of this point, see Fuller, Elmore, and Orfield (1996).

3. Thomas R. Oliver and Pamela Paul-Shaheen (1997) provide an excellent study of policy entrepreneurship and state health care reforms in the United States. In addition, there is growing discussion among international relations scholars of the advocacy techniques used by "norm entrepreneurs" who, for our purposes, can be thought of as policy entrepreneurs who engage in dialogue and coordinated action at the transnational level. See, for example, Finnemore (1996) and Keck and Sikkink (1998).

4. Donald Green and Ian Shapiro (1994) have launched the most comprehensive critique of rational choice to date. However, these criticisms have not gone unchallenged. In Jeffrey Friedman's (1996) edited collection, the doyens of rational choice and their acolytes take turns explaining everything that is wrong with what Green and Shapiro have to say.

5. During the 1980s and 1990s a flurry of books and studies emerged that emphasized problems with educational policy and educational standards in the United States. Prominent among these works were the report of the National Commission on Excellence in Education, *A Nation at Risk* (1983); Eric D. Hirsch's *Cultural Literacy* (1987); and Harold W. Stevenson's *The Learning Gap* (1992). Countering the claims of naysayers, David C. Berliner and Bruce J. Biddle produced *The Manufactured Crisis* (1995).

6. Henig (1994, ch. 5) reviews the early efforts to institute school choice in the U.S. that were spearheaded by Southern whites in the years after the United States Supreme Court's landmark school desegregation rulings: *Brown v. Board of Education*, 347 U.S. 483 (1954) and *Brown v. Board of Education*, 349 U.S. 2994 (1955). During this time state legislatures in Alabama, Louisiana, Mississippi, and Virginia adopted "freedom of choice" laws explicitly designed to promote racial segregation. Social sanctions against racial mixing, combined with laws allowing students to drop out of desegregation plans, had the effect of ensuring "separate but equal" (or, more precisely, separate and *un*equal) education, since black students would be encouraged

both officially and unofficially to remain in or return to their segregated schools. The U.S. Supreme Court struck down these plans in *Goss v. Board of Education*, 373 U.S. 683 (1963). However, several of these Southern states found another way to circumvent desegregation through making legislative provision of publicly funded vouchers for students to attend private schools. In a series of rulings made during the 1960s, the U.S. Supreme Court struck down these plans as in violation of desegregation court orders.

7. Ironically, Alum Rock is located a great distance from the inner cities that represented the original targets of voucher plans.

8. For an excellent discussion of the history of magnet schools, their distribution across the United States, and what makes them distinctive, see Blank, Levine, and Steel (1996).

9. The source of these figures is The Center for Educational Reform, Washington, D.C. The relevant website is www.edreform.com.

10. In some states, representatives of the Republican Party have also been attracted to public voucher plans because of the opportunity they present for weakening the power of teacher unions and, thus, their role in the political process (which has typically been to support members of the Democratic Party).

11. A statewide voucher plan was adopted in Florida in mid-1999. This plan allows students in failing public schools to use public funds to attend private schools, including religious ones.

12. The source of these figures is *Just Doing It 4: 1998 Annual Survey of the Private Voucher Movement in America*, published by the Children's Educational Opportunity Foundation of America. See also www.ceoamerica.org.

TWO

Explanations of Policy Change

In any system of power government manifests itself through the way it structures relationships among members of society. Of course, as individuals we relate to each other in multiple and complex ways, and many of our day-to-day relationships are neither explicitly nor implicitly affected by government. But whenever formal, public discussion takes place and collective choices are transformed into laws establishing appropriate modes of conduct, then government manifests itself. In combination, current laws in any jurisdiction and the activities government agents perform in support of those laws establish public policy.

Typically public policies relating to any area of social activity exhibit an aura of permanency. Think, for example, of the laws governing the attendance of children at school, or how we drive, or the respect we must pay to private property. Such laws and how they are enforced have significant influence on the structure of our lives and on how we choose to act. This has been the case for generations. Knowledge of the relevant laws is pervasive in society, and that knowledge is most often passed along by word-of-mouth or simply by people's observing each other's conduct. Thoroughgoing changes to public policy regarding public schooling, the laws of the road, property rights, and many other matters that are integral to our day-to-day practices would appear counterproductive. It is no surprise then to find that if policy change occurs at all, it occurs slowly. When changes are made to a particular area of public policy, they usually affect only portions of that policy—one or a handful of laws, not the whole set that structures relevant actions. There are times, however, when policy change represents a break from the past, when policy innovations are adopted.

How do we explain policy innovation? That is, how do we explain policy changes that appear to challenge, at least in part, established ways of doing things? This question motivates all that follows in this book. My answer in brief is that policy change can arise from a variety of causes. However, we should pay greater attention to the ways that particular individuals, termed policy entrepreneurs, act to promote changes in given policy areas. According to previous descriptions, policy entrepreneurs are individuals who, through their creativity, strategy, networking, and persuasive argumentation, bring ideas for policy innovation into common currency and thus promote policy change. In treating policy change as a variable to be explained, I place myself in a tradition of political scientists who have made it their task to explain facets of the policymaking process and the antecedents of new policy or policy reform. Of these scholars, quite a few have noted the apparent role that policy entrepreneurs play in promoting policy change. However, the extant literature too often leaves policy entrepreneurs in need of clearer definition.

Any line of argument used to explain the causes of policy change must, by necessity, be based on an understanding of the nature of the policymaking process. Therefore, to make a satisfactory argument that policy entrepreneurs can, and often do, serve to promote policy change, it is necessary to clarify how the policymaking process operates. Here I synthesize and build upon the work of several political scientists. These scholars include, but are not restricted to, Frank R. Baumgartner and Bryan D. Jones (1993), John W. Kingdon (1995), Charles E. Lindblom (1968), James G. March and Johan P. Olsen (1989), and Paul A. Sabatier (1988). As anyone familiar with the work of these scholars will recognize, in making an argument for the importance of policy entrepreneurs in promoting policy change, I assume that the policymaking process is complex and that participants, while intending to act rationally, often lack the information and cognitive skill needed to be "lightning calculators" of their own best interests.[1] Building upon the work of these scholars, I also come to the view that the process of policy deliberation found in liberal democracies can be extremely productive, leading participants to realize and reflect on policy approaches that, without such deliberation, may well have been overlooked. I completely agree with David M. Ricci when he observes that the policymaking process "is analogous to a very complicated political conversation" where "success is not solely a function of how many tangible resources one uses to push into the conversation" (1993, 205).

Conceptions of the Policymaking Process

Over the past few decades, many political scientists have presented conceptions of the policymaking process. Generally, these scholars have sought to clarify what factors serve to shape the development and administration of public policies. Like other social scientists attempting to construct positive theories to explain social processes, these political scientists have necessarily had to be highly selective about what entities and events to consider. The goal is to develop conceptions of the policymaking process that explain a lot about the policymaking process with as little information as possible. But while complexity is to be avoided, this does not mean that *simplify, simplify* should become a mantra. If, in pursuit of parsimony, we build input-output models to explain items of public policy and our models treat the process of policy development as an uninteresting black box, we will run two risks. First, many policy outputs might come to appear anomalous, inexplicable in terms of the given set of inputs. Second, we risk ignoring much of the politics that accompanies policy development. Given our interest in understanding the politics of policymaking, perhaps the best position to maintain is one where we remain curious about complexities but cognizant of the potential for theory (which necessarily involves simplification) to enlighten our understanding of a range of particularities.

A good place to begin conceptualizing the policymaking process is to think about boundaries. What political actors and political institutions routinely shape the policies that governments develop and administer? As recently as 1968, Charles Lindblom observed that the policymaking process was such a new focus for inquiry that "no one seems to want to answer the question of what is supposed to be included in the process and what excluded from it." David Easton, writing fifteen years ahead of Lindblom, managed to convey just how potentially all-encompassing our study of policymaking could be. According to Easton (1953, 128): "Political life consists of all those varieties of activity that influence significantly the kind of authoritative policy adopted for a society and the way it is put into practice." But to observe that all action in the political world is somehow intended to shape public policy provides little more than a starting point for serious thinking. Ultimately, we want to sort through the myriad details of political life and focus on those actors and institutions that routinely and significantly influence policy.

One popular approach to establishing boundaries when conceptualizing the policymaking process has been to divide it into steps or "stages" such as problem definition, agenda setting, policy adoption, implementation, and evaluation.[2] Inspired by Easton's (1953) application of systems analysis to political science, scholars have sought better understanding of political phenomena by assuming that the development and administration of public policy follows a linear path. Applying this approach, political scientists have developed bodies of literature focusing on each of the stages. How far do we get by narrowing the focus in this way?

Overall, use of the stages heuristic has been quite fruitful for policy scholarship. First, it has encouraged specialization, allowing scholars to dwell, for example, on the politics of policy adoption as a self-contained process. Scholars have developed a depth of understanding on such matters and gained insights that can be applied across a range of policy areas and jurisdictions. Second, it has facilitated a move away from traditional institutional analysis of policymaking with its tendency to treat such entities as the legislature, the presidency, and the bureaucracy in isolation from one another. This has led to a burgeoning literature examining the strategic interactions between actors in the policymaking process. Third, use of the stages heuristic has prompted scholars to direct increasing attention to pre- and postdecision processes. Considerable attention has been paid to how problems get identified and defined and how agenda setting occurs. Scholars have also contributed to the now-vast literatures on both policy implementation and policy evaluation. For the most part, the conceptions of the policymaking process that I find of most use in my work implicitly incorporate this approach of treating the policy process as a series of stages. These contributions are primarily concerned with the politics of problem definition, agenda setting, and policy adoption; they consider the politics of implementation and policy evaluation only tangentially.

Despite the obvious advantages of using the stages heuristic, Hank C. Jenkins-Smith and Paul A. Sabatier (1993, 3–4) suggest that it has brought with it several disadvantages. In their view, the major disadvantage is that the approach is descriptively inaccurate because it assumes linearity where this often does not exist. For example, rather than problem definition being confined to the start of the policymaking process, it is possible that some crucial aspects of problem definition are left up to bureaucrats during policy implementation. Similarly, policy evaluations might be used strategically within the agenda setting stage to demonstrate that problems exist in current policy settings and to argue that those problems be addressed in specific ways. Related to this apparent descriptive inaccuracy, Jenkins-Smith and Sabatier argue that this representation lacks a causal mechanism linking the various stages. These criticisms seem justified, but it is not at all clear just how they should be addressed.

Since any effort to achieve conceptual focus necessarily involves making exclusions, all efforts to conceptualize the policymaking process are potentially open to challenge. Drawing somewhat artificial boundaries around problem definition, agenda setting, policy adoption, implementation, and evaluation has its costs, but, in my view, there is much to commend this method of achieving greater focus in conceptual work. The method has led to the identification of relationships among entities and events that have unquestionably improved our understanding of the policymaking process. Next I review several efforts to conceptualize the policymaking process, noting where possible the cumulative nature of these works.

Proximate Policymakers and Incremental Policy Change

In presenting his conception of the policymaking process, Charles Lindblom (1968) argued that we should devote most of our attention to the behaviors of "proximate" policymakers. These individuals include legislators, political executives, appointed bureaucrats, and some party officials; that is to say, anyone with some policy decisionmaking authority. Typically, there is considerable specialization among proximate policymakers, and this ensures that relatively small groups of individuals are able to focus their attention on specific policy areas. Proximate policymakers operate within a "play of power" governed by institutional structures or the rules of the game that include the provisions of relevant constitutions, legislative acts, administrative rulings, executive orders, and judicial decisions. Policy choices therefore constitute a product of the structured interactions of proximate policymakers, and these choices do not emerge randomly. However, there is no deterministic linkage between the preferences and actions of any given participants and particular policy choices. Prior to formal decisions being taken, the proximate policymakers are subject to influence both from one another and from outsiders, such as interest group leaders and people with ideas to push.

The nature of democratic government and the separation of powers together force participants in the policymaking process to cooperate to achieve policy change. Lindblom characterizes formal procedures, like committee decisionmaking in legislatures, as "islands of formal organization in a sea of informal mutual adjustment" (1968, 93). Often, participants will try to consider their policy proposals from the perspective of those they seek to persuade, and they will make adjustments to ensure that the proposals are more attractive to others. Mutual adjustments constitute the major means through which cooperation occurs, and proximate policymakers are always interacting with each other in the hope of maximizing the chances that their particular policy preferences will prevail. This process of mutual adjustment often results in new policies that do not reflect anyone's original views. Where persuasion does not alter the views of others, coercion can sometimes be used—but for one proximate policymaker to coerce another, he or she must have some authority that can be used to the other's detriment. Since not everyone can work power asymmetries to his or her advantage, informal opportunities for seeking cooperation among policymakers are always more numerous than those based on coercion.

Lindblom rejects the notion that policymakers follow a rational choice strategy, in the sense of defining the problem, laying out alternative solutions, predicting the consequences, valuing the outcomes, and making a choice. Even if a unitary actor is required to make policy in response to a given event, complexity soon makes the exercise of rational choice impossible. If, for example, rioting occurs in several cities, the problem to be addressed is by no means self-evident. Thus, it is easy to imagine relevant solutions not even being considered and inappropriate policy choices being made, simply because of the ambiguity surrounding the nature of the problem in the first place. The potential for rational choice is further stymied because policy is made by many individuals who can be expected to hold divergent views about the nature of any given problem and how best to address it. Reasonable people will disagree about many aspects of a policy issue, making it most unlikely that bold policy responses will ever be adopted with complete unanimity.

In combination, the ongoing struggle for political influence and the perpetual fear that new policies or policy reform might create unfortunate and unpopular consequences virtually ensure that proximate policymakers change policy in an incremental fashion. Even though making changes through incremental steps might be easily dismissed as irrational, Lindblom suggests that such behavior represents a "shrewd, resourceful" way of wrestling with complex problems. No seasoned politician will seek policy changes that force large numbers of people to involuntarily depart from habitual actions and habitual ways of thinking, because the political risks would be too high. Thus, when viewed from a short-term perspective at least, policymaking typically appears conservative, perhaps even timid.

Who, besides the proximate policymakers, can have influence in the policymaking process? Lindblom suggests that policy advisors, interest group leaders, and ordinary citizens can all have influence. How much influence is gained is essentially a function of the way that arguments are made. Those who have more financial resources are better placed to make strong arguments for policy to mirror their preferences, but such resources are neither necessary nor sufficient for achieving influence. "Men who can bring relevant fact and analysis to bear on a political issue can, without holding office or heading an interest group, achieve influence disproportionate to their numbers" (1968, 111). Intellectual resourcefulness and a determination to participate are critical. Lindblom believes that many people are excluded from influence because they are not prepared to make the committed effort required to gain a hearing from proximate policymakers. "Policy making is laborious; there is no escaping its burdens . . . a big share in policy making is reserved to those who look at participation in the play of power not as a privilege but as a task, job, or career" (1968, 115).

In the years since Lindblom developed this conception of the policymaking process many scholars have incorporated his key insights into their work. Political scientists accept Lindblom's view that policymaking is predominantly incremental in nature, and they accept his reasons for why this is so. The question of who has the greatest influence on policymaking is not so settled. Nonetheless, the view is rarely contested that proximate policymakers have a significant amount of agency when deciding what policy issues to consider and what solutions to adopt.

Process Streams and Windows of Opportunity

John Kingdon's ([1984] 1995) interest in the policymaking process centers on how particular policy problems and solutions achieve prominence at certain times. Rather than dissect the politics of how policy choices are made, Kingdon examines the predecision stages of problem definition and agenda setting. Little, if anything, of what Kingdon says contradicts Lindblom's conceptual work. Yet Kingdon goes much further than Lindblom in terms of providing a coherent approach to understanding the complexities of the policymaking process. Kingdon argues that agenda setting and policy change emerge through a combination of the actions of participants and the operation of both formal and informal social processes. Many individuals can, through their various actions, call increasing attention to particular policy issues. However, it is primarily elected officials—key members of Lindblom's set of proximate policymakers—who decide which issues will become agenda items and, thus, the grounds for considering new policy or policy change.

Like Lindblom, Kingdon emphasizes the important role that informal communication channels play in supporting the rise to prominence of policy issues. Collectively, a range of individuals serve to make up specialized policy communities or networks: elected officials, bureaucrats, interest group representatives, researchers, and interested citizens. "The communication channels between those inside and those outside of government are extraordinarily open, and ideas and information float about through these channels in the whole issue network of involved people, somewhat independent of their formal positions" (1995, 45).

Kingdon's discussion of the various participants in the policymaking process and their social milieu is insightful. His key contribution to conceptualizing the policymaking process is his argument that policy issues emerge on government decisionmaking agendas as the result of developments in three separate process streams: the problem stream, the policy stream, and the political stream. He argues that advocates of policy change, whom he terms policy entrepreneurs, often serve to join the three independent streams through their efforts to bring prominence to particular problems and policy innovations. In this way they significantly raise the chances that particular policy issues will stimulate new policy or policy change.

Problem recognition occurs in the problem stream. At any given time many people, both inside and outside government, will be aware of social conditions that in their view constitute problems justifying government action. However, the facts of social conditions rarely speak for themselves. Those who would like to see new policy or policy change must work carefully to define conditions as problems. In doing so they use a range of strategies. These include using indicators or other evidence to demonstrate the magnitude of the problem, showing how the problem is changing, highlighting differences in the problem across jurisdictions, and drawing attention to "focusing events" or "crises." Focusing events provide excellent vehicles for bringing prominence to policy problems. When these events arise, attention to policy problems can shift rapidly.

Much is at stake when it comes to problem definition. Those benefiting from the status quo face incentives to convince others that no problem exists. Those seeking to highlight a problem, aside from demonstrating the problem's significance, must show that policy solutions are available. Thus problem definition is often undertaken with specific policy solutions in mind. Furthermore, solutions often chase problems. That is to say, people who believe that they have found a clever policy solution will work hard to "hook" it to various policy problems. To ensure that problem recognition occurs, people might use press releases, speeches, letters or visits to decisionmakers, expert testimony, or other means. Kingdon observes that "getting people to see new problems, or to see old problems in one way rather than another, is a major conceptual and political accomplishment. . . . The process of fixing attention on one problem rather than another is a central part of agenda setting" (1995, 115). For aspiring policy entrepreneurs problem definition is a key task.

The second process Kingdon highlights is the policy stream. This stream, populated by communities of policy specialists, is where ideas for policy solutions or viable policy alternatives are generated and debated. Within policy communities many ideas are considered. Occasionally people come up with new ideas for policy solutions, but for the most part they work with old ideas, thinking about ways to reformulate them or combine them with others. Even though ideas often sweep policy communities like fads, governments typically react quite slowly in response to them. To survive in the policy community, ideas must be workable and feasible, and must also be compatible with the values of a majority of specialists in the relevant policy community. Compatibility can be achieved both through the alteration of ideas and through efforts by their advocates to persuade others of their merits.

Kingdon suggests that interest group politics does not dominate the development and survival of ideas in policy communities. "If we try to understand public policy solely in terms of these concepts . . . we miss a great deal. The content of ideas themselves, far from being mere smokescreens or rationalizations, are integral parts of decision making in and around government" (1995, 125). Of course, power is not irrelevant, and elsewhere Kingdon suggests that "iron triangles" made up of legislative committee members, interest groups, and bureaucrats will make efforts to block or transform policy ideas that could potentially affect these entities. Meanwhile, those who have particular policy solutions to push tend to spread their ideas throughout policy communities by using a variety of means. Occasionally, when ideas catch on, policy entrepreneurs begin to build coalitions in their support, and, when this goes well, a bandwagon phenomenon can occur.

The third independent process that Kingdon identifies is the political stream. This is composed of things like election results, changes in administrations, changes in the partisan or ideological distribution of legislatures, interest group pressure campaigns, and changes in public opinion or the "national mood" (1995, 87). Changes in the political stream and occasional changes in the problem stream, like focusing events, provide the major opportunities for agenda changes in government. Agenda change can come quite rapidly at times, but it is important to remember that organized political forces can serve as a brake. It is also important to note that rapid, nonincremental change in the policy agenda need not produce rapid, nonincremental changes in actual policy. For even the possibility of nonincremental policy change to arise, serious amounts of bargaining and coalition building in the political stream typically must occur.

Agenda change emerges when the three process streams are joined. At critical times, dubbed "windows of opportunity," the conditions in all three streams favor a joining of problems, solutions, and political momentum. To join the three streams, policy entrepreneurs must judge that the time is right. They "lie in wait in and around government with their solutions at hand, waiting for problems to float by to which they can attach their solutions, waiting for developments in the political stream they can use to their advantage" (1995, 165).

Kingdon's conception of the policymaking process is rich in the sense that it guides us through the complexities associated with the development of policy agendas and alternatives without becoming encumbered with details. Yet there are also limitations to this conception. In particular, the argument that the problem, policy, and political streams are independent suggests that the emergence of opportunities for shifting the limited attention of decisionmakers and, hence, joining the streams is not readily controlled. The role played by chance here is unclear. On reflection, it seems reasonable to expect that individuals in a policy community are constantly, and *simultaneously*, working at problem definition, policy design, and politicking. Such effort can be expected to increase the likelihood that windows of opportunity will open. Presumably, those who advocate policy change see things this way. We should not expect eager policy entrepreneurs to patiently "lie in wait" until the timing for agenda change is propitious. Rather, we might see them as making deliberate efforts to draw the attention of decisionmakers to given problems and, wherever possible, to force agenda change.

Beyond questioning how much the timing of agenda change depends upon interactions among "independent" process streams, we might ask a more general question about how the formal and informal structuring of behavior in the policymaking process serves to promote or inhibit efforts to force policy change. By emphasizing the most fluid aspects of the policymaking process, Kingdon devotes little attention to questions of structure (other than those having to do with the timing of events in the political stream). However, a reading of Kingdon that is informed by insights from the new institutionalism literature can be illuminating. The question we would most like to address is this: How much can individuals or small groups deliberately manipulate the policymaking process to achieve desired policy change? To develop an answer to this question, it is necessary to think about the relationship between agency and structure in the policymaking process.

Agency and Structure

In a disparate body of literature termed the "new institutionalism," political scientists recently have begun to show increasing interest in questions of agency and structure, looking at the ways that institutions affect political behavior.[3] The starting point for theorizing here is the understanding that, on the one hand, individuals exhibit *agency* as they engage in purposive action with the goal of changing aspects of social relations. At the same time, individuals are embedded in sets of social relations that serve to guide and constrain, or *structure*, their behavior. Important questions therefore emerge: How much freedom do individuals have to alter the structures in which they exist? How do structures sustain themselves? How do structures shape or deflect efforts to secure change? Since public policy consists of the laws in any given jurisdiction, and these laws structure relationships among members of society, conceptions of the policymaking process and discussions of policy change should directly address agency and structure issues.

Theorists working in the rational choice tradition have sought to understand why legislators and other government agents follow formal and informal rules when making policy choices. These institutions, or rules of the game, could be altered, and such alterations potentially could allow the instigators to realize their desired policy outcomes more readily. Why so much stability?[4] In answering this question, contributors to this branch of the new institutionalism have borrowed heavily from the work of economists interested in explaining the internal organization of firms and, more broadly, the variety of contractual arrangements found in capitalist societies.[5] For this reason, rational choice theorists argue that institutions increase the certainty that given actions will lead to given outcomes. In turn, this increased certainty supports greater cooperation among participants, who recognize that a good turn today is likely to be rewarded in the future if the institutional structure remains stable. Although the formal rules could be changed, and, typically, it would be in the short-term interests of some participants to make such changes, empirical observation suggests that the rules of the game change slowly. An argument made for why the rules of the game remain stable over long periods is that at the time when the rules are chosen, it is uncertain what policy outcomes will be stable under them. Thus, over time, legislative procedures and informal norms of behavior among representatives remain fairly stable.[6] Policy outcomes can be interpreted as the result of the strategic interactions among participants, all of whom know the rules they are operating under and have a reasonably good understanding of how the rules affect their chances of realizing their policy preferences.[7]

This rational choice version of the new institutionalism has much to offer those interested in explaining how proposed policy changes are processed by legislatures and how policy implementation occurs.[8] Given a stable set of rules and the espoused interests of participants in the decisionmaking process, we might reasonably predict policy choices and provide explanations of them. Do some institutional features also influence the selection process that results in the items found on the policy agenda? Rational choice theorists are now beginning to consider questions of this sort (Krehbiel 1991). One possibility is that those proposing particular changes have already looked ahead and reasoned back to determine (or at least reduce the list of) proposals worth making. There is much of value that this branch of the new institutionalism adds to our understanding of policymaking.[9] Yet, it is also fair to say that little of the work in this tradition pays attention to questions of *process*. The many simplifying assumptions that must be made to facilitate mathematical modeling often remove from consideration everything other than preferences and policy settings.

Paralleling the work by rational choice theorists, other political scientists have also begun to take renewed interest in institutions. Drawing heavily on insights from organizational sociology, March and Olsen (1989) seek to explore how political institutions contribute to stability and change in political life. According to these scholars, individuals behave in ways that are influenced not only by conceptions of self-interest but also by conceptions of duties and roles. Given less than full information without some guiding structure, individuals would face daunting problems when determining how to act in a broad range of situations. Accordingly, institutions serve to provide cues to actors about how to understand events and behave in given contexts. Politics is not just about making choices, it is also about constructing interpretations and meanings. This conception of politics and its guiding institutions can be seen as complementing, rather than supplanting, the rational choice conception and Kingdon's process streams conception. In this section I consider how "rediscovering institutions," in the sense of paying attention to the political structures discussed by March and Olsen, can enhance our understanding of the policymaking process. March and Olsen suggest ways of better understanding who gets to have influence in agenda setting, how policy learning occurs, and why policy change is sometimes quite abrupt and nonincremental in nature.

March and Olsen argue that in the policymaking process decisionmakers require advice on a broad range of issues because the decisionmakers themselves can be experts in only a few things. The quality of the advice they receive is critical: bad or misleading advice could be politically ruinous—yet many would-be advisors might seek (deliberately or in ignorance) to give advice of this sort. Decisionmakers therefore require ways to screen those who seek to influence them. Given time constraints, comprehensive evaluations of others is all but impossible, so decisionmakers must use shortcuts or heuristics to make their assessments. As March and Olsen (1989, 44) explain:

> Most individuals in politics most of the time will not be eyewitnesses to most relevant events. Both what they "see" and what they "like" will be dependent upon available sources of information, which of the available sources they are exposed to, and which of those they are exposed to they trust. Learning under such conditions becomes dependent both upon processes like discussion and persuasion, and upon relationships like trust and antagonism. . . . Individuals under such conditions will tend to like what those with whom they most frequently interact like.

Observing the dynamics of the situation, trusted advisors who enjoy frequent access to decisionmakers will go to considerable lengths to ensure that their advice remains sound. This suggests that the advisors will mull over new ideas and seek evidence of their workability long before deciding whether and how to advise decisionmakers about them. Therefore, policy networks in and around government can be seen as filters, sorting out the list of ideas that become candidates for consideration on government agendas. With time, what is essentially an informal filtering mechanism becomes indispensable for decisionmakers and thus attains a status similar to a set of formal procedures. Since trusted advisors will seek to avoid taking risks, we should expect this system to have a bias favoring incremental policy adjustments. As March and Olsen note, "Outcomes can be less significant—both behaviorally and ethically—than process" (1989, 51).

To gain influence in policymaking circles, an advocate of policy change must earn the respect and trust of others. At a minimum this means knowing a lot about how to forge and maintain good social relations, and doing a lot to develop a reputation as someone with a depth of understanding about the relevant issues and a commitment to the positions taken. This conception of how and why the filtering mechanisms work in policy communities helps us to make sense of Kingdon's list of qualities marking policy entrepreneurs. According to Kingdon (1995, 180–181), to receive a hearing, to attain even a chance of influencing policymaking, policy entrepreneurs must have qualities of three kinds. First, they must have some level of expertise, be able to speak for others (as powerful interest group leaders do), or hold a decisionmaking position. Second, they must be known for their political connections or their negotiating skills. Third, they must be persistent. On reflection, we see that all of these qualities serve to signal understanding of the policy issues at stake and serious commitment to the positions espoused; matters that decisionmakers and others in policy communities will interpret as evidence of trustworthiness.

To this point, I have discussed how political institutions surrounding the policymaking process itself structure the behavior of individuals within it. Beyond this, March and Olsen also provide insights into how the stabilizing effect of political institutions relating to specific policy areas serves to promote learning in policy communities. We should construe political institutions here to consist of the set of laws, bureaucratic organizations, and behavioral norms that structure day-to-day actions in specific policy areas. Such political institutions provide a high degree of order, but they are constantly under pressure to change because groups that find the current rules of the game unsatisfactory will push for their own concerns to be addressed. If, in response to such pressure institutions can adapt in incremental ways, then there is no need for policymakers to think deeply about the nature of the system and how alternative systems may promote overall improvements in outcomes. Learning occurs through increased understanding of current institutional arrangements and how they can adapt, but no new learning occurs in the sense of developing new knowledge of alternative institutional arrangements. Incremental adjustments serve to eliminate the incentives for searches for more thoroughgoing solutions. Thus, so long as institutions can adapt in incremental ways, long periods of institutional stability should be observed. Policy changes, other than incremental adjustments, will not occur.

Despite the apparent calm that might be observed in specific policy areas for long periods, it is possible that incrementally adjusting institutions will eventually become the focus of abrupt, nonincremental policy change. Systems that are essentially stable and that allow for incremental adjustments might reach a critical point at which they can no longer adapt to their environment as they had been able to in the past. In such a case a significant need for new knowledge might develop among policymakers, and here learning about alternative institutional structures might take place. New knowledge, coupled with a political will for change, can provide the impetus for nonincremental change. Once that change takes place, the cycle of incremental policy adjustments in response to pressures in the environment will once again begin and the incentive to learn will once again disappear. Based on this portrayal of institutional adaptation and change, March and Olsen suggest that political institutions "tend to produce relatively long periods of considerable stability punctuated by rather substantial, rather abrupt changes" (1989, 170). They argue that such stability punctuated by short bursts of abrupt change represent a highly efficient use of knowledge in policy communities.

In sum, the new institutionalism as presented by March and Olsen provides some useful insights into the nature of the policymaking process. However, these authors do not present a conception of the policymaking process rivaling the works of Lindblom (1968) and Kingdon (1995). Rather, March and Olsen's work constitutes a set of refinements of earlier studies that draw our attention to the ways that formal and informal rules help to structure behavior. In terms of thinking about the policymaking process, March and Olsen's arguments concerning trust and learning in policy communities and the antecedence of rapid institutional change are nonetheless quite valuable.

Policy Images and Policy Venues

Taken in total, scholarship on the policymaking process has provided a range of insights that advance our understanding of how the process operates. Frank Baumgartner and Bryan Jones (1993) show how a synthesis of these various contributions is both possible and enlightening, and in so doing present a conception of the policymaking process that accounts for stability punctuated by abrupt change. While essentially echoing March and Olsen's account of stability and change, this telling gives greater attention to the actual behaviors of the individuals who promote policy change. Baumgartner and Jones also delineate the incentives faced by participants in the policymaking process, explaining why individuals might seek to contribute to or resist nonincremental policy change.

Baumgartner and Jones argue that policy change will typically emerge when large numbers of people alter their views of particular issues relevant to the subsystem. "Issue definition . . . is the driving force in both stability and instability, primarily because issue definition has the potential for mobilizing the previously disinterested" (1993, 16).

The potential for change in policy is endemic, but when we look across the range of public policies in place at any time stability is the defining characteristic. Baumgartner and Jones explain this by noting two things. First, decisionmakers who could force policy change through enacting or amending legislation have limited concentration and can pay close attention to only a few issues at a time. Second, the political system is highly variegated, and within it there are many policy subsystems, or communities, made up of individuals and groups that have various (not necessarily shared) interests in specific areas of public policy. These subsystems are defined by the relevant laws and organizations that support the day-to-day administration of given policies. Hence, for the most part, within any subsystem, policy change occurs incrementally.

Those who exercise decisionmaking and administrative power within subsystems are said to be in control of "policy monopolies." These monopolies have two characteristics. They are built upon a set of institutional arrangements that limit access to policymaking in the relevant policy area. As well as this, the institutional arrangements are supported by "policy images" that can be communicated directly and simply through symbols and rhetoric. By way of formal structure, policy monopolies are akin to the "iron triangles" noted earlier in this chapter. However, "iron triangles" is a term that denotes the combined political power of legislative committee members, bureaucrats, and interest groups associated with particular policy areas and has a narrower definition than Baumgartner and Jones intend to convey. The specific roles of the individuals holding a policy monopoly can differ across policy areas and jurisdictions. Therefore, the nature of each of two policy monopolies operating at the local government level might be distinct from each other, and both might also be distinct from policy monopolies at the state or national government levels.

Under policy monopolies, members of the broader polity defer to the judgments of the "experts" who have specialized knowledge of the particular policy area. This knowledge might include a full understanding of the scope and limits of the relevant laws, the organization and allocation of power within the supporting bureaucratic structures, and relevant technical issues. Deference of this sort ensures that policy monopolies are immune from ongoing interference by the broader polity. But this system of deference and noninterference is largely contingent on the broader polity's members' continuing to receive positive images regarding activities in the policy subsystem. Negative images can serve as cues to alert politicians that policy reform is needed. Such reform is expected to manifest itself through nonincremental policy change, and this will typically bring a policy monopoly to an end.

Given their argument that policy images serve as the keys to stability and change in the policymaking process, Baumgartner and Jones devote much attention to how such images can be changed. This leads them to view problem definition as a central aspect of politics. In their telling, success in getting an item on the policy agenda is very likely to herald nonincremental policy change. "In the process of agenda-setting, the degree of public indifference to given problems changes dramatically. Since this is the structure on which policy subsystems are based, it should not be surprising if periods of agenda access are followed by dramatic changes in policy output" (1993, 20). The significant role ascribed here to problem definition and agenda setting calls for a careful explanation of how these predecision policy processes operate.

Baumgartner and Jones argue that policy entrepreneurs engage in problem definition with the express goal of changing policy. Those who find a particular set of policies unsatisfactory will strive to put a new interpretation on various activities and events. Argumentation and the creation of new understandings of issues are critical here. Policy entrepreneurs can be expected to devise new "causal stories" designed to draw attention to aspects of public policies and their effects that previously have been largely ignored.[10] The goal of such efforts is to attract the attention of potential allies in a struggle for policy change. If policy entrepreneurs can successfully win new allies who can help outsmart and vanquish opponents, then the possibility arises for bringing policy monopolies to an end. However, efforts of this sort are likely to meet with countermeasures from those who benefit from the status quo.

Baumgartner and Jones argue that advocates of policy change who find themselves stumped by supporters of the status quo can sometimes improve their chances of success by switching the venue in which debate occurs. Action of this sort, while difficult to engineer, has the potential to alter the alignment of power by drawing new sets of individuals or groups into the policy battle. Moving the debate from the legislative committee room to the public domain through media efforts can disarm opponents who have previously won battles through technical expertise, insider contacts, and skills at working the system. Also, venue change can increase the chances that a policy image, cherished by those benefiting from the status quo, might now change. In a new venue a new conception of a policy problem might catch on, producing a bandwagon of support for significant policy change.

Scholars who have developed conceptualizations of the policymaking process commonly claim that policy is often made within subsystems. The need for participants in policymaking to have high levels of expertise necessitates this kind of compartmentalization across policy areas. In the 1960s and 1970s discussion of iron triangles was common. However, following Hugh Heclo's (1978) introduction of the notion of "issue networks" and Jack L. Walker's (1981) discussion of "policy communities," increasing interest has been given to examining how loosely connected collections of individuals and groups work together to create and support stable, issue-specific policy settings. I now turn to reviewing a prominent representation of the policymaking process that has emerged from this new tradition. There is much here that serves to improve our understanding of policy communities and their internal dynamics in ways that complement insights offered by Kingdon and by Baumgartner and Jones.

Advocacy Coalitions

The Advocacy Coalition Framework is a concept developed by Paul Sabatier and a number of others in a series of articles and book chapters (especially Sabatier 1988 and Jenkins-Smith and Sabatier 1993). Sabatier defines an advocacy coalition as "people from a variety of positions (e.g., elected and agency officials, interest group leaders, researchers) who share a particular belief system—i.e., a set of basic values, causal assumptions, and problem perceptions—and who show a nontrivial degree of coordinated activity over time" (1988, 139). The "glue" that holds an advocacy coalition together is its members' shared beliefs over core policy matters. The framework assumes that members of coalitions will often disagree on minor matters, but that disagreement will be limited. Sabatier rejects the view that "coalitions of convenience" motivated by "short-term self-interest" can have lasting impact on policy directions. Once formed, coalitions seek to translate their shared beliefs into public policies or programs. Thus the actions and interactions of the advocacy coalitions are viewed as important for shaping policy. The site for these activities is the policy subsystem.

Sabatier describes a policy subsystem as a network of individuals from a variety of public and private organizations who are actively concerned with the maintenance and evolution of policy in a particular area. Policy subsystems are broad in scope, and at any given time may contain a number of advocacy coalitions—perhaps one dominant coalition, and one or two subordinate ones. According to Sabatier, policy subsystems consist of more than interest groups, administrative agencies, and legislative committees at a single level of government. They also contain journalists, researchers, and others who generate and disseminate policy ideas.

Within the framework nonincremental policy change is conceived as stemming from events outside the policy subsystem. These can include changes in socioeconomic conditions, changes in the systemic governing coalition, and the impacts of policy changes in other subsystems. Incremental policy changes can result from policy learning within the subsystem, and the learning can arise when the introduction of new ideas alters the beliefs of members of the advocacy coalitions. But there are other possible sources of change.

The Advocacy Coalition Framework provides a useful guide to thinking about the context in which policy changes take place and directs our attention to thinking about the ways that belief structures arise and adjust over time to bring stability to a policy subsystem. Although the framework identifies exogenous shocks as the potential sources of nonincremental policy change and policy learning as a potential source of incremental policy adjustment, it does not direct our attention to exploring the processes that determine when policy change will actually take place. Clearly, not all exogenous shocks and not all instances of policy learning translate into policy change. Thus we need to better understand why particular policy changes materialize. Another weakness of the framework is that it does not help us to explain changes in the composition of advocacy coalitions and how collective action problems are managed by coalition members. These limitations aside, however, the Advocacy Coalition Framework provides a useful addition to our understanding of how policymaking occurs.

An Emerging Consensus?

The works reviewed here, taken as a group, present a reasonably coherent portrait of the policymaking process. Of course there are differences in orientation and emphasis, and, given the amorphous and complex nature of policymaking, we should expect this. Yet frequently the scholars whose work I have discussed reach consistent conclusions about the types of interactions that support the development and maintenance of public policies. Thus we can distill an emerging consensus.

While all public policies, by definition, are ultimately based upon laws and authoritative decisions that are binding on all in society, their actual impacts are often quite circumscribed. Therefore, it makes sense that most citizens and most proximate decisionmakers most of the time give their attention to a limited range of public policies. We can expect that the greatest attention paid to any policy area will come from those who believe the quality of their day-to-day lives or their political futures are closely bound up with specific policy settings. The upshot of this is that, within any jurisdiction, there will be a large amount of fragmentation in terms of policy involvement. Realizing this, scholars commonly argue that each area of public policy is dominated by relatively small gatherings of actors. These gatherings have been variously described as iron triangles, issue networks, policy monopolies, or advocacy coalitions. Each description has a distinctive meaning. For the most part, these distinctions reflect the decisions that scholars have made over where to draw the boundaries separating off those actors whose involvement or interest in specific policy areas merits close study.

No matter what the area of policy, actual policymaking can take place at a number of levels. Legislators establish enacting legislation, but this usually becomes a source for the creation of even more policy. This additional policymaking might take place at the legislative level or at a more operational level.[11] As decisionmaking moves from the most general levels to the most specific, we can expect two things to happen. First, the number of actors attempting to influence policy will diminish. Second, policymaking will advance in an incremental fashion. Another way of conceptualizing this is to say that legislatures deal primarily with the establishment of the political institutions that broadly set policy directions in particular areas. These political institutions include the relevant laws and the supporting bureaucratic organizations. Establishing these political institutions or fundamentally altering how they operate constitute instances of policy change that are nonincremental in nature. That is to say, they are policy changes intended to disrupt established ways of doing things. Once in place, the political institutions generate their own policy through administrative rulings and through incremental decisions concerning day-to-day operations. As these political institutions mature, the collection of actors paying ongoing attention to policymaking will decrease to a small, stable set.

The maturation of political institutions is reflected not only in the stability of policy settings and organizational routines, but also in the emergence of specific policy images. These images can be thought of as summary evaluations of the policy area and its broader meaning. When maturation occurs it is possible to say that a policy monopoly exists. This means that the purposes of the given sets of policies and the conduct of those charged with administering them are widely accepted as reasonable and worthwhile. This does not mean that conflict disappears. However, under policy monopolies most conflict can be managed and defused without the need for significant policy change. Those who have a strong stake in maintaining the policy monopoly will work hard to ensure that the image associated with the policy area remains positive. Thus, when disagreements over policy emerge and threaten to adversely affect the relevant policy image, these individuals can be expected to make serious efforts to accommodate the demands of those calling for change.

Across all areas of public policy there is typically a lot of agreement about policy goals and a lot of stability in policy settings. Most policymaking involves nothing more than securing incremental policy adjustments. This is all to the good. Since public policy establishes appropriate modes of conduct in society and there are high costs associated with changing the rules of the game, long-term policy stability has many benefits. Still, all this stability suggests that much about the policymaking process is somewhat dull. Where do we look if we want to find policymaking characterized by intellectual discourse, screaming matches, head-banging efforts to achieve compromise, and the development and approval of significant policy innovation?

The most exciting aspects of the policymaking process come into play when new problems arise that cannot be addressed within preexisting policy settings or when fundamental disagreements arise over policy direction. At these times the relative calm normally surrounding a given policy area is disturbed. The policy conversation changes. Accepted policy images are challenged. Government actions or inactions that once seemed benign become the focus of penetrating questions. Such changes in the policy conversation are engineered by individuals and groups who, for any number of reasons, have become disenchanted with the old ways of doing things. Often in the literature on the policymaking process, these individuals or groups are said to be led by policy entrepreneurs. Although it is generally accepted that such actors cannot single-handedly prompt policy changes that reflect their policy preferences, well-planned efforts to change the policy conversation definitely appear able to set the scene for agenda change and, potentially, of policy change as well.

Efforts to change public policy in nonincremental ways require that the areas of interest become the focus of unusual amounts of attention. Those who ordinarily do not get involved in specific areas of policy join the debate and help define battle lines. The actions necessary to promote agenda change and create conditions favoring policy change are substantial. Occasionally, of course, little effort may be required to generate a consensus view that change is needed. However, more often we might expect that change comes only at the end of a long period in which policy entrepreneurs work hard to bring other people around to sharing their views about policy problems and how they can be solved.

Policy Entrepreneurs as Change Agents

The scholars whose representations of the policymaking process I have reviewed all make the point that there is room in this process for energetic, creative individuals to help stimulate or redirect debate about policy issues. They also emphasize that such people need not hold any particular position inside government. Kingdon (1995) and Baumgartner and Jones (1993) have gone even further on this point. In their conceptions of the policymaking process they suggest that change is often the product of the actions of a specific class of individuals, actors they term "policy entrepreneurs." As Kingdon tells us, policy entrepreneurs "could be in or out of government, in elected or appointed positions, in interest groups or research organizations. But their defining characteristic, much as in the case of a business entrepreneur, is their willingness to invest their resources—time, energy, reputation, and sometimes money—in the hope of a future return" (1995, 122). Over the past two decades, many other scholars have also made reference to the importance of policy entrepreneurs as agents of policy change. Thus, drawing upon a variety of discussions, it is possible to construct a general description of what it is that these policy entrepreneurs are said to do in the policymaking process. Ultimately, though, we want to develop a more nuanced description and critically explore the usefulness of the concept of the policy entrepreneur. This task is left for later chapters. For now, a general description is sufficient for establishing the focus of this study.

Among the activities that policy entrepreneurs engage in, the most important include identifying problems, networking in policy circles, shaping the terms of policy debates, and building coalitions to support policy change. Policy entrepreneurs can play a key role in identifying policy problems in ways that both attract the attention of decisionmakers and indicate appropriate policy responses. Yet, the task of problem definition is made all the harder when individuals and groups in positions of power have previously taken care to establish and maintain a given policy image. The policy entrepreneur must define problems in ways that are not readily dismissed by those who benefit from current policy settings.

This might mean highlighting specific aspects of the problem that others have previously noted, but arguing that these problems are closely related to others. To do this, new causal stories might need to be told about why these problems have been emerging.

Policy entrepreneurs must develop strategies for presenting their ideas to others in ways that will ensure they are taken seriously. This is why policy entrepreneurs spend large amounts of time networking in and around government. In so doing, they learn the "worldviews" of various members of the policymaking community and make contacts that can help build their credibility. Making these contacts allows policy entrepreneurs to determine what arguments will persuade others to support their policy ideas. For policy entrepreneurs operating at the state or local level, networking across jurisdictional boundaries can also be important for a few reasons. First, through these contacts they can learn more about the details of policy innovations elsewhere. Knowing these details can increase the credibility of policy entrepreneurs because they can then more readily give authoritative-sounding responses to questions or objections raised concerning a proposed policy innovation. Second, policy entrepreneurs may draw upon experts from other jurisdictions to give testimony on earlier experiences with the policy innovation. Third, networking across jurisdictions allows policy entrepreneurs to learn what strategies for selling a particular policy innovation have met with success elsewhere.

Policy entrepreneurs also work to shape the terms of the ensuing debate surrounding their proposed policy innovation. Steven Kelman suggests that "often . . . the face of the issue that people see—and hence the policy alternatives they support—is up for grabs" (1987, 28). While this might present opportunities for policy entrepreneurs, it also means that at any given point in a debate other individuals and groups might try to move the debate in new directions. In seeking support for their policy innovations policy entrepreneurs face choices about which issues to push and how to push them. Thus, arguments in support of policy change will sometimes have to be crafted in different ways for different audiences. The policy entrepreneurs must also be prepared to make adjustments to their policy proposals that take account of the interests and expectations of others. Doing this successfully while maintaining an image of integrity is clearly a task for the politically savvy.[12]

Crafting arguments in support of their proposed policy innovations is critical for policy entrepreneurs if they are to successfully sell their ideas to potential supporters. Frequently, policy entrepreneurs seek to assemble and maintain coalitions to support specific policy innovations. These can prove valuable political resources for a variety of reasons. A coalition can allow a policy entrepreneur to rapidly spread the word on a particular policy innovation among a policy community. But the communication flow here goes both ways. Therefore the coalition can serve as a useful device for gathering information on the views of others. Within the coalition, deliberation and debate can occur over how to ensure that the policy innovation is widely accepted as important and desirable. Finally, a coalition can serve as a vital resource when moving from the step of getting a policy issue on the government agenda to actually having it considered and adopted by a legislature.

The success of policy entrepreneurs in any one of these activities will influence their success in others. Policy entrepreneurs who carefully define policy problems and who make good use of networks of contacts will be better placed to make winning arguments in support of their proposed policy innovations. This, in turn, can give them leverage when it comes to coalition building. And the more effectively this is done, the greater the chances that their ideas will be accepted by decisionmakers.

This general description of policy entrepreneurs as derived from discussions in the literature on policymaking suggests that policy entrepreneurs may well play a significant part as agents for change. However, there are limits to previous treatments of policy entrepreneurs, and reasonable grounds exist for taking a somewhat skeptical view regarding their significance in the policymaking process. More work is needed to make the term "policy entrepreneur" into a useful concept and one that improves our understanding of the politics of policy change. Next, I provide a distillation of my thinking about policy entrepreneurship as it emerges in this book. I then present portraits of three individuals who appear to have served as policy entrepreneurs promoting the school choice idea in three states during the 1980s and early 1990s.

Keys to Policy Entrepreneurship

The discussion and evidence presented in this book suggest that policy entrepreneurs cannot simply assume that their actions will produce the outcomes they desire. Yet there are things that policy entrepreneurs can do to improve their chances of having a policy impact. Below I list six keys to policy entrepreneurship. Extracted from my broader discussion, these statements necessarily appear bald and devoid of nuance. This is intentional. These keys should be read both as the distillation of topics and ideas examined more closely throughout the book and as an invitation to further reading.

1. Policy entrepreneurs must be *creative* and *insightful*, able to see how proposing particular policy innovations could alter the nature of policy debates.
2. Policy entrepreneurs must be *socially perceptive*, able to see problems and issues from a range of perspectives, so that they can propose policy innovations that hold broad appeal.
3. Policy entrepreneurs must be *able to mix in a variety of social and political settings*, so that they can readily acquire valuable information and use their contacts to advantage in pursuit of policy change.
4. Policy entrepreneurs must be *able to argue persuasively*; often this will mean making different arguments to different groups while keeping the overall story consistent.
5. Policy entrepreneurs must be *strategic team builders*, able to determine the type of coalition best able to support their pursuit of policy change.
6. Policy entrepreneurs must be *prepared to lead by example*, to create "prefigurative forms" of the policy innovations they seek to introduce.

Policy Entrepreneurs and the Rise of School Choice

The introduction of school choice represents an important policy change. However, some advocates of the idea interpret the changes so far as being of little significance. Terry M. Moe argues that "when choice-based reforms actually get adopted, they tend to be limited. Although often touted as revolutionary, they are in fact incremental changes that, of political necessity, are simply grafted onto the existing system without altering its fundamentals" (1995, 7). To the extent that the school choice initiatives put in place over the past decade or so have not transformed the whole system of public education in the ways that Moe favors, this argument is correct. However, Moe fails to recognize that these policy changes represent an acceptance by politicians that the old ways of doing things are problematic. Further, as evidence from many states now demonstrates, small steps like the introduction of open-enrollment plans have been followed by the introduction of other choice-based reforms, like charter schools. At every step these changes have developed constituencies prepared to go into political battle to keep them in place and to extend their reach. Therefore, these limited steps represent a challenge to previous practices in the area of public education and they are most appropriately viewed as nonincremental changes.

To what extent have policy entrepreneurs been active in promoting the school choice idea and articulating it so that it gets onto state legislative agendas? Some existing evidence suggests that policy entrepreneurs have done much to promote the school choice idea. Of course, instances can be observed where little effort has been required to have the idea considered and even adopted by a state legislature. As Ted Kolderie, a close observer of the school choice movement, has said to me, "I think you have some people that are just copying. They've heard about this . . . idea and they say, 'Let's have one of these too,' get hold of it, lump it through, but whoever's in charge of it said, you know, 'Don't make any waves.' " Here, I present portraits of three people who have worked at the state level to secure the adoption of school choice legislation. Each has done a lot more than just copy the ideas of others, and all have been prepared to rock the boat. Perhaps not surprisingly, then, their actions have led to important policy changes, and many other individuals and groups frustrated with the current system of public education have turned to them for advice on how to build support for the school choice idea.

Joe Nathan in Minnesota

Joe Nathan is a former Minnesota public school teacher who currently serves as the director of the Center for School Change at the University of Minnesota's Hubert H. Humphrey Institute of Public Affairs. Nathan came of age intellectually in the late 1960s when he became active in the civil rights movement. Thus he views educational liberty as a matter of civil rights. During the 1970s Nathan honed his educational and political skills in the alternative schools movement (Cookson 1994, 43). With others he worked to develop the St. Paul Open School, the sort of school envisaged by Mario Fantini in his proposal for public school vouchers. The idea of the St. Paul Open School was to promote learning by shaping teaching to the needs of the individual students and giving them careful guidance and feedback.

Nathan started out believing that this sort of education would be good for everyone. However, some students and parents felt that they needed a stricter program. A fundamental school was then set up as well, and some of the teachers who agreed on the value of a stricter program transferred there from the open school. Through this process Nathan came to realize "there is no one *best* program for all students—or all teachers." Of the open school and the fundamental school, Nathan has said: "The parents and the educators of the two programs . . . disagreed almost totally on how schools should be organized and instruction provided" (Nathan 1989, 12). However, he strongly believed that both groups had the right to develop educational approaches that best matched their preferences. This insight was the impetus to his further work to extend educational choice in Minnesota. Nathan's work with open schools helped to develop a strong support group for alternative education, and this proved politically useful as he began to work toward achieving school choice for Minnesota.

During the early 1980s Nathan started working with several others in Minnesota, like Ted Kolderie of the Citizens League, and university professor and state legislator John Brandl. Together they pushed for legislative changes that would permit school choice. According to Nancy C. Roberts and Paula J. King (1996), this team of policy entrepreneurs worked closely for several years to support the school choice idea. Writing and generating ideas were more than intellectual exercises for this group: during the 1980s they developed positions that would convince policymakers of the feasibility of a school choice approach. Having their ideas read, heard, debated, and accepted by as many people as possible was extremely important (see King 1988, 260). The entrepreneurs also lobbied Minnesota state legislators, helped with the development of bills, set up testimony, and served on advisory taskforces. They also linked their efforts in Minnesota with efforts on the national educational scene. They did this by writing reports, giving speeches, networking, and working with members of the National Governors' Association (see King 1988, 398).[13]

Early on in their efforts to secure school choice, Nathan and his allies decided that there was little point in getting others to change their views through compliance or passive acceptance. Rather, they sought to convince people by teaching them new ways of looking at education issues. To this end, they deliberately worked at transforming people's "worldviews" by "challenging the premises—givens—on which the education system was based" (King 1988, 221). In pushing for public school reform

Nathan did not deny that the state's education system was among the best in the nation, judged by such objective measures as graduation rates and test scores. His concern was that public education had grown complacent, resistant to creative thinking about improvement, and, above all, demanding of increased financial support during a time of austerity (Elmore 1991, 60).

In pushing for school choice Nathan made a number of important points. First, he argued that choice would stimulate competition and motivate schools and districts to pursue productive reforms and enhance their course offerings. Second, he said that choice would create programs that were more responsive to student needs and would increase parental participation and loyalty. Finally, he argued that a state choice initiative would improve educational equity by extending to poorer families an option that already existed for families who could afford to move to better districts or send their children to private schools.

Adoption of school choice in Minnesota occurred in several steps. At each step Nathan and his allies pushed for more radical changes than they eventually won, but they used each success as a basis for moving a few more steps in the direction of the goals they sought. The most heralded piece of legislation came in 1987, when the School District Enrollment Options program was authorized.[14] This interdistrict enrollment option allows families and students to apply to enroll in any school district other than the one in which they reside. Along with the interdistrict school choice authorized by the state, local districts have also been encouraged to allow intradistrict school choice, and many have made such arrangements. Most important, since 1989 all students residing in Minneapolis and St. Paul must actively choose the schools they attend. Following the adoption of school choice in Minnesota, Joe Nathan has often testified in legislatures across the country in support of the school choice idea. Increasingly, he has become associated with the charter schools movement and he was a key player in achieving the passage of the nation's first charter schools law in Minnesota in 1991.

Polly Williams in Wisconsin

Polly Williams is an African American from Milwaukee who has been a Democratic assemblywoman in the Wisconsin legislature since the early 1980s. Williams gained national prominence in 1990 when she successfully sponsored the bill introducing publicly funded vouchers to enable children from low-income families currently enrolled in Milwaukee public schools to attend private schools. Since then many articles and opinion pieces on Williams have appeared in the national media.[15]

Often portrayed as controversial and outspoken, Polly Williams was inspired to push her school choice plan partly as a result of her experiences as a parent. She describes herself as a fighter. At one time Polly Williams was a single mother raising four children and depending on welfare. Williams has often recalled an episode from her child-rearing days: When she was notified that her daughter would be bused to a public school across town, Williams grew angry because busing to her meant exchanging one bad school for another. Williams requested an exemption but it was rejected, and when she went to the school board to make an oral appeal she lost. She did not leave the building, but walked into the superintendent's office and left a note for him on his desk. She wrote: "My name is Polly Williams, and I live on Burleigh Street. My daughter will stay home before I'll let her be bused. You may send the police to arrest me." Finally the transfer request was approved.

As a mother, Williams was determined to provide her children with the best possible education. Consequently, she went to considerable effort to save enough money to send them to private school through the eighth grade. But because she could not afford private high school tuitions, her children later transferred to a public school. These experiences inspired Williams to fight for changes that would help other poor parents obtain quality education for their children. As she has quipped, "We have desegregation, integration, and transportation. We still don't have education."

When Williams wrote her school choice bill she spread the word in church basements and neighborhood beauty salons. She told the parents that she rallied, "We want school choice, and we will have it." When the bill was moving slowly through the legislature, Williams brought many parents to attend legislative hearings at the Milwaukee public schools administration building. She was determined that if the education establishment was to deny parents the right to choose, then it would do so facing those people directly. Before this time, Williams had believed that state education administrators took the view that poor African-American families needed to be protected from making inappropriate decisions regarding their children's education. However, as she learned more about how the public school system worked, she came to believe that much of the talk about caring for parents and their children was really a cover for bureaucratic self-interest.

To push her bill through the legislature, Williams teamed up with conservative Democrats, Republicans, and other African American members of the assembly. Williams and her supporters then had the bill approved as part of the biennial budget process, which meant that the bill avoided the floor attention that might have made its passage more difficult. In previous years, Wisconsin Governor Tommy Thompson had proposed fairly broad-based private school voucher plans for the state and he had also endorsed open enrollment (see Witte and Rigdon 1993, 108). These efforts went nowhere, in part because of strong opposition from teachers' unions. With the teamwork Williams promoted, things were different. As one commentator has observed, "Unlikely alliances like these don't happen every day. When they do, you can feel the ground under the status quo start to shake."

Paul DeWeese in Michigan

Paul DeWeese is an emergency room physician who lives in Lansing.[16] He became interested in the school choice issue as a result of his experiences living in a poor area of Detroit around 1980, when he was doing a medical residency. At that time he observed the closing of a small private school in his neighborhood. From what he could tell, the school was very good. The school closed, however, because of lack of funds, and the children in the school then had to attend the local public school. DeWeese has observed that "this was very frustrating to the parents because the local public schools within that area were everything that this local independent school was not. There was violence in the halls. . . . The teachers didn't seem to care. The parents did not feel involved."

This episode led DeWeese to ask why public policy was organized in a way that prevented parents from exercising school choice, even when they had a lot of information about what works well for their children. DeWeese also began to question the way that we distinguish between public and private schools. "What we've done as a society is we've arbitrarily said that a school is public, not by how well it serves children, but if it's owned and operated by the government." DeWeese thought a lot about these issues but he did not do anything about them at that stage.

Five years after seeing the small private school close DeWeese began looking to buy a home in Lansing. He had children who would soon be attending school and he remembers telling the realtor to "just show me the homes where there are good schools." According to DeWeese, this is when things came full circle for him from what he had observed in Detroit. "I began to realize how very important it is to me as a parent to have a kind of sense of control. That somehow this system just doesn't assign my kids to a school. . . . That if the school system isn't meeting their needs, I can take them out, I can move to a different location, or I can get them into private school."

DeWeese began to talk to others about this experience and realized that it is common for middle- and upper-middle-class people to choose their residential location with the quality of the local schools in mind. This made him desire to seek changes for people who could not exercise such choice, people like his friends from his old neighborhood in Detroit. In 1987 he began to talk seriously with others about changing public policy. He began to volunteer to talk to various groups about the kinds of strategies that could be used to bring about change in Michigan.

Paul DeWeese went on to construct a coalition called TEACH Michigan.[17] This coalition was intended to promote the introduction of a full voucher program in the state, a policy change that would require voter-supported constitutional change. Partly due to the networking efforts of DeWeese and other coalition members, an open-enrollment school choice plan was first considered by the Michigan legislature in 1989. In 1990 legislation was passed that made provision for interdistrict public school choice. However, DeWeese and his allies did not see this legislation as providing the opportunity for demonstrating the workability of a voucher program. Hence they continued to work toward their original goal. When the idea of charter schools was adopted in Minnesota and California, people in Michigan began expressing interest in the idea. While also falling short of the program DeWeese desired, the charter schools approach did appear to provide an excellent vehicle for making the voucher idea more acceptable to the wider public. Charter schools could serve to introduce school choice "in an incremental kind of way, a non-threatening kind of way, so that [members of the general public] could look in their own community or their own region of the state, and they could identify choice schools that were getting government money, they could see them working, they could see the parents choosing, and the parents happier because their kids were in schools they thought were better." Thus DeWeese and others from TEACH worked closely with

Governor John Engler to achieve the legislation necessary for charter schools to begin in the state. The bill was originally introduced in the legislature in 1992, but no action was taken until 1993, when the charter schools legislation was passed.

Emerging Questions

The three individuals discussed here appear to have promoted the school choice idea to the point where it gained sufficient support to be considered and adopted as a policy by the relevant state legislatures. Thus they could be said to be school choice policy entrepreneurs. However, we might question whether other factors were also at play here that, in combination, mattered more than the efforts of these individuals. Further, even if we could satisfy ourselves that Joe Nathan, Polly Williams, and Paul DeWeese were policy entrepreneurs who really made a difference, we might worry that they represent exceptional cases. How sure could we be that other instances of state legislative consideration and adoption of the school choice idea were also caused—at least to some reasonable degree—by the actions of individuals identifiable as policy entrepreneurs? And how sure could we be of the reliability of our identification methods?

Summary

The previous conceptions of the policymaking process presented here, and the explanations they provide for how policy change occurs, indicate that a role exists for policy entrepreneurs in drawing attention to policy ideas and, thus, stimulating policy change. But seeing policy entrepreneurs as primarily identifiable by the arguments they make—and how they make them—actually takes us only a short distance when thinking about the relationship between policy entrepreneurs and policy change. Using these identifying criteria, someone could almost always be found to fit the bill of change agent. Further, since policy change emerges only after a consensus has formed that change is desirable, an incentive exists for various individuals to take the credit for prompting such change, even if they did not. Thus, in light of a policy change, we should expect not only that a "policy entrepreneur" could be found but that various individuals will be claiming that they were the ones who mattered. Many participants in the policymaking process will want to be able to say that without them and the arguments they made to those around them, nothing would have happened. Given the complexity of the process, potentially many people would, in fact, be justified in making such a claim. For this reason we need to ensure that we define policy entrepreneurs in a manner that discriminates as clearly as possible among those who should and those who should not be conferred with the title.

I am confident that Joe Nathan, Polly Williams, and Paul DeWeese represent a class of actors who can, and often do, make a difference in the policymaking process. However, to make a convincing argument that individuals like this constitute policy entrepreneurs and that they often serve to promote policy innovations, significant effort must be put into theory construction and empirical testing of that theory. In what follows, I seek to do that.

Notes

1. Thorstein Veblen ([1898] 1919, 73) is the source of the description of man as "a lightning calculator of pleasures and pains." Veblen believed this description, which is implicit in much orthodox economic theory, to be impoverished and inaccurate.

2. I borrow this description of the approach from Hank C. Jenkins-Smith and Paul A. Sabatier (1993).

3. See Hall and Taylor (1996) for a useful review of alternative approaches.

4. This question is the title of an article written on the subject of policy stability by Gordon Tullock in 1981.

5. For a useful review and discussion, see Eggerttson (1990), especially chapter 3.

6. For a complete discussion of this matter, see Shepsle (1979).

7. Others, especially Terry Moe (1991), have argued that the institutions of democracy are essentially counterproductive. In creating uncertainty about future power relations and forcing policymakers to compromise with their opponents, these institutions are construed as the source of agencies and, more broadly, policy rules that are destined to be at best inefficient and at worst "organizational nightmares."

8. Murray J. Horn (1995) provides a good review of the literature.

9. For example, discussions of the origins of regulatory regimes and of congressional oversight as a check on bureaucratic discretion are quite insightful. See, for instance, essays in McCubbins and Sullivan (1987) and Banks and Hanushek (1995).

10. Baumgartner and Jones borrow the notion of "causal stories" from Deborah Stone. See Stone (1988, 1997).

11. For a discussion of policymaking during implementation, see Goggin (1987).

12. For a discussion of applied political strategy in the policy realm, see Bardach (1972).

13. King's evidence is used as the basis for much of the discussion presented in Roberts and King (1996).

14. Information regarding the political and policy issues surrounding the Minnesota school choice plan, the details of the plan itself, and evidence of its impact on student performance have been presented in many reports, articles, and book chapters. See, for instance, Boyer (1992, 51–55), Brandl (1989), Chubb and Moe (1990, 210), Elmore (1991, 59–61), Montano (1989), and Nathan and Jennings (1990).

15. The information provided here draws in particular from portraits of Polly Williams presented by Kraar (1991) and Norquist (1993).

16. Information and quotes that follow are taken from conversations with Paul DeWeese conducted in 1994 and 1995. With his permission the conversations were recorded.

17. TEACH stands for "Towards Educational Accountability and Choice."

THREE

Entrepreneurs and the Market Process

Increasingly, political scientists discussing agenda setting, the legislative process, policymaking, and policy change have come to note the importance of actors whom they often refer to as public entrepreneurs, political entrepreneurs, or policy entrepreneurs. But throughout these discussions the meaning of entrepreneurship in political settings has frequently been left vague. Typically, the terms public entrepreneur, political entrepreneur, and policy entrepreneur are treated as interchangeable. Further, while the political importance of particular actors has been emphasized, little effort has been made to explain just *why* they should be labeled as *entrepreneurs*. What makes them worthy of the description? Why not call them innovators or leaders or strategists? Are these political actors *literally* entrepreneurs in the sense that economists and scholars of business use the term? Or are there key differences in usage? Most previous discussions of entrepreneurs in politics have been conducted without as much as an acknowledgment of these questions.

In contemplating the behaviors of various actors in political settings, I have come to think that referring to them as entrepreneurs is, in fact, reasonable. I hold the view that entrepreneurial actors exist and can be identified in politics, and that they are appropriately named since they share important characteristics with their counterparts in the marketplace. However, more effort must be made to clarify precisely what role entrepreneurs play in politics and why it is appropriate to label various individuals as entrepreneurial. In collaboration with Mark Schneider and

Paul Teske, I have gone some way in this direction by exploring the actions of individuals in the local political setting whom we termed "public entrepreneurs" (see Schneider and Teske with Mintrom, 1995). But much work remains to be done.

In this chapter and the one to follow, I provide a discussion of the concept of the entrepreneur as a key figure in the market process and how that concept has been developed over time. The description that I construct of the entrepreneur is designed to provide a solid foundation upon which to subsequently develop a clearer description of policy entrepreneurs. Of course, the idea of leaping over this initial discussion of entrepreneurs in the market process and plunging directly into a discussion of policy entrepreneurs holds some appeal. But the basis for that appeal is shallow, and I think such an approach would be mistaken. At best, it would avoid discussion of a few points that relate only to the role of entrepreneurs in the marketplace. At worst, it would open the possibility for our discussion of policy entrepreneurs to be fraught with conceptual blind spots. This, I would argue, is the very source of the weakness of previous discussions where the term *entrepreneur* has been poorly defined.

Thinking initially about the activities of entrepreneurs in the marketplace makes it all the easier to systematically discuss the parallels and overlaps between entrepreneurship here and entrepreneurship in the policymaking process. The reward for working through a discussion of entrepreneurs and market processes is a strengthening of our understanding of policy entrepreneurship. Such strengthening holds the promise of making the concept of the policy entrepreneur a more valuable tool for social scientists and policy scholars to work with. That, I suggest, is a reward worth seeking.

Theorizing about Entrepreneurs

Over the centuries many economists have discussed the role and importance of entrepreneurs as actors in the market process. Of these discussions, several are generally held to be significant contributions. However, as Mark Casson (1982) has noted, these contributions do not reflect a cumulative effort. The economic literature concerning entrepreneurs has not produced a coherent body of theory. The disjointed nature of these discussions of entrepreneurs starts making sense when we note the very different concerns that have motivated each of the major contributors. Lack of coherence can also be attributed to the fact that mainstream economic theorists, who for the most part have engaged in cumulative explorations, have all but ignored the role of the entrepreneur for well over a century. It is no wonder then that theories of the entrepreneur appear almost as fugitive pieces within the broader body of economic literature.

Richard Cantillon is generally credited with introducing the term *entrepreneur* into economic discourse in his essay concerning "the circulation and exchange of goods and merchandise" published posthumously in 1755. Writing in French (although he was, in fact, of Irish origin), Cantillon explored the actions of the merchants or middlemen who go between agricultural producers in the countryside and consumers in the towns. These entrepreneurs buy goods for a prearranged price but sell at a price that cannot be arranged in advance. Hence, as suppliers of certainty to others with whom they contract, Cantillon suggested that entrepreneurs stand to gain if their foresight is correct and to lose if they are wrong. Only if they sell goods at prices above contracted fixed costs do they gain. Cantillon went on to argue that anyone who willingly accepts uncertainty regarding the return on activity constitutes an entrepreneur. Even though his discussion focused on the merchants who go between producers and consumers, the implication was that all economic actors could be divided into two broad groups: those who receive fixed incomes and those who receive uncertain incomes. According to Cantillon this second group, the entrepreneurs, were central actors within market economies.

From the fifteenth century, several English terms were used to describe economic actors prepared to engage in transactions for uncertain returns, such as land speculators, farmers, and directors of public works projects. These terms also included "adventurer," "projector," and "undertaker." Of these terms, the one that came into most common parlance was undertaker, and this is the term that was used in translating Cantillon's term entrepreneur into English. By the time Adam Smith wrote *The Wealth of Nations* in 1776, the term undertaker had come to mean any ordinary businessman. Smith suggested that a more appropriate term would be "capitalist." This is perhaps not surprising, since in Britain and elsewhere at this time, ownership of capital was required for anyone to engage in the sort of speculative activities associated with entrepreneurship. For the most part, this practice of associating the entrepreneur with the business owner has stuck, but over time theorists have come to see that the same individual may play multiple roles, and that entrepreneurship per se might be a small part of the general activities of an economic agent (see, for example, Schumpeter 1934 on this point). As William J. Baumol laments, it is unfortunate that the term "adventurer" went out of currency as a descriptor of the individuals we have come to term entrepreneurs (1993, 12). After all, it is those economic agents who are sufficiently imaginative and adventurous to willingly engage uncertainty, step outside day-to-day routine, and have the courage of their convictions that have typically been seen as quintessential entrepreneurs.

Jean-Baptiste Say (1821) is credited with giving the entrepreneur prominence in economic discourse. According to Say, the identifying feature of the entrepreneur was the ability to make good judgments concerning the estimation of needs and ways of satisfying them. Say did not consider uncertainty of income to characterize the entrepreneur. Following Say, the economic theorists who have made the most significant contributions to our understanding of entrepreneurship include Knight (1921), Schumpeter (1934), Kirzner (1973), Leibenstein (1978), Casson (1982), and Baumol (1993). I will now briefly discuss the main themes of the contributions of each of these theorists. I offer more detailed discussion of these themes and their implications later in the chapter.

The principle focus of Frank H. Knight's contribution was the management of uncertainty. In the presence of uncertainty Knight argued that "the actual execution of activity, becomes in a real sense a secondary part of life; the primary problem or function is deciding what to do and how to do it" (1921, 268). Knight claimed that it is entrepreneurs who make these decisions in the face of uncertainty and carry responsibility for them. To that extent, the entrepreneur attempts to manage uncertainty and, in making decisions, displays confidence in his own ability by assuming the risk of loss. The decisions made by the entrepreneur go beyond selecting product types and identifying markets to enter. They also have to do with the details of management because, given uncertainty, internal organization of the firm can no longer be construed as a matter of indifference or of mechanical detail.

Joseph H. Schumpeter (1934) presented a view of entrepreneurial activity that was at odds with Knight's. According to Schumpeter, the defining characteristic of entrepreneurs is their penchant for innovation, for developing the "new combination of means of production" (1934, 74). Because this function may be performed by any number of people in and around a business firm, Schumpeter argued that risk bearing could not be construed as an identifying characteristic of the entrepreneur. In his view innovation could take place in different areas of activities, and any new approach that contributes to profit was seen as the domain of the entrepreneur. Thus the entrepreneur could develop and market new products or improve the quality of an existing good. The entrepreneur could also introduce a new method of production, or open up a new market (either on the supply side or the demand side), or create a new type of business organization to increase profit. Through these actions the entrepreneur engages in what Schumpeter termed "creative destruction." In opening new opportunities for profit and making old approaches uncompetitive, the innovations introduced by the entrepreneur in each of these areas all destroy older ways of doing things, and incessantly create new ones.

Working out of the Austrian School of economics, Israel M. Kirzner (1973) has taken the view that the defining characteristic of the entrepreneur is neither risk taking nor innovation, but alertness to profit opportunities. The hallmark of Austrian economics, as exemplified in the works of Friedrich A. von Hayek and Ludwig E. von Mises and their followers, is the emphasis given to the study of market process. In the Austrian approach the possibility of equilibrium in specific markets is treated as suspect, as, of course, is the broader notion of general equilibrium. Therefore, contributors focus on exploring the effects of change, error, and imperfections in markets and in human ability to acquire and process relevant information. Profit opportunities arise only in a state of disequilibrium. Hence, according to Kirzner, through their creative acts of discovery entrepreneurs play a vital role in bringing markets closer to equilibrium. One criticism that is readily made of this perspective is that it tends to emphasize the arbitrage function of the entrepreneur rather than the innovation, organizational, and leadership functions.

Harvey Leibenstein (1978) shares Kirzner's view that the defining characteristic of the entrepreneur is alertness to profit opportunities. However, he came to this view through the development of his general X-efficiency theory, which portrays inefficiency as a normal state of affairs, even in markets that appear to be in equilibrium. According to Leibenstein, we must distinguish between the allocation of inputs and the effective use of these inputs in decisionmaking units. X-inefficiency arises from differences in motivation levels across individuals. These differences mean that no unique production function will emerge in an industry, an outcome that is at odds with a key assumption of neoclassical microeconomics. Pervasive inefficiency provides many opportunities for entrepreneurial activity. Leibenstein argues that innovative entrepreneurs attempt to determine efficient production processes and coordinate productive activities across different markets. Establishing effective channels for communicating relevant market information and improving the motivation of employees are thus seen by Leibenstein as potential sources of reward for entrepreneurial behavior.

Mark Casson (1982) developed a theory of the entrepreneur that he attempted to embed in the tradition of neoclassical microeconomics. To do so, Casson suggested that entrepreneurs are characteristically different from other economic agents in that they have more information. Hence, according to Casson, "an entrepreneur is someone who specializes in taking judgmental decisions about the coordination of scarce resources" (1982, 23). In Casson's view a judgmental decision is one where different individuals, sharing the same objectives and acting under similar circumstances, would make different choices. The differences arise because the individuals have different perceptions of the situation arising from different access to information, or different interpretations of it. In seeing the entrepreneur as someone who makes decisions about the coordination of resources, Casson sought to emphasize that the entrepreneur is an agent of change.

In the most recent effort of an economist to theorize about entrepreneurs, William Baumol (1993) argued that the role of the entrepreneur is to locate new ideas and put them into effect. To do this entrepreneurs must lead and inspire others, and they must not become complacent, because the ideas that will bring additional profits today will receive only normal profits in the future. Baumol describes the entrepreneur as

> any member of the economy whose activities are in some manner novel, and entail the use of imagination, boldness, ingenuity, leadership, persistence, and determination in the pursuit of wealth, power, and position, though not necessarily in that order. In other words, the term is meant to encompass all ***nonroutine*** activities by those who direct the economic activities of larger or smaller groups or organizations. (1993, 7–8)

For Baumol entrepreneurs are much like the Schumpeterian innovator. However, Baumol construes "innovator" more broadly than Schumpeter and, in so doing, improves our ability to identify entrepreneurial action across a range of business activities.

In theorizing about entrepreneurs the scholars mentioned here have all made contributions that, through triangulation rather than cumulative effort, give us important insights into the role of the entrepreneur in the market process. As I mentioned earlier, however, in developing their theories all these scholars have either implicitly or explicitly challenged key assumptions associated with mainstream microeconomic theory. In fact, in standard economic treatments of the market and the market economy, it is difficult to find any discussion of the entrepreneur at all. As Baumol has said, in neoclassical microeconomics "the entrepreneur has been read out of the model" (1993, 13). To find out why this is the case I next discuss the approach to theorizing about the market process embodied in mainstream microeconomics.

Theorizing without the Entrepreneur

The entrepreneur disappeared from mainstream economic theorizing as contributors attempted to produce elegant, formal models of the operation of markets and the decisionmaking processes of households and firms. In the British tradition Adam Smith (1776) set the climate for this development. Like Richard Cantillon (1755), Smith was interested in producing a general understanding of the market economy, the circular flow of income, and interdependences within the system. But the approach Smith used was distinctive. Intimately acquainted with the work of Sir Isaac Newton, in developing his theory Smith attempted to emulate Newtonian physics. In Newton's system universal order is given one fundamental motivational force, gravity. In constructing a counterpart theory to explain the workings of the market economy, Smith argued that self-interest should be taken as the fundamental motivational force. Of course, this need not rule out the role of the entrepreneur. However, because Smith associated entrepreneurship with the role of the capitalist owner of the firm, he reserved no special place for the entrepreneur in his theory. Indeed, Smith's focus on discovering the systematic or persistent forces that lead all prices to be "continually gravitating" to their "natural" levels, drew attention away from distinguishing among types of capitalists.

The influence of Newtonian physics, so prevalent in Smith's theory, became more pronounced in subsequent efforts to develop economic thought into a science. In particular, the practical expression of Newtonian physics in the mathematics of classical mechanics proved enormously important for Alfred Marshall and his continental contemporaries as they attempted to bring greater precision to the theories of their classical predecessors. In this emerging body of work, summarized to considerable degree in Marshall's *Principles of Economics* (1890), emphasis was placed on establishing the conditions under which equilibrium could be expected to emerge both in a single market and in the economy as a whole. Although Marshall recognized the interrelated and dynamic nature of market processes, for the purposes of model building and developing deductive intuitions he worked within the comparative statics framework.[1]

Since Alfred Marshall applied mathematical techniques to explore concepts developed by the classical economists, it has become common practice in the discipline of economics to develop models involving either optimization analysis or equilibrium analysis. In building models of behavior economists typically identify the agents of interest, such as households or firms, and then specify the choices that are feasible for them and how the choices of other agents serve as constraints.

To be at all useful, any model requires the use of facilitating assumptions to isolate the essential features of the phenomenon under investigation. In the neoclassical tradition, a number of key assumptions have typically been made concerning the characteristics of the agents of interest and the nature of the market. For the purpose of understanding how the entrepreneur was expunged from the neoclassical framework, I next briefly note and discuss the implications of some of the assumptions frequently found in neoclassical models. I do not wish to imply that all models in the neoclassical tradition contain all of these assumptions. In fact, much of the effort that economists have put into theory construction and model building over the years has concerned relaxing one or more of these assumptions and assessing the impacts of these changes in terms of the behavior of economic agents and equilibrium outcomes. That said, however, the preponderance of efforts to employ the neoclassical market model to assess microeconomic phenomena embody all or most of the following assumptions. Frequently, other assumptions are also made. Hence the listing that follows is incomplete, but I believe it contains the major assumptions associated with the neoclassical market model as it has been applied to a staggering array of economic activities.

The neoclassical model assumes a steady-state or stationary economy. It is designed only to explore the effects of small changes in quantities and prices, referred to as changes at the margins. The model is not equipped to deal with major changes. There is no potential for the creation of new products or new markets or, indeed, for any creativity on the part of economic agents. For the purposes of understanding the workings of well-established markets, incorporating this steady-state assumption into a model is entirely reasonable. However, this assumption removes the potential for exploring how new markets for new goods and services develop.

Relatedly, the neoclassical model assumes perfect competition among economic agents. By definition, then, under perfect competition there can be no sustainable above-normal profits. No incentive exists for economic agents to adjust their buying or selling plans other than, perhaps, to occasionally engage in brief periods of arbitrage activity to take advantage of minor perturbations in prices. The model also assumes that the costs of exchange are zero. As a result, contact between buyers and sellers is assumed to be readily organized. The act of seeking out buyers and sellers and the search costs that such activity incurs are not taken into account in this model. Hence entrepreneurial actions designed to reduce these costs have no place here.

Next, the neoclassical model assumes that all goods are homogeneous and that they can be defined by just two attributes, price and quantity. Further, buyers in particular markets are assumed to be homogeneous. As a result, there is no possibility for modeling the actions that agents take to differentiate their products and to engage in market segmentation. No personal relationships are allowed for by these models. Yet, as Friedrich A. von Hayek ([1946] 1948, 97) observed, much of actual market behavior involves competition among sellers for the loyalty and trust of buyers.

Finally, the neoclassical model assumes perfect information among producers concerning the production function for the homogeneous product traded in the perfectly competitive markets. The model also assumes ease of entry and exit from markets. Given this, the model does not provide any way of thinking about barriers to competition and differences in the organization of firms and how these affect market performance. Of course, it does not take much reflection to realize just how important differences in production processes, technology, labor relations, and wage structures can be in influencing the competitiveness of firms in actual markets. These are precisely the areas where entrepreneurial actions can have considerable influence on market outcomes. Once we admit the possibility of differences across firms, we also see that the neoclassical model has no way to take account of differences in property rights or the broader legal framework on the relative performance of firms. Again, these are areas where we would expect entrepreneurs to exert considerable influence and where differences in entrepreneurial talent could strongly affect outcomes.

As these observations indicate, by assuming that the markets under investigation are already established and that the decisionmaking processes of buyers and sellers follow simple, easily deduced rules, the neoclassical model leaves little room for the unconventional behavior of the entrepreneur. For these reasons, George L.S. Shackle (1955, 91) described it as an "inhuman model" because it is incapable of conveying the full range of economic activity. Still, much was gained from severely limiting the range of economic activity explored within the neoclassical model. While obviously limited in the extent to which it can explain many empirical phenomena in markets, the model provides a solid starting point for thinking about the behavior of economic agents across a range of circumstances.

In recent years efforts have been made to relax some of the assumptions made in neoclassical microeconomics concerning the nature of the key building blocks of the neoclassical market model, like the household, the firm, and the operation of markets. Some economists have explored choices and allocation decisions within households (e.g., Becker 1976). Others, inspired by cognitive psychology, have looked at preference formation within the individual (e.g., contributions in Kahneman, Slovic, and Tversky 1982). The theory of the firm has recently developed into a rich literature that goes beyond modeling the firm as a production function and looking at the firm as a nexus of contracts established to economize on information costs and other transaction costs associated with market activity (for a review, see Eggertsson, 1990). Finally, some efforts have been made in recent years to explore more closely how markets operate in situations of less-than-full information (e.g., Akerlof and Yellen 1985; Banerjee 1992; Ellison and Fudenberg 1995). Among these efforts, some have attempted to explore the dynamics of markets with the same mathematical rigor that has been applied to static market analyses. In breaking through the previous assumptions of behavior of households, firms, and markets, these recent developments acknowledge differences in information acquisition and use. To the extent that they demonstrate the importance of perception, strategic decisionmaking, and organizational skill, these new efforts at theory construction raise the possibility that the role of the entrepreneur will at some point be accorded far greater significance than has traditionally been the case in mainstream economic theorizing.

Market Equilibrium and Market Process

In this section I review differences in the ways that economists have conceived of the market process, focusing in particular on the distinctions that can be drawn between neoclassical and Austrian approaches. This review is important because it sets the stage for the following chapter, where I explore what Casson (1982) terms the "market-making" activities of the entrepreneur. But for now we must consider the broader contextual issues of market equilibrium and market process.

Market equilibrium is said to occur when agents face no incentives to revise their behavior, given the behavior of all other market participants. This notion of market equilibrium is most relevant when we attempt to explain observed stability and tendencies toward stability in markets. Because much stability does in fact obtain in market societies, the neoclassical market model repeatedly serves as an appropriate tool of analysis. That is to say, despite the unrealistic facilitating assumptions, given stable market conditions, the neoclassical model can frequently provide predictions concerning the actions of agents and equilibrium outcomes that accord well with market observations. What the model is unable to do is provide a detailed explanation of the process of adjustment that occurs to keep markets in equilibrium.

The problem that arises here is fairly clear. In combination, the facilitating assumptions that work so well in allowing us to determine the optimal behavior of agents and equilibrium outcomes serve to make nonsensical any story that might be told about actual market adjustment processes. If our interests lay solely in calculating optimal behavior of agents and equilibrium outcomes in given markets, then the neoclassical model would not be problematic at all. It is only when we seek to understand adjustment processes that the limitations of the model manifest themselves. Significantly, these limitations occur even when we attempt to explain the process by which infinitesimal adjustments take place near the equilibrium point of a market. It is no surprise, then, that the neoclassical model has been heavily criticized by theorists most interested in explaining what Schumpeter described as "a change in the channels of economic routine or a spontaneous change in the economic data arising from within the system" (1934, 82).

When we turn from the neoclassical tradition to begin a search for satisfactory theories of market process, with few exceptions it is economists of the Austrian School who have made the most important contributions. Unlike those working in the neoclassical tradition, the Austrian economists have been concerned to ensure that their theoretical discussions remain closely informed by observation of actual market processes. This desire for realism has resulted in theories that contain much description of the nature of markets but that lack the predictive precision of those of their neoclassical counterparts.

As Bryan J. Loasby (1983) reminds us, in Austrian School economics interest lies in understanding processes of market adjustment as a sequence of human decisions that improve knowledge. In the adjustment process the role of the entrepreneur is paramount. Motivated by the possibility of pure profit, he is continually working to adjust production to meet what he anticipates will be the most urgent demands of buyers. He makes and revises his plans on the basis of past experience, current knowledge, and expectations regarding the future. Although often disruptive, entrepreneurship is an attempt at greater coordination. Thus, a market in which prices and quantities are out of equilibrium offers profit opportunities to entrepreneurs, who formulate plans to buy and sell particular quantities at particular prices on the basis of their expectations. These plans are then tested in the market, and the results may confirm plans and expectations or cause them to be modified. In this way the economy is said to move toward equilibrium of both plans and prices.

As I noted earlier, Kirzner (1973) argued that the defining feature of the entrepreneur is an alertness to opportunities for profit in the market system. Of course, assuming perfect competition and perfect information, no such opportunities for profit would exist in the first place. Thus, Kirzner's argument relies on a view of the market that is characterized by uncertainty. In this context an entrepreneur who observes and responds to a profit opportunity serves the role of helping to bring the market into an equilibrium state. Others, also observing opportunities for profits, as well as the actions of the entrepreneurs who have observed them already, will also put their energies into exploiting these opportunities. However, if enough people take such action, the opportunities for profit will soon be fully exploited, and the disequilibrium state that allowed them in the first place will be led back to equilibrium.

Schumpeter (1934) argued that the entrepreneur, rather than promoting equilibrium in markets, actually promotes disequilibrium. In Schumpeter's view, the entrepreneur is a far more creative individual than that portrayed by Kirzner. But there must be limits to the amount of disruption that the entrepreneur can cause. In thinking about this issue, we see that the views of Kirzner and Schumpeter need not be construed as contradictory. Suppose a Schumpeterian entrepreneur develops an innovative production process, allowing him to attain above-normal profits in a market that has previously been characterized by normal profits and, hence, equilibrium. The actions of the entrepreneur will initially lead the market away from the equilibrium position. He may have the good fortune to temporarily be alone (and happy) on the disequilibrium path, bringing with him his previous customers and those of his competitors. However, this action will not go unchecked. First, we might expect that other producers in this market will attempt to use a variety of means to discredit the actions of the entrepreneur. According to Baumol (1993), we might even expect that, where necessary, other producers will engage in counterproductive entrepreneurial activity designed entirely to stymie this entrepreneur's approach to making above-normal profits. Second, even if the entrepreneur can break through these encumbrances, we should expect that other entrepreneurs will seek to imitate this entrepreneur in taking advantage of the profit opportunity that he or she has identified. But these secondary responses are, of course, precisely the sort of actions that Kirzner anticipates in his work.

By synthesizing the views expressed by Schumpeter and Kirzner, we come to see that the actions of entrepreneurs can have both disequilibrating and equilibrating effects on the market process. What is most important, however, is that we now see that any effort to take the market from the equilibrium path will ultimately be met with subsequent efforts to take it back to equilibrium. It should also be noted that, while many entrepreneurs might be expected to attempt to take a market off the equilibrium path to obtain above-normal profits, these actions will frequently be unsuccessful. In such cases, the entrepreneur finds himself alone (and disappointed) in a state of disequilibrium, with the market remaining in equilibrium. But the incentives structure established in a market economy ensures that entrepreneurs who make mistakes of this sort will quickly learn and adjust their behavior accordingly.

As the foregoing discussion makes clear, in thinking about the market process, I have found it useful to draw primarily upon insights from the Austrian School economists. However, I should note that our choice among economic approaches to embrace when thinking more generally about the market process and entrepreneurship need not be this stark. As mentioned earlier, Casson (1982) has attempted to develop a theory of the entrepreneur that is intended to maintain close linkages to the neoclassical framework. Such theory construction is enabled primarily by relaxing the full information assumption that typically accompanies the neoclassical market model, and by assuming that entrepreneurs have better or more relevant information than other economic agents. In the next section I follow closely Casson's discussion of the entrepreneur as market maker. I take a somewhat more eclectic approach to working with the theoretical perspectives of others in the following chapter, where I enter into more specific discussion of the actions that entrepreneurs take and how these can affect market outcomes.

The Entrepreneur as Market Maker

A key problem for economic theorists involves explaining how change, especially significant change, occurs in market economies. Like the Austrian School economists, Casson (1982) argues that the figure of the entrepreneur provides the missing link in the process of market adjustment. But Casson pursues this argument vigorously, taking care to work through various logical implications. In so doing, he suggests a broad role for the entrepreneur, including perceiving opportunities for gain and organizing others in order to take advantage of those opportunities. Taking this approach, Casson develops a theory of the entrepreneur that complements and, more important, integrates insights from other approaches to theorizing about entrepreneurs. According to Casson, the entrepreneur, by having better information than others, is better able to "effect a trade" (1982, 158). However, effecting a trade requires considerable skill and effort, and demonstration of this skill and effort also serves to distinguish the entrepreneur from other economic agents. In encountering and overcoming obstacles to trade, the entrepreneur serves to make markets. Here I discuss the elements of market making identified by Casson and note how he sees them as relating to one another.

Having better information than others, the entrepreneur is more able to perceive opportunities for profit. But what gives rise to this informational advantage? Casson suggests that entrepreneurs must have the ability to both synthesize and interpret information. Thus, the information advantage can be seen as stemming from individual talent and intellect on the one hand, and the social position of the entrepreneur on the other. An individual who can relate well to others and who can identify ways of matching resources to wants will have the ability to see opportunities for profit where others do not. However, these talents only become valuable within a social context. Therefore the entrepreneur must have access to people and situations to use these talents to advantage. Casson suggests that this access is gained through both formal and informal channels.

Having better information, the entrepreneur gains opportunities for making contacts between potential buyers and sellers and, thus, effecting a trade. Typically, an entrepreneur will have to make a decision about what opportunities for profit to pursue. Given uncertainty, it is always possible that potentially more profitable opportunities will be passed up for less profitable ones. The risk of this happening is high because establishing trade among buyers and sellers always involves a range of organizational tasks. These tasks require the use of scarce resources, which, once expended, become unrecoverable, sunk costs. So, whether the chosen trade returns profits that exceed those that could have been earned by engaging in alternative trades or other forms of employment is ultimately affected by the ability of the entrepreneur to minimize the use of those resources. Some of the ways that the entrepreneur can minimize the use of scarce resources are obvious. But many are not.

Establishing contact between buyers and sellers can be achieved through a range of market-making activities. All of these, including advertising, can be thought of as types of search. Here, the ability of the entrepreneur to take advantage of the information provided to him through formal and informal channels becomes vital. An inefficient search procedure could prove extremely costly. Reducing the potential for inefficiency will involve synthesizing information with intellectual insight. Part of the task here involves ensuring that the reciprocal wants of the buyers and sellers are clearly specified and communicated among the relevant parties. Determining how much information is provided to these potential parties to a trade requires sound judgment. Spending as little as possible on providing information would be a good thing, in terms of minimizing the costs of establishing trade. However, expending insufficient effort to ensure that all parties have a clear understanding of reciprocal wants may jeopardize the prospects of a trade actually occurring.

The initial steps toward effecting a trade can be seen as requiring the entrepreneur to display a range of skills, from quotidian aspects of time management to more complex endeavors to elicit information from people who may, for strategic reasons, be unwilling to make relevant details known. Where the trade involves introducing an innovative product, the ability to carefully manage communications among buyers and sellers is vital. Although some elements of the trade may be routine, and previous procedures may be used for establishing negotiations, by definition an innovative product will require the adoption of new procedures and new ways of doing business. Even among trading partners who are familiar with each other and have established a track record of good relations, new situations of this sort can be the source of misunderstandings and, perhaps, disagreements. The skill of the entrepreneur in avoiding problems of this sort can greatly affect the overall success, and hence profitability, of a trade.

Assuming that an entrepreneur can identify buyers and sellers and establish reciprocal wants, the next aspect of effecting the trade involves organizing these people so that the specified trade actually occurs. At a minimum, the entrepreneur must ensure that the exchange of the good actually takes place and that the good corresponds to specifications negotiated between the parties. Casson argues that all of this essentially boils down to appropriately structuring the flow of information. This can be done either informally or formally. Frequently, however, because of the complexity of the products being traded, formal approaches are used. Much of this organizational work can be thought of as involving the writing and administering of contracts, and, as writers on the nature of the firm (Coase 1937; Williamson 1975, 1985) make clear, contracting always involves the expenditure of resources. Thus, the vast range of different organizational forms that are used to facilitate production and trade in market economies can be seen as the result of the efforts of entrepreneurs to economize on information and other transaction costs.

Because the organization costs of effecting a trade are likely to be considerable, entrepreneurs face incentives to ensure that the relationships they establish between buyers and sellers are carefully maintained. Entrepreneurs also face strong incentives to reduce the opportunities for competitors to gain from the trade that has been effected and the information generated as a by-product of that trade. In this connection entrepreneurs can be expected to pursue a number of strategies for reducing market-making costs. First, an entrepreneur will attempt to engage in repeat trading. This can be advantageous since the partners to the trade and their reciprocal needs will already have been established, contracting will be easier after the initial round, and opportunities will be afforded for improving the quality of service. Second, an entrepreneur will attempt to establish a reputation for dealing fairly with all partners to a trade. This can be good for extending the number of trades an entrepreneur is engaged in. Finally, an entrepreneur may be expected to actively seek to control various assets associated with the production process. This can reduce the possibility of losing trade, and hence profit opportunities, to competitors.

Casson's portrayal of the entrepreneur as market maker led him to define the entrepreneur as someone who not only looks out for new trading opportunities, but who also engages in much that could often be thought of as straightforward business management. Given this, we might wonder whether most organizers or directors of business firms are entrepreneurs. Casson's response is clear. When it comes to the firm as market-making organization, Casson (1982, 178) sees only the choice of structure and the establishment of that structure as being entrepreneurial acts. Once the appropriate organizational form has been established, decisions can be delegated to those in managerial positions.

Casson's theory of the entrepreneur serves to establish broad linkages between the somewhat diverse activities that can reasonably be thought of as the preserve of the entrepreneur in the market process. This theory explains how entrepreneurs serve to effect new trades that may often involve some type of product innovation. It also establishes why entrepreneurs might be associated with the founding and leadership of firms. There is much in Casson's theory that is useful and suggestive about the role of the entrepreneur. However, there is considerably more to be said about the actions of entrepreneurs in the market process.

Summary

The entrepreneur is best thought of as a market maker. The entrepreneur attempts to respond to unmet needs, or to meet needs that are currently being met, but to do so in a way that leads to greater satisfaction at the same cost, or the same level of satisfaction at lower cost. The entrepreneur acts most obviously as market maker by seeking to coordinate resources in novel ways and to create new combinations. In so doing, the entrepreneur allows trade to take place between previously separate individuals. Less obviously, the entrepreneur also serves as a market maker when working purely with existing production functions. In attempting to meet presently met needs in a more satisfactory manner (either through improvements in product quality or through reductions in product cost), the entrepreneur again allows trade to take place between previously separate individuals. In this case, new trade arises because new buyers are now willing to purchase the product that was heretofore judged to be out of the buyers' price range or simply not delivering enough value for money. New trade may also arise between new sets of buyers and sellers. In any event, trade is effected between parties where previously there was none.

The motivation for the entrepreneur to serve as a market maker comes from the expectation that, in effecting new trades, opportunities for above-normal profits will be realized. That opportunities for above-normal profits exist is dependent solely on the condition of imperfect information. The entrepreneur seeks to profit from introducing new information to buyers and sellers, letting them know that opportunities for trade exist. Still, given the uncertain operating environment, the entrepreneur might well be wrong. Breaking out of routine trading practices, breaking into unknown territory, the entrepreneur seeks to gain from this action but inevitably runs the risk of losing. Given this, entrepreneurs face strong incentives to attempt to make decisions concerning opportunities for gain that are right more often than they are wrong. They also need to pay attention to a range of details having to do with the production process.

Note

1. Indeed it was Marshall who introduced the idea of assuming "other things equal," the *ceteris paribus* condition, which has subsequently become the hallmark of the partial equilibrium approach to economic analysis. Marshall's work was extremely influential. Combined with the insights that emerged contemporaneously from Léon Walras's (1874) general equilibrium model, Marshall's work laid the foundations for the emergence and refinement of all subsequent neoclassical microeconomic theory construction and modeling. Marshall expected that the use of static models would be only a temporary phenomenon until a satisfactory mathematics emerged to deal with the dynamics of economic life. However, even today the mathematics of economic dynamics remains at an elementary stage.

FOUR

Aspects of Entrepreneurship

It is one thing to understand *what* role entrepreneurs play in the market process. But it is also vital to consider *how* they play that role. Here I explore more closely *how* entrepreneurs organize their activities in pursuit of their goals. I have distilled this overview of entrepreneurship from a fairly broad body of literature. The discussion is divided into four main parts, each of which is designed to explore distinct aspects of entrepreneurship: perceiving opportunities for gain, developing innovations, devising strategies and working the system, and organizing others and providing leadership. These topic headings each capture the most important and distinctive aspects of entrepreneurship. Of course, empirically, these apparently separate aspects of entrepreneurial activity will often merge into each other.

After discussing these aspects of entrepreneurship I will present a summary statement concerning the actions of entrepreneurs in the market process. The description of entrepreneurial activity that emerges here is one where social interactions are paramount. Perhaps more than anything else, entrepreneurs appear here as individuals who succeed because they are adept at making the most out of a range of social situations. This does not mean that they are cynical manipulators of those around them. In fact, good reason exists for believing that cynical manipulators might quite quickly come up against serious limits to achieving ongoing success. Contrary to that famous line by Yeats, that "The best lack all conviction, while the worst are full of passonate intensity," in the world of entrepreneurship the best *do* exude conviction, and it is the *best* who are full of a passionate intensity. They couple this conviction and intensity with a shrewd sense of their operating environment and a decidedly humanistic interest in finding out what other people are searching for.

Perceiving Opportunities for Gain

Perception occurs as the product of two quite distinctive processes. The first process involves receiving relevant information. The second involves interpreting that information. The entrepreneur can exercise considerable control (albeit not absolute control) over what information is received and how that information is interpreted. Given this, through the choices they make concerning the process of perception, entrepreneurs can strongly influence the odds that the actions they take will lead to gains or losses. The literature on entrepreneurship, as we might expect, contains many discussions of the role of information and perception. Here I discuss four elements of perceiving opportunities for gain.

Receiving Relevant Information

Entrepreneurs can receive relevant information by actively seeking it or by simply paying attention to the flow of information passing by them in their formal or informal positions. Although not fully able to control information flow, entrepreneurs can structure their activities or interactions to ensure that the information they receive is most likely to alert them to opportunities for gain. Among previous theories of entrepreneurship, little attempt has been made to specify the sources of the information that entrepreneurs will work with. Only Casson's (1982) observations mentioned in the previous chapter suggest that a mixture of formal and informal information channels will be used. Harvey Leibenstein's (1978) discussion alerts us to the ways that entrepreneurs might structure relations—in his case, relations in organizations—to increase opportunities for receiving information about opportunities for gain.

Recent studies by business anthropologists shed more light on this issue. In particular, these studies emphasize the importance of the position of the entrepreneur. Close proximity to relevant information is crucial. Thus Don Lavoire argued that "entrepreneurship is not so much the achievement of the isolated maverick who finds objective profits others overlooked as it is of the culturally embedded participant who picks up the gist of the conversation" (1991, 36). Lavoire went on to suggest that "his ability to read new things into a situation is not primarily due to his separateness from others but, indeed, to his higher degree of sensitivity to what others are looking for" (1991, 49). In their discussion of entrepreneurship and innovation in small manufacturing firms, Ruth D. Young and Joe D. Francis (1991) have provided support for claims of this sort. High-quality information about unmet needs and the methods that are potentially available to meet those needs were found to be important for the entrepreneurs they studied. This information had led the entrepreneurs to believe that a special niche existed that the larger manufacturing concerns they had been associated with had no intention of filling. Howard Aldrich and Catherine Zimmer (1986) have discussed the importance of informal, social networks for facilitating entrepreneurship.[1] In their view, "Successful entrepreneurs will be found in positions with weak ties to people who are in positions to provide timely and accurate information, to people with the resources to act as customers, and/or to people with resources to invest" (1986, 20).

Interpreting Information

How entrepreneurs interpret the information they receive is decisive in determining whether or not they perceive opportunities for gain. It is possible to imagine, for instance, two entrepreneurs both acquiring the same highly accurate information concerning an opportunity for gain, but, because of differences in the ways that they interpret that information, one might perceive an opportunity for gain while the other does not. In the literature on entrepreneurship there have been several discussions on this theme. Thus Lawrence H. White has argued that "entrepreneurial projects are not waiting to be sought out so much as to be thought up. The entrepreneur's plans must be based on expectations, and these must be created by him: an image of future markets is available not through sight but through insight" (1976, 7).

This statement accords with Lavoire's (1991) suggestion that entrepreneurs are distinguished not by the nature of the information they receive but the ways that they choose to interpret or "read" it. In each case we are reminded that entrepreneurship has much to do with subjective judgment, imagination, and creativity. Thus, we might wonder how entrepreneurs can consciously act to ensure that their methods of interpretation allow them to extract clues from available information and, hence, best perceive opportunities for gain.

This discussion brings us to essentially the same point that Thomas S. Kuhn (1970) made concerning the role of paradigms as means of organizing the behavior of scientific communities. According to Kuhn, "Something like a paradigm is prerequisite to perception itself. What a man sees depends both upon what he looks at and also upon what his previous visual-conceptual experience has taught him to see. In the absence of a training there can only be, in William James's phrase, "'a bloomin' buzzin' confusion.'" (1970, 113).

If economic agents can be thought of as being like scientists in that they all seek to predict and control, then we might go on to say that most economic agents are engaged in what Kuhn called "normal science." Operating in mature markets in equilibrium, they do not need to be particularly reflective upon their ways of interpreting the world. Kuhn's central argument also appears relevant here—that scientists will adopt a new paradigm on faith that it will prove more fruitful than the old paradigm that was found to come into crisis. We might expect that entrepreneurs will reject old ways of interpreting information if those ways have led to poor judgments being made about opportunities for gain. Further, we might expect that much of the task of entrepreneurs seeking to take advantage of opportunities for gain is to persuade others that their interpretations of information are sound, and that others should share these new interpretations.

Assessing Whether Opportunities Will Produce a Gain

Beyond establishing that opportunities for gain exist, entrepreneurs need to think critically about such opportunities. Typically opportunities for gain could be assessed according to several criteria. Among other things, these might include the likely duration of the opportunity, the likely barriers to securing the gain, the likely interest of potential rivals, and the likely responses of rivals to the opportunity. Peter F. Drucker (1986) discussed issues of this sort at some length and made specific suggestions for how entrepreneurs can better assess the merits of apparent opportunities for gain. These suggestions tend to revolve around ensuring that opportunities and their implications for action are well understood. Drucker also recommended that entrepreneurs take time to talk with others about opportunities for gain, listening to how others respond to the concept. If other people do not agree that an opportunity exists, even when presented with a range of arguments in favor of pursuing the opportunity, this may well be a sign of potential problems in the future. After all, because all entrepreneurship is strongly dependent on the ability of the entrepreneur to work with and coordinate others, it is vital that others share the perception that a valuable opportunity exists. In terms of filling a currently unmet need, assessment involves ensuring that all potential trading partners agree that grounds exist for mutual exchange. In terms of doing a better job of filling a need that is currently being met, the entrepreneur must ensure that the essential aspects of the opportunity for gain can be readily conveyed to all concerned. This is particularly important because many people may be affected by a process change, and the entrepreneur must be confident that these people will support any attempt to exploit the opportunity.

Assessing Capabilities for Exploiting Opportunities

Entrepreneurs who perceive opportunities for gain and desire to exploit them must initially engage in careful analyses to determine whether they have the necessary resources at their command, or could gain access to such resources. This often involves considering how other people could be persuaded to join the entrepreneur in attempting to secure the perceived gains. It might well be the case that many opportunities for gain are perceived, but the process of assessing capabilities leads to a passing up of these opportunities for others that appear within the entrepreneur's grasp. Clearly, a large amount of self-knowledge is required at this point. The entrepreneur needs to honestly assess his or her strengths and weaknesses and candidly compare these with those of likely competitors. The value of good contacts, trusted associates, and the ability to listen closely to the opinions and suggestions of others become vital at this stage. While potentially having more information than others, entrepreneurs still operate in an uncertain world. All the uncertainty surrounding a potential opportunity for gain can never be removed. However, entrepreneurs can avoid many mishaps and possible disasters by attempting to make clear-eyed assessments of their capabilities for exploiting opportunities before they take the plunge.

Developing Innovations

Having perceived an opportunity for gain and determined to pursue it, entrepreneurs must next take action. This means developing an innovation that either meets a presently unmet need or better satisfies an existing one. But how does the process of developing innovations work? And what distinguishes innovation from invention on the one hand and imitation on the other? Developing innovations should be construed as a process where the initial input is completely conceptual and the final output is a new product or a new form of production. Of all the contributions that entrepreneurs make to this process, Schumpeter (1934, 88–89) argued that the most important is leadership, which can be understood as involving a mixture of communication and organizational skills. In Schumpeter's view, such leadership was more important than inventiveness—for lack of leadership many fine inventions would never be brought to market as innovations. Leadership qualities allow an entrepreneur to establish a set of agreements and arrangements that ensure successful exploitation of opportunities for gain. However, we should not rate these skills over judgmental decisionmaking—the sheer ability to think carefully and to reflect upon the implications of embarking upon various courses of action (see Knight 1921).

Having made these preliminary observations, I now want to consider in more detail the steps in the process of developing innovations, working through an example as I do so. Suppose an entrepreneur, who has very good knowledge about an industry, has good contacts within it, and continually receives high-quality information about industry developments, decides to exploit a perceived opportunity for gain. This opportunity involves working with established firms in the industry to show them how to improve the efficiency of their production processes through better integration of their information management systems. In particular, the entrepreneur believes that many firms in the industry could improve their profitability by ensuring that routinely generated information on customer satisfaction, customer suggestions, and customer complaints is used to provide rapid performance feedback to production units. However, he also believes that the possibilities for improving profitability in this way could be numerous. Therefore starting out with a "sure thing" holds the promise of generating further business. Once the entrepreneur has perceived this opportunity for gain, he must go from the conceptual level to the point of delivering a new product. The product in this case is expertise and guidance that results in firms doing things differently, and more profitably, than in the past. The product is a type of system "reengineering" where the entrepreneur intends to be the agent of change.

Innovation as a Social Process

As a prelude to generating business, the entrepreneur must target specific customers and think about how he will approach them and sell his concept. To do this, the entrepreneur must consider the situation of potential customers and think of ways to bring them around to sharing his perspective on the concept. The entrepreneur must establish a context within which potential customers, through their own reasoning, come to discover and acknowledge the previously vague or unrealized needs that the entrepreneur's product could satisfy. Ultimately this acknowledgment must involve the realization that the current situation is unsustainable; that without purchasing this product the potential customers will face the possibility of a crisis of some sort. (This is frequently treated as the domain of marketing and advertising, with both new and established markets.) In determining how to approach potential customers the entrepreneur's concerns go well beyond those of marketing. The thinking that occurs at this stage will result in further shaping of the concept. Innovation development, then, is not simply a matter of invention augmented by marketing; it involves a series of steps throughout which the concept is refined in response to anticipated customer needs.

In the case of our example, the entrepreneur might seek to make an argument that leads the potential customer to conclude that the sort of product he can deliver is vital for ensuring the continued rate of sales of the firm. Because of the technical nature of the product he plans to sell, the entrepreneur knows that his marketing strategy has to involve working very closely with potential clients. Most likely these are senior figures in the targeted firms. To gain access to those people the entrepreneur knows that he must come across as being highly credible. Two characteristics work in his favor here. First, he has a record of doing top-quality work in several firms in the industry. He knows that he can speak with authority about his previous activities and the ways that he managed to achieve, on a more limited scale, the sort of changes that he now proposes to carry out at a broader level. Second, he knows that he has a good reputation among contacts in the industry, and that these contacts may be able to help him secure his first chance to deliver his new product. But is this enough? Perhaps to demonstrate his confidence in his own abilities, the entrepreneur will have to devise some way of signaling his commitment to this initiative and to delivering a top-quality product. One means for doing this might be to propose to potential customers that the bulk of the payment for the product being delivered be contingent upon success of the system the entrepreneur proposes to create. This raises the issue of how the entrepreneur will support himself (and any employees) during the initial stages of the venture (see Barzel 1984). But for our purposes we should note that in working through the process of considering how to capitalize on his previous successes, and how to exploit and maintain his industry reputation, the entrepreneur is further led to refine the concept for the innovation he intends to sell.

Once the entrepreneur develops a relationship with a particular customer and tacit agreement is reached that a trade can occur, the next step involves writing a contract. Although a contract can never cover all possible contingencies (Williamson 1985), the contract-writing stage is important because it forces many otherwise implicit elements of the trade and the specification of the product to be made explicit. During the lead-up to the contract and the contract writing itself, it is likely that further product innovation will occur. Thus it is inappropriate to think of the entrepreneur as the person who both establishes a trade and who comes to the situation with "all the answers." While coming to the situation with an innovative idea and a particular point of view, a way of "reading" situations that is unique, a successful entrepreneur must be prepared to accommodate customer needs, to bend and shape the proposed product so that it best meets the expectations of customers. In this sense innovation can never be thought of as the sole domain of the entrepreneur. Some component of innovation is collaborative.

With preliminary work to win a customer completed, next comes the production process itself. Although we typically think of production processes as involving little more than a well-defined, mechanical transformation of inputs into outputs, in fact the production stage is also vital for innovation development. During production, the entrepreneur reaches many decision points that present opportunities for carefully managing customer relations. How these relations are handled significantly affects customer expectations and perceptions of the product. It is possible to imagine a scenario in which the entrepreneur leads customers to expect much more from the product that can eventually be delivered. Such a strategy would lead to disappointment on the part of customers, and this would be extremely damaging for the entrepreneur. Yet it is just as possible to imagine a scenario in which the entrepreneur is careful to manage customer expectations and perceptions of the product. Most innovations that entrepreneurs introduce are subsequently refined. This suggests, of course, that most new products could be dramatically improved upon. Or, in other words, most new products have a range of attributes, some of which are very good and are difficult to improve upon and some of which are quite poor. Given this, through customer relations, provision of information, and development of instructions, the entrepreneur has considerable scope to shape the way the final product is received. The key goal of the entrepreneur is to ensure that customers are excited enough by the core elements of the product that they are prepared, at least initially, to discount (or perhaps not even notice) product weaknesses and design problems. Maintaining close relations with customers during the production process allows opportunities for readily apparent product weaknesses and design problems to be tackled and eliminated. For these reasons the production process itself can be thought of as yet another phase of innovation development.

Innovation, Invention, and Imitation

So far, I have deliberately attempted to make the point that developing innovations proceeds in a series of steps—frequently small, and not necessarily linear—that continue right through the production process. Thus, I have suggested that innovation should be seen as emerging from social relations rather than from the entrepreneur's ability to spot an invention and take it to market. In making these points, I see myself taking a position that is similar to that presented by Baumol (1993). In his discussion of entrepreneurship, Baumol argued that Schumpeter drew too sharp a distinction between invention and innovation. If we conceptualize innovation as a process that proceeds in a series of small steps, then it becomes difficult to see where invention ends and innovation begins. Of course Schumpeter's point stands that if an invention does not attract the attention of entrepreneurs, then it is irrelevant. But to the extent that this point suggests that all invention takes place before the entrepreneur arrives on the scene, then it is unhelpful. A better interpretation is to see that in striving to be innovative and bring "new combinations" to market, the entrepreneur must be continually inventive. Further, this ability to be inventive must be tethered to customer relations.

This interpretation of the development of innovation raises the possibility that imitation is also a form of innovation. Schumpeter viewed imitation as springing from two sources. First, imitation might occur as a result of competitors scrambling to catch up with the entrepreneur. Second, imitation might be the deliberate strategy of those who wait for an initial entrepreneur to develop an innovation and establish the market for it before they enter the scene and attempt to win away some of the entrepreneur's above-normal profits. Although these actions are reactive rather than proactive, Schumpeter saw them as important because they ensure that the innovation eventually trades at a price that maximizes the sum of consumer and producer surplus. Baumol argues that imitation is actually more important than this. In particular, he claims that where it involves transferring an innovation from one firm or geographic location to another, imitation serves to promote economic development in ways that can far outstrip the contribution made by the initial development of the innovation. Further, because it is rare that an imitator can simply take an innovation from one location and introduce it without refinement to another, imitation often involves some form of invention. Through this process of adaptation, the imitator might perceive a need to make product refinements that constitute genuine improvements for all users, even those where the innovation was initially introduced.

Devising Strategies and Working the System

Entrepreneurs can be thought of as operating within a set of institutions. These can be both formal, such as the legal system, as well as informal, such as relevant social norms. Given these institutions, entrepreneurs must determine how best to establish organizational arrangements that allow them to make the most of the opportunities provided. But, given imperfect information and differences in talent and resources, many possible approaches can be taken to working within a given set of institutions, just as many different approaches can be taken to playing a game or a sport with long-established and well-understood rules. Sometimes, through the strategies they use and the organizations they develop, entrepreneurs force changes in institutional arrangements.

I think of devising strategies as the task of figuring out how best to achieve desired goals, given available resources and the constraints imposed by the operating environment. In many cases, and especially when an innovation is being introduced, it is not at all obvious how goals, resources, and constraints interact. Taking time to consider such issues might lead to the identification of resources that were previously ignored. And knowing the relevant constraints requires sound ability to identify and distinguish among aspects of the operating environment.

Some of these aspects might be represented by binding constraints that are difficult to change, while others might be represented by slack constraints, that suggest readily exploited opportunities. A key to working the system is the ability to read the operating environment and form accurate judgments about relevant resources and constraints and how they can be managed.

Considering the Immediate Operating Environment

Suppose an entrepreneur has determined to effect a new trade or develop a new innovation. Any action of this sort, because it is intended to bring about change, will inevitably prove disruptive. The disruption will be greeted with a variety of responses from people in the immediate environment—those who know and who already have some relations with the entrepreneur. In devising strategy, entrepreneurs must seek to determine who will be immediately affected by their actions and to anticipate likely responses.

Schumpeter (1934) touched on this matter in his discussion of the difficulties associated with being an entrepreneur. Beyond the ingenuity and decisionmaking ability required to succeed, Schumpeter argued that the ability to anticipate and manage resistance and hostile reactions from others was critical. Max Weber (1930) also noted the resistance that the entrepreneur is likely to encounter in the immediate environment. To understand why such resistance can be so acute we must recognize that, for the most part, people prefer stability and routine to change. As previously noted, in pursuing their goals entrepreneurs must be ingenious and make well-judged decisions. But by creating (or threatening to create) change, entrepreneurs also force other people out of their comfortable routines; those people, too, must now think differently about things and make new decisions. Only, unlike the entrepreneur who engaged in this activity voluntarily, those who are subjected to the effects of their actions must engage in thinking and making new decisions under duress. Typically they would rather stay with their comfortable routines, but entrepreneurs' destabilizing activities make the old ways of doing things unsustainable.

According to Weber (1930, 69), entrepreneurs can do much to improve their ability to successfully introduce a new innovation. The focus here is on developing "ethical qualities." By working over time to build their reputations as hard workers and people of good character, entrepreneurs reduce the likelihood that their change-forcing activities will be met with hostility. Weber and Schumpeter both emphasized the role that social norms and sanctions serve in placing constraints on entrepreneurs as change agents. This suggests that in devising strategies, entrepreneurs must think carefully about the relationship between what is legally permissible and what is socially permissible. Or, we might say that in seeking to reduce possible opposition to their efforts, entrepreneurs must consider both the letter and the spirit of the laws that characterize the immediate operating environment. This does not mean that entrepreneurs must resort to slavishly following conventions. It means, rather, that they must reflect upon how different combinations of actions taken in pursuit of their goals will be received by others. Using such reflection, entrepreneurs might come to some decision about how best to act to reduce the likelihood of being opposed by others. It is possible, of course, that such reflection leads entrepreneurs to think up strategies for promoting their innovations that turn possible sources of opposition into sources of support.

The business management literature provides us with a general analytical framework that can help us think about how entrepreneurs might devise strategies and think of ways to work the system. S.W.O.T. analysis is used to identify and then scrutinize a firm's internal strengths (S) and weaknesses (W) and the opportunities (O) and threats (T) that are posed by the external environment. As Peter Wright, Charles D. Pringle, and Mark J. Kroll (1992, 70) have noted, S.W.O.T. analysis is designed to enable firms to position themselves to take advantage of particular opportunities in the environment and to avoid or minimize environmental threats. In doing so these firms attempt to emphasize their strengths and moderate the impact of their weaknesses. The analysis is also useful for revealing previously underutilized strengths and identifying weaknesses that could be rectified. Matching information about the environment with a knowledge of the capabilities of a firm can enable managers to formulate realistic strategies for attaining their goals.

Thinking in terms of the entrepreneur and immediate relations to other people and firms, it is clear that a careful S.W.O.T. analysis could prove valuable for helping the entrepreneur whose goal is to launch an innovation. For example, the entrepreneur's moral character and reputation as a sound worker—features emphasized by Weber—could be seen as strengths that could help the entrepreneur to secure the otherwise difficult-to-obtain goodwill of potential financiers, employees, and customers. In contrast, lack of understanding of the details of the legal environment and how to work the system to one's own advantage could be a weakness. In terms of opportunities, changing social norms might allow the entrepreneur to undertake an activity that, while always having been legal, may have previously been frowned upon and considered improper. Finally, threats might include the possibility that competitors will launch innovative countermeasures that effectively block the entrepreneur's ability to attain his goal. Ultimately, the more effort that entrepreneurs put into understanding the nature of their immediate operating environments and their comparative strengths and weaknesses in these environments, the more likely they are to succeed in launching innovations.

Considering the Industry and the Macrolevel Operating Environment

Beyond the benefit of clearly understanding their immediate operating environment, entrepreneurs can also gain from having a good grasp of the workings of the broader industry to which they belong. The greater the knowledge that entrepreneurs have of their industry, the legal environment, who is who, industry norms, and broad industry trends, the more likely they are to devise successful strategies. For example, an entrepreneur with a sound knowledge of the industry in which he or she operates is more likely to have a clear sense of who will be likely rivals, what tactics they might use, and how strategies might be devised that mitigate the efforts of rivals to stymie the launch and success of the innovation. In contrast, the entrepreneur who has only a rudimentary knowledge of how the system works in the first place is unlikely to be able to figure out how to survive in it, let alone effect significant changes. Having the ability to conceptualize the broader, industry-wide, operating environment is also important because it can help the entrepreneur assess whether the conditions he or she is well acquainted with at the local level are particular or general. This in turn can guide the development of strategy. If the conditions producing opportunities for gain are localized, then the extent to which the entrepreneur must anticipate the reactions of others is reduced. Of course, this might also mean that the opportunities for gain are relatively limited.

Finally, in devising strategies and working the system the entrepreneur can gain insights from considering the macrolevel operating environment. This environment is shaped by broad social and political trends and the institutions and organizations that support them, such as the legal system and the manner in which it is enforced. For many entrepreneurs these matters might seem irrelevant. However, it is also possible that entrepreneurs can realize above-normal profits by correctly extrapolating from current trends and, hence, determining a more profitable way to introduce their innovation into the market. For example, an entrepreneur might note that changes in information technology and concomitant changes in the attitudes of ordinary people toward it opens new possibilities for his or her innovation and how it might be marketed. Similarly, the entrepreneur might gain from exploring ways that the structure of the legal system and enforcement procedures provide opportunities and threats regarding the launch of an innovation. As Yoram Barzel (1989) and Gary D. Libecap (1989) have emphasized, most goods have multiple attributes. Measurement for the purposes of writing and enforcing contracts typically involves paying attention to the most salient aspects of these goods. This suggests that there are frequently margins available for exploitation by sharp-eyed profit seekers. Further, because laws are typically made in reaction to change rather than in anticipation of it, entrepreneurs can often gain from the poor specification of property rights in their areas of activity. Thus, taking a broader view of the operating environment can potentially be quite beneficial to entrepreneurs as they devise strategies and seek ways to work the system to their advantage.

Organizing Others and Providing Leadership

Beyond the activities mentioned already, to be successful entrepreneurs must devote significant amounts of time and energy to the coordination of others. Potentially, coordinating activity for the production of any good or service could be conducted completely within the market setting. However, exclusive reliance on markets can be costly due to the ongoing need for all contributors to the production process to find appropriate trading partners, write contracts with them, and monitor their performance. As Ronald H. Coase (1937) pointed out, coordinating production in markets can often become prohibitively expensive. In the face of this, entrepreneurs who wish to exploit perceived opportunities must take considerable care in choosing a means of organizing production that makes efficient use of inputs and that economizes on the costs of organization. In recent years, a large body of literature has emerged exploring the transaction-cost economizing rationale for observed differences in firm-like arrangements.[2] Much of this literature, following Armen A. Alchian and Harold Demsetz (1972), has stressed the team aspects of many production processes and the need for firms to be established to reduce team shirking. This, of course, is a manifestation in the private domain of the collective action problem that is pervasive in the public domain (see, for example, Olson 1965; Ostrom 1990; Sandler 1992).

Here I explore how entrepreneurs coordinate others to realize their goals. In considering this aspect of entrepreneurship, it is important not to stray from discussing entrepreneurial activities and wander into the domain of management. But can we readily distinguish these domains? Contributors to the literature on entrepreneurship have often wrestled with this issue. Schumpeter argued that a clear line of demarcation could be drawn between entrepreneurship and management. Thus, he claimed "everyone is an entrepreneur only when he actually 'carries out new combinations,' and loses that character as soon as he has built up his business, when he settles down to running it as other people run their businesses" (1934, 78). In this definition managing others is an entrepreneurial activity only if it supports the promotion of change. More recent contributors to the literature on entrepreneurship have argued that any line of demarcation between entrepreneurship and management is likely to be somewhat arbitrary. Thus, according to Casson, the entrepreneur must pay attention to a range of "less glamorous" activities that would typically be thought of as managerial rather than entrepreneurial (1982, 392). Casson suggests that, among other things, entrepreneurs must develop organizational arrangements that delegate decisions to subordinates in ways that ensure the subordinates face incentives to act in the best interests of the entrepreneur. Baumol also takes this view. However, he adds that the development of organizational arrangements is not a one-shot deal; instead, the entrepreneur must be constantly on the lookout for new ideas and ways to implement them. "She must lead, perhaps even inspire; she cannot allow things to get into a rut and, for her, today's practice is never good enough for tomorrow" (1993, 4). We might say that to some degree all entrepreneurs need to be managerial. Further, while all managers need not be entrepreneurial, entrepreneurship does have its place in the echelons of management and it can facilitate important contributions to organizational goals. So, questioning the relevance and appropriateness of drawing a clear line between entrepreneurship and management allows us to gain further insights into the contribution of the entrepreneur to the market process.

Choosing Production Functions

In the neoclassical model of the firm the production function stands as the central component. It serves as an expression of how given combinations of inputs generate the outputs that firms produce. In fact it is no exaggeration to say that in this model the production function *is* the firm. Jerry Evensky captured the essence of this representation in the following statement: "Factors of production are allocated to and then combined in processes of production that apply techniques chosen from the available technology in order to produce goods and services" (1990, 22). In typical expositions of this model, the assumption is made that all economic agents know the available technology and all relevant prices. Given this, they then choose the most efficient, or least cost, means of combining inputs. In a world characterized by perfect information, this would be a reasonable assumption. However, as Richard M. Cyert and James G. March (1963) noted in their behavioral theory of the firm, except in the most trivial instances, the complex nature of decisionmaking tasks and the limits to the cognitive capabilities of decisionmakers inevitably obscure the most efficient means of production. We might add that because entrepreneurs seek to develop innovations, by definition they tend to operate in a twilight zone where their own actions serve to generate information about available technology and relevant prices.

To accurately portray the process by which entrepreneurs choose production functions, we must consider both the inclusions and the exclusions of the neoclassical model of the firm. In so doing, we see that while in theory there will exist a production function that most efficiently transforms given inputs into a given output, typically firms that all ostensibly produce the same output do so using a range of production functions. Because many production functions can produce the same output, and the most efficient production function is not immediately apparent, considerable scope exists for entrepreneurs to engage in search behaviors designed to identify production functions appropriate for creating their innovations. Alternatively, the search behavior of entrepreneurs might involve identifying production functions that are, in themselves, innovations. Such production functions allow for more efficient methods of combining inputs to produce outputs than those that are already known. Notice that in both cases the actions of entrepreneurs serve to extend the range of available technology.

Entrepreneurs who decide to develop innovative products often use their knowledge of the talent pool and production technologies in the relevant industry when, among other things, they decide on the mixture of labor and capital they will use in the production process. Although it is the case that entrepreneurs can use contractual arrangements and the development of organizational culture to influence the behavior of people they work with, making appropriate decisions in the first place about the composition of the production workforce can have a huge bearing upon subsequent productivity. Similarly, in theory capital investments can readily be transformed, but in practice such change can be expensive, and avoiding unnecessary changes is important for maintaining profitability. This suggests that the process of selecting a production function consists of making a large number of microlevel decisions, some of which will be made only occasionally, others of which will be ongoing. As with other aspects of entrepreneurship, being an adept reader of social situations, figuring out whom to approach for technical advice, and having a clear sense of how to appropriately structure interactions among contributors to the production process can be vital for ensuring the effective attainment of goals.

Establishing a Nexus of Contracts

Choosing a production function involves thinking analytically about the appropriate relationship between a set of inputs and the creation of an output. But knowing the details of an efficient production function provides only the starting point for determining an appropriate way to organize production. Recipe books can be thought of as lists of production functions for the creation of food because they tell us in a purely technical fashion how to combine inputs to create outputs. However, they tell us nothing about the organization of cooks, how many cooks might be optimal, or where production should occur. When choosing a particular production function the entrepreneur seeks to establish an efficient relationship between inputs and outputs. In contrast, when choosing how to coordinate production the entrepreneur seeks to achieve an efficient relationship among input owners. Distinguishing between these activities is conceptually possible and useful from the point of view of discussing entrepreneurship. Observationally, however, such a distinction would be more difficult to make.

In devising efficient relationships among input owners, entrepreneurs must seek to minimize a range of costs. Among these the three most important types of cost to consider are production costs, management costs, and transaction costs (Demsetz 1991). Production costs involve the costs of inputs and their combination to create new outputs. Inputs can here be seen both as raw materials and as the wages of workers and the fees paid to contractors. Management costs are those incurred while directing others to perform their designated tasks. By contrast, transaction costs come from efforts to arrange aspects of production through markets, thus including the search costs of finding appropriate trading partners, the costs of writing contracts with potential partners, and the costs of monitoring contract compliance. In a complex production process where many individuals are contributing components to the final output, both management costs and transaction costs could be extremely high. An entrepreneur must decide what components of the final product to produce "in house" and which to purchase across markets. In-house production incurs management costs; production across markets incurs transaction costs. The resultant nexus of contracts will reflect the entrepreneur's judgment regarding efficient organizational forms.

Establishing a nexus of contracts among input owners that efficiently supports the production process is a vital aspect of entrepreneurship, but there are limits to what can be achieved through the design of formal contractual arrangements. Many aspects of informal human relations also serve to affect the value of any given trade. For this reason, the entrepreneur must take care to ensure that informal as well as formal relations among contributors to the production process function smoothly. Alchian and Demsetz made this point succinctly in their discussion of firms and team production. While their interest lay primarily in explaining formal differences across firm-like arrangements, they nonetheless observed: "Every team member would prefer a team in which no one, not even himself, shirked. . . . If one could enhance a common interest in nonshirking in the guise of team loyalty or team spirit, the team would be more efficient" (1972, 790). Increasingly, informal aspects of organization have received attention from contributors to the literature on the firm, business strategy, and organization theory. Taking insights from this diverse set of contributions, I next discuss how the entrepreneur can improve the effectiveness of a production process by working to establish an appropriate organizational culture.

Establishing an Organizational Culture

For entrepreneurs, establishing a supportive organizational culture holds the promise of improving cooperation among group members, giving people a clear sense of the values and general practices of the organization and ensuring the lines of communication remain open. Without informal norms of cooperation it is highly unlikely that cooperation will emerge. As Gary J. Miller has pointed out, "People do not have a dominant strategy to cooperate; rather, cooperation is rational only when each player has a great deal of confidence that others are cooperating. Cooperation can unwind very quickly" (1992, 186). Therefore, it is helpful for the productivity of an organization if its members share the view that their cooperative actions will be met with similar responses. Without getting a clear sense of the values and general practices of an organization, members are unlikely to respond to given contingencies in consistent ways. Lack of coordination of this sort can reduce the likelihood of an organization responding rapidly to changes in the operating environment, and productivity is likely to be harmed. Finally, without open lines of communication it can be difficult for vital information to be rapidly disseminated when the need arises. Thus, in defense of idle talk James G. March and Guje Sevón (1988, 433) have argued that "gossip maintains links among people . . . during those long periods when communication is unneeded, so that communication links will be easily available should they be needed."

Cooperation, clear values, and open lines of communication in an organization may appear desirable, but the question remains of just how much control an entrepreneur can have over these things. Is it possible to build a supportive organizational culture? According to a range of observers the answer is *yes*. Further, for reasons that will soon become clear, it is also the case that the actions of the initial leader of an organization, that is, the entrepreneur, can be hugely influential in shaping the subsequent character of an organizational culture. In seeking to develop a supportive organizational culture entrepreneurs can take several actions, each of which reinforce the others. I discuss here three types of action. My intention is not to provide an exhaustive list, but rather to suggest the possibilities that are open to an entrepreneur who seeks to establish a supportive organizational culture.

First, to promote cooperation among members of the organization, it is important for the entrepreneur to extend their expectations of how long they will remain associated with one another. When people perceive that their interactions with others are for the short term, they face few incentives to engage in cooperative action since the possibility of future reciprocity is low. Miller (1992) argued that one way the leader can extend time horizons is to make credible commitments to the survival of the organization and the well-being of members over the longer run. Yet when the entrepreneur is just starting out with a new venture, making commitments of this sort can be difficult. But possibilities exist for signaling commitment. One is to make it known that the failure of the venture would be seriously damaging to the entrepreneur's own livelihood. Another possibility involves getting the backing and support of individuals who have strong records of success. Finally, the entrepreneur may demonstrate a "future orientation" by regularly discussing next steps for the organization, perhaps in the context of reporting quarterly or annual successes.

Second, to promote particular organizational values, and encourage high levels of informal communication, the entrepreneur can attempt to lead by example. Entrepreneurs can set up organizations in ways that convey a sense of team spirit. This might involve encouraging members of the organization to eat meals together regularly, or supporting efforts by others to help particular members of the organization when bottlenecks or pressing deadlines arise in part of the production process. Leading by example is possible in instances like this. Management books often stress the importance of leaders creating "myths" about themselves, such as stories about how they have gone out of their way to be helpful to particular employees when they have faced problems. Often, the importance of "management by walking around" is stressed as a key to promoting organizational values and encouraging informal communication (see, for instance, Peters and Waterman, 1982). Management by walking around allows leaders to communicate the importance of certain values and demonstrate directly their commitment to team work. Striking up spontaneous conversations and encouraging members of an organization to do this can be very good for keeping open the lines of communication.

Finally, the entrepreneur can attempt to build a reputation for fairness with employees and a commitment to maintaining a high-quality product. David M. Kreps has argued that a key element of building a reputation for operating according to a given "principle" involves applying the principle at all times, "even when its application might not be optimal in the short run" (1990, 93). Where possible, the entrepreneur could try to ensure consistency between informal efforts at reputation building and adjustments to formal organizational systems. For example, giving rewards for innovative thinking could become part of the system of employee compensation used in the organization. Similarly, adopting a policy of ensuring complete customer satisfaction, even in cases where this might require providing additional services at no cost, sends a strong message both to customers and to members of the organization about business integrity. This is another way of helping to promote and maintain a performance-enhancing organizational culture.

The development of organizational culture is path dependent. What happens in the early stages of an organization comes to have a strong influence on what happens later. A key aspect of developing an organizational culture involves conveying expectations to members and giving them a sense of what constitute appropriate forms of behavior in any given set of circumstances. For example, cultures might differ significantly with respect to the amount of time and effort people put into their work, the way they communicate with those around them, and so on. Ultimately this should lead people to take certain actions by default, in an essentially "unconscious" fashion. Two implications follow. First, how the entrepreneur behaves when first building up the organization will matter greatly for subsequent developments. Second, once an organizational culture has been set on a particular path, the habits of mind and knee-jerk responses of members will not be easily altered.

An additional point is worth making here. Annalee Saxenian (1994) has suggested that the culture of informal work groups, management by walking around, and spontaneous conversations that were deliberately encouraged in Silicon Valley companies like Hewlett Packard ultimately had a spillover effect in the whole community of computer engineers in the region. "Entrepreneurs came to see social relationships and even gossip as a crucial aspect of their business" (1994, 33). Although we should question the extent to which the entrepreneurial climate in Silicon Valley was shaped by other forces, the thought is appealing that the actions of the entrepreneurs in a handful of pioneering companies ultimately influenced the way that many other companies came to organize their day-to-day activities. In fact, this outcome is not dissimilar to what we see happening when an entrepreneur introduces a new production process or brings a new product to market. Done well, these actions force others to change how they do things.

Entrepreneurs and the Market Process

The defining characteristic of entrepreneurs is that they seek to create and bring to market products or services that represent innovations. Entrepreneurs seek to establish trade among people where before there was only an absence, a void, and thus distinguish themselves by venturing into new territory in the marketplace and serving as market makers. By definition, in this new territory they cannot rely on maps that others have drawn and they cannot follow familiar directions. They must imagine new possibilities and then take actions intended to support the realization of those possibilities. All the actions of entrepreneurs, including the imagining of new possibilities, require significant levels of social interaction. Entrepreneurs must be engaged enough in relevant social activities to achieve an acute sense of what others want in order to persuade others that what they have to offer is a useful innovation. Yet these entrepreneurs must also achieve enough distance from their society and the marketplace so that they are able to see things differently from those around them. They must be able to question the contemporary order of things, seeing, for example, the arbitrariness of how we construct our sense of satisfaction within the current range of products and services.

Many people might think they see opportunities for gain; and many people might believe that they have come up with inventions that could do wonders for improving human lives. However, out of these hordes only a relative few go on to actually attempt to develop innovations, attempt to devise strategies for action, and attempt to organize others to effect new trades. It is these relative few who merit being described as entrepreneurs. Whether or not they succeed in their efforts is immaterial. For the purpose of description, what counts is that an individual attempts to bring an innovation to market and does so in a fashion that, given available information, appears at least *intendedly* rational.

Entrepreneurship involves several aspects. First, entrepreneurs must perceive opportunities for gain. This requires them to develop a clear sense of what others are looking for, and determine the likelihood that they themselves could come up with a product or service that would successfully fill a given need. Second, entrepreneurs must develop innovations. Although they might start out with particular ideas or inventions that they intend to work with, entrepreneurs must always consider how potential customers will respond to what they have to offer. For this reason the development of innovations is always a social process. Even outright imitation—taking an idea observed in one context and bringing it to another—will typically require the entrepreneur to think carefully about how to present the innovation to others. Consequently the nature of the innovation will likely change then too. Third, entrepreneurs must devise strategies and work the system. The more intimate information they have of their operating environment the better they are positioned to introduce their innovations. Correctly anticipating how others will respond can be a critical determinant of the success of an innovation. Finally, entrepreneurs must organize others and provide leadership. Rarely can individuals develop innovative products and services in isolation. They must find ways to work with others. This requires thinking carefully about how to organize production processes, how to structure contracts among participants in these processes, and how to ensure relations among all members involved in production operate smoothly. Among these aspects of entrepreneurship, the development of innovations is the one that is unique to the entrepreneur. But the development and introduction of innovations cannot occur without the entrepreneur undertaking the other, supporting actions.[3]

My discussion in this chapter serves to highlight the extent to which entrepreneurs must be unusually sociable individuals. Entrepreneurship cannot occur outside a social setting. Every aspect of entrepreneurship involves the social construction of meaning. To shape the meanings that others attach to particular objects or actions, entrepreneurs must be excellent communicators. This means taking the time to listen to what others are saying, as well as thinking carefully about how to present ideas and arguments to others. The combination of these skills is rarer than we might think.

In everyday parlance it is occasionally said that, in a given instance, "so-and-so was quite *entrepreneurial*." What might this mean? Typically, such a comment is made when an individual has acted in an unusually forward manner, seizing the day, seizing an opportunity, when others might have been content to let it pass. Given what I have said here, this everyday use of the term "entrepreneurial" is not inconsistent with my definition of entrepreneurship. Yet a distinct impoverishment of the notion of the entrepreneur occurs when we describe things like somebody's academic grantsmanship or another's efforts to beat out the competition for a promotion as entrepreneurial. Such actions are entirely consistent with the nature of the game that has previously been established by others. Such actions do not represent challenges to the status quo; if anything, they simply serve to reinforce it. In contrast, even though entrepreneurs also seize opportunities, they do so with the intention of changing the current structure of things. They strive to generate something new, to introduce an innovation. More often than not such action will upset the status quo. Doing this requires a great deal of thought and energy and a lot of social interaction. Compared with this, most of what we routinely term entrepreneurial involves little more than striking a pose.

Summary

Entrepreneurs act as market makers. Through their efforts to bring innovations to market, they permit various individuals to engage in trade with each other where previously no such trade occurred. Yet these creative actions of the entrepreneur can also be destructive. They offer new possibilities for trade, but they also challenge old ways of doing things. Those who have benefited from the old ways, and who stand to lose from entrepreneurial challenges, cannot be expected to passively accept changes wrought by innovative upstarts. Given this, entrepreneurs must pay attention to a range of details in their operating environment if they are to achieve success. Further, entrepreneurs can rarely act single-handedly, and so they must be very good at listening to and working with others.

In describing the actions of entrepreneurs, my purpose throughout has been to set the stage for thinking more carefully about the merit of referring to certain actors in the policy process as policy entrepreneurs. Political scientists frequently use the terms entrepreneur and entrepreneurial to describe political actors and the things they do. But how literally should we take such descriptions? Usually little or no effort is made to explain the use of this market-based metaphor. Apparently the "logic of the imagination" can freely transport us from the realm of markets to that of politics. But the shift is not so smooth, and important questions emerge. Are some political actors behaving in a manner that is consistent with that of entrepreneurs in the marketplace? Or could we just as readily describe them using other words? To answer such questions in a systematic manner, we must first have a clear understanding of just what it is that entrepreneurs do. Hence our excursion into the world of entrepreneurs in the market process.

Now we can return to politics. The description of the entrepreneur that I have presented offers a starting point for careful thinking about entrepreneurship in political contexts. If the image of the entrepreneur in the market process is suitable for use as a metaphor by scholars interested in the behavior of policymakers, then how far can we extend this metaphor? How can use of this metaphor lead us to think in new ways about what goes on in the policy process? Are there points where the metaphor breaks down? An understanding of market entrepreneurship enables us to respond directly to such questions. Thus, in the next chapter I shift from the world of markets to the world of politics and I offer a theory of policy entrepreneurship.

Notes

1. To develop their discussion Aldrich and Zimmer (1986) used Mark S. Granovetter's (1973) model of social relations, which suggests that social relations are represented by strong ties and weak ties. A family member or a close friend can be considered as a strong tie. A friend of the family or a friend of a friend can be construed as a weak tie. In emphasizing the "strength of weak ties," Grannovetter suggests that weak ties can often serve as vital conduits for channeling relevant information to an individual on a variety of matters. In terms of entrepreneurship weak ties can serve to alert an individual to potential opportunities for gain.

2. For reviews, see Williamson (1985) and Eggertsson (1990).

3. For some readers it might appear strange that I have not emphasized risk bearing as the distinguishing characteristic of entrepreneurs. But many individuals bear risks in the marketplace, even when not serving as entrepreneurs. Risk bearing is not unique to entrepreneurs. That said, it is clear from many facets of this discussion that entrepreneurship is a risky business. There are many easier ways to make a living. In choosing to pursue a particular opportunity for gain, the entrepreneur passes up other possibilities. To that extent all entrepreneurial activity has opportunity costs. Further, almost all of the relationships that entrepreneurs establish have the potential to fall apart. As a result entrepreneurs run the risk of losing customers and suppliers. This, in turn, can harm their reputation, both in the short term and the longer term.

FIVE

Policy Entrepreneurs and the Policymaking Process

In the marketplace entrepreneurs reveal themselves through their efforts to introduce innovations. To increase their chances of success with such efforts, they must understand their operating environment and they must have the ability to listen closely to others. Only then can entrepreneurs begin to argue and behave in ways that alter the interpretations that others bring to given situations. As in the marketplace, in the world of policymaking promoting policy innovations can be arduous. Successfully advocating policies that signal a break with the past requires huge amounts of social activity. To make successful arguments for policy innovation, advocates must understand their audience and they must recognize the limits and opportunities presented by their operating environments. Introducing policy innovations requires intelligence, social acuity, and endurance.

Here I follow past practice among political scientists and define those who seek to introduce policy innovations as policy entrepreneurs. But I do so to start—rather than foreclose—careful scrutiny. In this chapter I set out a theory of policy entrepreneurship. I explore the extent to which we can draw parallels between the actions of entrepreneurs in the marketplace and what their counterparts might be expected to do in the policymaking process. This effort holds the promise of improving our ability to appropriately identify actual policy entrepreneurs and to then consider how their actions conform to or depart from theoretically derived expectations.

Policy Innovation as a Form of Policy Change

Policy change can have many causes. When we observe the outputs of any policymaking forum, we see an ongoing series of policy changes. Indeed, the very term "policymaking" implies the production of change. Because policy change is the output of policymaking, everyone involved in the policymaking process contributes in some sense to making change possible. In light of this, it would seem curious to claim that some actors are sufficiently different that they deserve a special name, that they deserve to be called policy entrepreneurs. But what distinguishes policy entrepreneurs from the rest of the crowd is their penchant for introducing innovations.

As in the world of policymaking, in the marketplace change frequently occurs. However, the introduction of *innovative* products and the development of *innovations* in the production process appear distinctive. Consider, for example, the market for higher education. Observed from year to year, the range of courses offered by universities for credit and the degree requirements might change in routine ways through established procedures. But if a university introduces a degree program or group of courses aimed especially at increasing revenues by attracting new groups of people into the student body, then this can be seen as an *innovation*. The introduction of not-for-credit summer courses involving travel or study abroad for art lovers, gardening buffs, or cycling enthusiasts represents such an innovation. The new courses present a challenge to conventional understandings of what a university is meant to do. They change the behavior of a certain group of people (in this case people who, in the past, might never have thought of universities as offering leisure opportunities). The new courses also require people in the university to adjust their perceptions of the role of faculty members. This is what innovations do. Innovations represent changes that are deliberately designed to lead or force people to break out of particular routine behaviors and come to new understandings of their environment. Seen in this way, it is possible to think of innovations as changes that have the potential to trigger a chain reaction of related changes.

Two additional points should be made here. First, the distinction between innovations and other forms of change is *not* equivalent to the distinction between fundamental and incremental change. Although typically it is the case that fundamental changes embody at least some amount of innovation, innovations can be facilitated through incremental steps. Consider the example of universities offering leisure-oriented summer courses. This innovation could well be introduced in an incremental way, beginning with just one course and then growing to involve courses offered by many departments.

The second point to make is that entrepreneurs can be thought of as people who work to introduce innovations, but the introduction of an innovation need not always depend on the actions of an entrepreneur. Again, consider the university example. Suppose that there is a university where leisure-oriented courses have never been heard of, let alone tried. Also, suppose that this university currently enjoys sound and sustainable financial health. Under these conditions, anyone interested in introducing the innovation would most likely have to make a major effort to persuade others of the merit of the idea. A range of entrepreneurial skills, such as the ability to work with others and make convincing arguments, would help increase the chances of the innovation being adopted. Now consider an alternative scenario. Suppose that the idea of enhancing university revenue through leisure-oriented courses had been introduced in many places and had come to be accepted among university administrators as a useful moneymaking innovation. Suppose, further, that the university of interest is experiencing declining enrollments and financial difficulties. Under these circumstances it would be much easier to introduce the innovation at this university. (Of course, it would still take significant organizational effort to put the innovation in place.) We might now expect high levels of receptiveness to the innovation, thus reducing—and perhaps eliminating—the need for an entrepreneur to push for its adoption. The innovation would still represent a deliberate break from the old way of doing things, but resistance might be limited, making adoption easier.

The Milieu of the Policy Entrepreneur

Whenever we seek to explain variation among individuals who perform ostensibly identical tasks, we must consider both contextual and individual factors. By ignoring contextual factors, we might unduly conclude that one individual is better suited to a task than another. Our ability to explain performance differences is further complicated by the tendency for individual and contextual factors to interact in significant, but not necessarily obvious, ways. Entrepreneurship involves perceiving opportunities for gain and then organizing others and bringing innovative products to market. Therefore, while entrepreneurs assuredly have considerable scope to influence outcomes, their actions are nevertheless socially embedded. The nature of the local context or operating environment affects both the likelihood that entrepreneurs will perceive opportunities for gain and their ability to successfully develop appropriate innovations. Therefore, we can improve our ability to explain why entrepreneurs are found more often in some places than in others by taking the time to focus entirely upon context, or the milieu of the entrepreneur.

Opportunities for Entrepreneurship in the Marketplace

Across a range of market settings, we can expect to find many unique entrepreneurial milieus. In the United States opportunities for entrepreneurship in the film industry tend to be found primarily around Hollywood, opportunities for entrepreneurship in computer technology are found primarily around Silicon Valley, and so on. When attempting to discuss the milieu of the entrepreneur in any general way, we must inevitably make simplifications. I delineate here four general scenarios, each characterized by a combination of the extremes of two variables. The first variable is the pace of change in the milieu, as measured in terms of consumer preferences, technology, and management techniques. The second variable is industry concentration, as measured by the number and size of the firms currently operating in the milieu. The cases are depicted in Table 5-1.

When the pace of change in an industry is fast and the concentration of firms is low many opportunities exist for entrepreneurship. This is Case 1. The fast pace of change ensures a high demand for people to come up with creative solutions to problems. The by-product of this demand for creativity is the development of an intellectual ferment. This in itself can be vital for prompting learning in the milieu and stimulating people to generate and discuss new ideas that could potentially lead to innovations. The low concentration of firms in the industry raises the possibility that people who seek to bring an innovative product to market will be able to do so through starting up their own businesses. Saxenian's (1994) discussion of the milieu in Silicon Valley suggests that innovation there has been propelled by this combination of fast change in the computer technology industry and low concentration among firms in the region.

Table 5-1. ***The Milieu of the Entrepreneur***

Industry Concentration	*Pace of Change*	
	Fast	Slow
Low	*Case 1* Many opportunities	*Case 2* Conditional opportunities
High	*Case 3* Conditional opportunities	*Case 4* Few opportunities

Case 2 arises when the pace of change in a milieu is slow and the concentration of firms is low: fewer opportunities for entrepreneurship exist than in Case 1. This is an instance of conditional opportunities. The low concentration among firms provides opportunities for people with ideas for innovation to succeed through starting their own businesses. However, the slow pace of change in the industry reduces demand for innovation. The emergence of brew pubs in recent years represents an example of innovation occurring in a fairly stable, slow-paced industry. Entrepreneurs surmising an opportunity for gain by combining microbreweries with bars were able to open up the market for beer and introduce innovative products.

Sometimes a milieu is characterized by a fast pace of change and high firm concentration. This is Case 3. This is another instance where opportunities for entrepreneurship are conditional. Although the pace of change creates a demand for innovation, the high firm concentration can serve to limit the opportunities for entrepreneurs to bring their innovations to market. As a result, entrepreneurs might find it most profitable to launch their innovations under the auspices of one of the established firms in the industry. This was the case for many years when the telephone industry in the United States was dominated by AT&T.

Case 4 depicts the most limiting conditions for the entrepreneur. These arise when there is slow pace of change in a milieu and high firm concentration. Not only is there little obvious demand for innovations here, but the high firm concentration can block the path of entrepreneurs seeking to launch new products. The airline industry in the United States is representative of this kind of milieu. For many years, the technology of air travel and its marketing has remained the same, several airlines have continued to dominate supply of services, and consumer preferences have been based overwhelmingly on price consideration. This makes it difficult for would-be airline entrepreneurs to perceive opportunities for gain, let alone develop innovations to capture them.

The four cases discussed here represent distinct milieus, each of which is likely to influence the amount and nature of the entrepreneurial activity found there. Because it greatly simplifies reality, this way of thinking about the milieu of the entrepreneur necessarily overlooks many details, some of which could be seen as more crucial to entrepreneurship than the pace of change and the level of industry concentration. Nonetheless, this taxonomy provides a straightforward and plausible way to think about how different conditions in a milieu influence entrepreneurship.[1]

The Policy Milieu and Opportunities for Entrepreneurship

Just as the relevant milieu can be thought to shape the opportunities faced by entrepreneurs in the marketplace, so we might expect policy entrepreneurs to be affected by their context. Knowing about contextual effects can thus help us understand why policy entrepreneurs and other actors in the policymaking process engage in specific actions. Following the approach used above I again discuss four cases, each representing a combination of two variables. These variables are similar to those used for thinking about entrepreneurship in markets. The first variable is the pace of change in the policy milieu. This can be measured in terms of citizen and interest group preferences and the introduction of public-sector management reforms in and around a given jurisdiction. The second variable concerns venues for political participation. These venues include the town hall in a city and the legislature in a state. Some venues for political participation are relatively more open or closed than others. For example, a venue characterized by direct democracy is relatively open, allowing a broad range of citizens to voice their ideas and preferences during the process of public policymaking. By contrast, a venue dominated by a few powerful interest groups can be thought of as relatively closed. Table 5-2 depicts the four cases.

First, consider Case 1. Policy change is often infectious. Significant policy change in one or two areas of government can generate support for additional change in other areas. A city or state government, for example, might be going through a period of general change in the organization of service delivery. More services might be getting contracted

Table 5-2. ***The Milieu of the Policy Entrepreneur***

Venues for Political Participation	*Pace of Change*	
	Fast	Slow
Open	*Case 1* Many opportunities	*Case 2* Conditional opportunities
Closed	*Case 3* Conditional opportunities	*Case 4* Few opportunities

out to private suppliers, or there may be a general trend to have government agencies play a direct role in service delivery. Such widespread change can generate a lot of discussion and exchange of ideas about approaches to policy design. When combined with an open venue for political participation, these conditions can create a milieu for policy entrepreneurs characterized by many opportunities. In such a milieu, we should expect that policy entrepreneurs will frequently perceive possibilities for the introduction of policy innovations. The openness of the venue also gives them scope to generate support for their proposed policy changes. Case 1 therefore represents the best conditions in a policy milieu for policy entrepreneurship.

Case 2 represents a milieu that, like Case 1, is characterized by an open venue for political participation. However, in this case, the general pace of policy change is slow. We can think here of a sleepy New England town where there is plenty of scope for participation in policymaking, but where nothing much ever seems to happen. Under these conditions, a policy entrepreneur would face fewer opportunities to introduce policy innovations than when the general pace of policy change is fast. The major task facing the policy entrepreneur here is to convince other people that change is necessary, a task that is relatively more difficult to accomplish when there are few other examples of change taking place.

Case 3 also represents a milieu with conditional opportunities for policy entrepreneurs to promote policy innovation. Although the pace of change is fast, the venues for political participation are relatively closed. We might think of a state government in which established interest groups dominate the policymaking process, reducing the possibility for individuals or newly formed groups to influence policy deliberations. To gain access to the policy debate, a policy entrepreneur might have to closely align with a political party or long-established interest group and attempt to influence the policy debate through the channels of that organization. This requires convincing other members of the organization itself that the idea for a policy innovation is a good one before trying to influence others.

Finally, Case 4 represents the milieu offering the least opportunities for policy entrepreneurship. The pace of change is slow, and the venues for political participation are relatively closed. Under such circumstances, it is difficult for a policy entrepreneur to argue that the introduction of a policy innovation is necessary, simply because so few other instances of policy change are available to demonstrate the possibility and value of change. Furthermore, gaining a hearing is difficult under these conditions, because the entrepreneur has to work closely with established organizations, who themselves may face few incentives to support a policy innovation.

This effort to classify policy milieus suggests that policy entrepreneurs can be helped or hindered by the nature of the politics in their locales. Over the past few decades various political scientists, beginning with Theodore J. Lowi (1964), have produced taxonomies relating distinctive types of politics to the making of distinctive types of public policies. As Barbara Nelson has observed, "The problem with this research is not that the typologies lack power to explain political actions, but that there are a goodly number of them, each developed to deal with a different question of governance" (1996, 572). Since I am suggesting yet another way of thinking about the political conditions affecting policymaking, here I note the points of intersection that can be found between my approach and two others.

James Q. Wilson (1973, 1989a) developed one of the earliest and most prominent typologies of the politics of policymaking. According to Wilson, policies could be classified in terms of the concentration or dispersion of their perceived benefits and costs. Taking this approach, it is possible to generate a two-by-two table, where the distribution of perceived benefits is treated as one variable and the distribution of perceived costs is treated as the other. According to Wilson, the expected incidence of the benefits and costs of particular policies can help us to explain the politics surrounding them. In presenting this typology, among other things, Wilson argued that policy entrepreneurs can often have important effects on policy outcomes.

Table 5-3. ***Wilson's Classification of the Politics of Policy Issues***

	Perceived Costs	
Perceived Benefits	Distributed	Concentrated
Distributed	*Case 1* Majoritarian politics	*Case 2* Entrepreneurial politics
Concentrated	*Case 3* Client politics	*Case 4* Interest group politics

When benefits and costs are both distributed, the result is "majoritarian politics." This is Case 1 in Table 5-3. There is little incentive for interest groups to form to influence policy direction. The key players in this kind of policymaking are the proximate decisionmakers and their advisors. Policy entrepreneurs might seek to change the ways that people perceive of benefits and costs, but such influence must be achieved through the making of arguments rather than the organization of interest group muscle. Wilson suggested that policy debates concerning antitrust regulation and social security are characterized by this type of politics.

Case 2 arises when perceived costs are concentrated and perceived benefits are dispersed. Wilson suggested that in this case, policy entrepreneurs face incentives to develop interest groups to secure specific benefits for group members. Efforts to secure consumer protection can be seen as falling into this category. Wilson observed the following:

> When measures such as these become law, it is often because a policy entrepreneur has dramatized an issue, galvanized public opinion, and mobilized congressional support. Sometimes that entrepreneur is in the government (a senator or an outspoken bureaucrat); sometimes that entrepreneur is a private person (the best known, of course, is Ralph Nader). The motives of such entrepreneurs can be either self-serving or public-spirited; the policies that they embrace may be either good or bad. (1989a, 439)

Wilson's Case 3 represents "client politics." According to Wilson, such politics emerges when powerful, concentrated interests are able to petition the government to develop and maintain policies that confer benefits upon them, to the cost of the broader society. Efforts by manufacturers to influence trade policies and efforts by service providers to limit competition by regulation of supply represent types of client politics. Wilson argued that instances of client politics can be challenged by policy entrepreneurs if they dramatize the costs of the present policy settings, demonstrate how benefits accrue to a select group, and call into question the motives of the politicians allowing this to happen.

Finally, Wilson's Case 4 emerges when policies have concentrated costs and concentrated benefits. In such instances, both those who benefit from and those who bear the cost of the policy face strong incentives to organize and to fight for or against the status quo. Wilson asserted that there is little demand or scope here for policy entrepreneurship. Politics takes on a business-as-usual nature, involving "a tedious process of mediation" to strike bargains between preexisting associations, interspersed with electoral efforts to change the relevant decisionmakers (1973, 336).

Although we are considering somewhat different questions, my approach to thinking about the milieu of the policy entrepreneur appears fairly consistent with Wilson's discussion of the politics of policy issues. My interest lies in considering how the policy milieu serves to support or stifle the actions of policy entrepreneurs who seek to promote policy innovations. Wilson's interest is in how different kinds of policy issues generate, and are thus accompanied by, different types of politics. According to Wilson, many opportunities for policy entrepreneurship exist when asymmetries between the perceived incidence of costs and benefits suggest that unorganized individuals could potentially gain from coalition formation.

I differ from Wilson in how I think about the development of policy innovations. In particular, while Wilson sees asymmetries in the distribution of perceived costs and benefits as likely sources of policy change, I argue that more general conditions in a policy milieu might alert a policy entrepreneur to the merits of introducing a policy innovation. Perceptions of the costs and benefits of current arrangements might often trigger the pursuit of policy change, but they are not the only things that matter. I have suggested that the pace of change in a policy milieu represents a key variable likely to stimulate the development of ideas for policy innovation. Some of this change might be driven by efforts to alter perceptions of costs and benefits. But the pace of policy change might also be driven by concerns about policy effectiveness, or new perceptions about what phenomena constitute problems, or what problems deserve public attention. In short, I suggest that in focusing on the milieu of the policy entrepreneur I tend to give more emphasis than Wilson to the importance of ideas, arguments, and the intellectual ferment for motivating efforts to secure policy change.[2]

Over recent years, a growing body of policy scholars has emphasized the importance of ideas and argumentation in the politics of policymaking. (For a discussion, see Majone 1996.) For example, in developing an alternative typology of the politics of policymaking, Anne Larason Schneider and Helen Ingram (1997) highlight how the social construction of target groups produces political opportunities and risks for politicians. According to these authors, politicians can avoid risks by delivering benefits to "stronger, deserving" groups ("the advantaged") or by imposing costs on "weaker, undeserving" groups ("deviants"). Significantly, by emphasizing that group identity is socially constructed, Schneider and Ingram suggest that rhetorical efforts to alter the demarcation of groups and the labels placed on them can have important material implications. For our purposes, Schneider and Ingram's discussion suggests that entrepreneurial efforts to reconstitute group identity might alter participation in policymaking. In other words, this work implies that policy entrepreneurs can potentially change the milieu in which they find themselves. This, in turn, might smooth the way for the introduction of various policy innovations.

Context Matters

Like other actors in society, policy entrepreneurs are not completely free agents. There are limits to what they are able to do, and these limits emerge from the combined effects of, among other things, the institutional structures governing policymaking, current policy settings, and the behaviors and expectations of other groups and individuals around them. This milieu shapes the opportunities and the actions open to policy entrepreneurs, but not in a deterministic fashion. A given milieu will not necessarily support or inhibit a given set of actions on the part of policy entrepreneurs. We can, however, talk about tendencies. By paying attention to the characteristics of a given milieu, we can form some expectations about the possible role that policy entrepreneurs might play in generating support for specific policy innovations.

Next, I shift my focus from the policy context to the characteristics and actions of policy entrepreneurs. This shift also takes us from *locus* to *process*. In general, policy entrepreneurs, like their counterparts in the marketplace, should be expected to behave as highly efficacious individuals. We should expect them to utilize their talents and resources to make the most of perceived opportunities.

Social Perceptiveness

Entrepreneurs in the marketplace must exhibit high levels of social perceptiveness. They cannot possibly survive if they show little interest in listening to others and identifying their needs. Therefore, social perceptiveness can be thought of as the starting point for entrepreneurial creativity. Once entrepreneurs have gleaned relevant information through observation and conversation, they can begin to interpret and understand that information. What is curious about the role of the entrepreneur is that, while being able to listen closely to others, he or she must be able to keep some critical distance from what is learned, avoiding the tendency to follow conventional ways of thinking. Understanding the needs of others is vital, but so too is the ability to interpret those needs in unique ways, coming to a novel understanding of how those needs might be met. This ability to be both close to others and yet maintain perspective on the situation places entrepreneurs in frequent danger of isolation, of being ostracized for coming up with ideas that run counter to, and that could readily be interpreted as challenging, conventional wisdom. This again suggests the importance of social perceptiveness on the part of the entrepreneur. Knowing when to avoid market engagement might be as valuable as knowing when to act.

Like entrepreneurs in the marketplace, policy entrepreneurs must also be creative individuals who exhibit high levels of social perceptiveness. The goal of the policy entrepreneur is to place an issue on the policy agenda and then have a preferred policy approach, a particular policy innovation, adopted. This requires policy entrepreneurs to blend creative thinking with the desire and ability to find out what other people want in terms of public policy, and how other people might be motivated to pursue particular policy goals. In contrast to their counterparts in the market policy entrepreneurs operate entirely in the realm of ideas. Even the innovations that they help to produce—new policies—are essentially abstractions until the point at which they are implemented by the relevant government agencies. Policy entrepreneurship involves making arguments about the causal relationship between government activities and real-world outcomes. For example, the policy entrepreneur Ralph Nader (1972) made the argument that cars lacked safety features and that more stringent government regulation of car design specifications could reduce the number of injuries and fatalities associated with road accidents. Similarly, over recent years various policy entrepreneurs have argued that our public schools are not performing effectively. These people have then proposed the introduction of various types of school choice, claiming that this policy innovation could make schools more responsive to the needs of students and their parents (see Nathan 1989, 1996).

Policy entrepreneurs must be socially perceptive if they are to identify social problems, draw attention to them, and gain support for remedial policy innovations. Often social problems might not even be recognized as such, requiring the policy entrepreneur to think creatively about how to make arguments that bring other people to agree that a problem exists and that it requires government action. But this creative thinking must be grounded in an awareness of the social context, and informed by a sophisticated understanding of how to make arguments that other people in that context find convincing. Absent social perceptiveness, the creative thinker whose mind turns to politics risks being labeled a crank. Anyone who rails against the present state of the world and the actions of the government but who shows no interest in taking constructive steps toward achieving change is doomed to be forever a voice in the wilderness.

In thinking about a problem, the policy entrepreneur must consider ways to demonstrate to others, particularly policymakers, that it is worthy of government attention and that a given policy innovation would represent a suitable response. This again requires social perceptiveness. Policy entrepreneurs cannot hope to have influence on the policymaking process if they are ignorant of the broader concerns of the times and the ways that their particular concerns and prescriptions for policy change complement or contradict them. This is not to say that policy entrepreneurs must somehow kowtow to broader policy fashions. Rather, with an awareness of the broader context and the concerns of policymakers, policy entrepreneurs can shape their proposals to improve the likelihood that their ideas will be taken seriously. We should expect that the greater the ability of the policy entrepreneur to perceive the needs of others and how they can be addressed, the greater the chances of having an impact on the policymaking process.

I have discussed social perceptiveness as a characteristic of the policy entrepreneur that can be isolated from other characteristics and from social position. Analytically, this separation is worthwhile because it allows us to focus closely upon specific features of the policy entrepreneur that are likely to influence success. However, empirically it might be extremely difficult to separate social perceptiveness from other characteristics. In particular, social perceptiveness would appear to be closely bound up with social connectedness. If you have a lot of contacts with other people, it is likely that you will be more socially perceptive than if you have few such contacts. Yet it is also the case that someone can have a lot of contacts with other people and—for a range of reasons—be quite limited when it comes to perceiving their needs and desires. Eventually we might expect some sort of equilibrium to be reached. That is to say, people who lack the skills of social perceptiveness are likely after some time to become more socially isolated, while those who have an abundance of such skills are likely to become increasingly central amid social groups.

Social Connectedness

Social and professional contacts represent vital resources for entrepreneurs in the marketplace, and we should expect this to also be the case for policy entrepreneurs. Later in this chapter, I will discuss at greater length some of the specific ways that policy entrepreneurs might use their social and professional contacts to advantage. For now, however, my intention is to focus upon and discuss the ways that they can develop their social connections and how such connections might be maintained for rapid and effective use when necessary.

For the entrepreneur, a well-developed set of social and professional contacts can make the difference between success and failure in the launch of an innovation. But developing such contacts in just one particular group is unlikely to be sufficient to sustain entrepreneurship. The likelihood that an entrepreneur will perceive opportunities for gain where others do not will be enhanced by his or her movement across various social and professional communities. Of course, most people who strive to live well-rounded lives will also tend to move across various social and professional communities, and think nothing of the dissonance between their conversations and actions in one setting compared with those in another. Any academic with children, for example, is likely to routinely participate in a broad, transnational professional community, a university and department community, a local service group, a group of parents based on the friendships of their children, a network of old friends from high school and college, and, of course, an extended family made up of parents, siblings, and cousins. In each social setting, the person will know or quickly learn the norms of behavior and how to be accepted by others. For entrepreneurs, aside from the latent resources represented by contacts in multiple settings, the value of such participation across social and professional communities is the potential it offers for "making strange" or defamiliarizing any given set of circumstances and social relations.

It is through the ability to disengage from the immediate situation and recognize the arbitrariness of many of our everyday practices and assumptions that the entrepreneur can better perceive the unmet or poorly met needs of others and hit upon possible ways to fulfill them or, at least, improve upon the present situation. Often, the very act of seeing the potential for forging productive linkages between previously separate individuals and groups represents the entrepreneurial "spark" from which innovations emerge and spread. Having the social dexterity to feel at ease across a range of distinctive social settings can be of great value to the entrepreneur, just as a talent for speaking a variety of languages can be a huge asset to an international traveler.

For entrepreneurs who seek to introduce change in the form of innovations, the key social task is to establish sound connections and relationships of mutual trust with those they need to work with, while recognizing that their very interest in promoting change is likely to mark them out as distinctive and potentially threatening. In light of this, what actions can they take to increase the likelihood of acceptance in the group and, hence, to also increase the likelihood of being able to change the ways that those around them think about and interpret given situations? Perhaps the best thing that entrepreneurs can do is attempt to minimize points of difference and disagreement between themselves and those around them. This means becoming hypersensitive to "the presentation of self" in daily interactions (Goffman 1956). Entrepreneurs must find ways to "fit in" with those around them, taking pains to speak in ways that make sense to the relevant group, and allow those around them to feel at ease with their presence.

Much of what I have said here applies equally to the policy entrepreneur as to the entrepreneur working in the market setting. Now, however, I will discuss in somewhat more specific terms the reasons why a policy entrepreneur would do well to develop and maintain social and professional contacts across a range of communities. For the policy entrepreneur the most crucial group to influence is decisionmakers. Thus, at the level of state government, for example, a policy entrepreneur must find ways to influence the thinking of key elected officials, such as members of the state legislature and the governor. This means that the entrepreneur must develop the sensibility of a political insider, learning the nature of the political game, learning who the most influential actors are, and learning how to make arguments in ways that will bring others to view a proposal for a given policy innovation as worthy of serious consideration. One way for policy entrepreneurs to do this is to work to establish contacts with a few people who, over time, will feel comfortable introducing them to others. Time spent building social and professional contacts in and around the decisionmaking body with the power to produce policy changes is essential.

Aside from building social and professional contacts around the center of power, policy entrepreneurs can improve their ability to spearhead policy change through taking other action some distance from the seat of decisionmaking. Two sites for building contacts appear most valuable: broader associations of policy specialists and advocates and local groups of people having some interest in the policy entrepreneur's issue areas.

Broad associations of policy specialists and advocates represent an important resource for policy entrepreneurs. It will often help for policy entrepreneurs to spend time making contacts with people in other localities who share their policy interests. For example, policy entrepreneurs interested in making changes to education policy in their state would do well to establish contacts with other people interested in education policy issues across the nation. Hugh Heclo's (1978) discussion of issue networks emphasizes the importance of contacts that span a range of jurisdictional boundaries and that, as such, establish a policy community. Having access to this broader community can give policy entrepreneurs many opportunities for learning about ideas and innovations that have been developed elsewhere and how they might be relevant to their own jurisdiction. Further, contacts with this broader policy community can serve as a good way to learn about and discuss "what works" in terms of political strategies for "selling" policy ideas to key decisionmakers. Having access to the views of insightful and trustworthy "outsiders" can be a special asset to a policy entrepreneur who, in the midst of politicking in his or her own jurisdiction, might find the support and the critical distance of others especially important for maintaining the energy and strategic sense to keep going.

The other key peripheral site for building social and professional contacts can be at the local or grassroots level. It is here, rubbing shoulders with both the potential supporters and enemies of policy change, that policy entrepreneurs can gain many insights into particular policy problems and come to an understanding of the sort of policy solutions that might address those problems. The ability to talk with others who have different worldviews and to learn from them can be honed through establishing contacts at the local level. As well as this, taking the time to get to know and understand those people who will be most affected by a given policy change can prove valuable for establishing a powerbase of supporters. This can be crucial when the time comes to make arguments for policy change to decisionmakers. We might expect that through building up social and professional contacts at the local level, policy entrepreneurs can come to determine which particular groups will be easiest to work with, and how to make arguments that would allow several distinctive groups to come together in a coalition to support a particular policy innovation.

Problems and Solutions

In devising innovations entrepreneurs can be thought of as problem solvers. However, they are unusual problem solvers because they are prepared neither to accept problems as others present them nor to offer easy, business-as-usual solutions. Thus, prior to developing innovations, entrepreneurs must reflect upon given situations and make informed guesses about the sort of innovations that might be welcomed. In this phase of the entrepreneurial process, the insight, alertness, and creativity of the entrepreneur manifest themselves in ways similar to those of the artist or the scientist engaged in the process of creative discovery. That is to say, the entrepreneur must be willing to hold skepticism in abeyance, dare to be adventurous, and break away from established approaches to working with incoming information.

Among policy scholars a range of efforts have been made to document the process by which policy innovations come to be developed. Typically, these scholars construe policy innovations as the *solutions* that policymakers adopt to address given policy *problems*. The relationship between problems and solutions is contested, however. In particular, questions have been raised about the accuracy of a portrait of policymaking that assumes that policymakers first become aware of a particular problem and, having paid attention to it, then embark on a "problem-directed search" that, by and by, leads them to hit upon a given policy innovation (cf. Cyert and March 1963). An early critic of this view, Robert Eyestone argued that "the issue translation process rarely proceeds step by step from issue definition to the choice of a public policy solution, even though it is convenient to analyze the process in these discrete steps. More commonly, the definition of an issue is influenced strongly by the available means of response" (1978, 51). Consistent with this view, Aaron Wildavsky (1979) suggested that efforts to wrestle with a problem will only occur if people believe that a solution can be found. Thus, according to Wildavsky, problems and solutions come intertwined, and our understanding of a given solution will inform our perception of—or perhaps even give us the ability to perceive—a putative problem. Viewing the world of policymaking through his model of process streams, John W. Kingdon (1995) made the even more radical claim that problems and solutions come out of distinctive and largely independent processes. Differences in the ways that people perceive connections between problems and solutions are indicative of a more general phenomenon. That is, just as group identity is socially constructed and open to political contestation and manipulation (Schneider and Ingram 1997), policy problems are always socially constructed (Cobb and Elder 1983). My interest here lies not simply in acknowledging that policy problems are always socially constructed, but in exploring the implications this realization holds for how we view the practice of policy entrepreneurship.

When we observe that policy problems are socially constructed, we implicitly bestow an enormous amount of power to the role that language plays in politics and in the policymaking process. Of course, the world consists of more than just language and our interpretation of things. There are stubborn facts that must be addressed. But to recognize the importance of language in the definition of policy problems and the emergence of acceptable solutions is to remind us of the malleability of our perceptions of given situations. For the policy entrepreneur language is the key to opening up new opportunities in the policy space. Thus, we might expect that policy entrepreneurs will seek to increase the likelihood that their preferred policy innovations will be adopted through argumentation and efforts to *re-present* conditions as specific types of policy problems. To even hope to have influence of this sort on the policymaking process, however, a policy entrepreneur must be a communicator of the highest rank. This means having the ability to carefully judge the needs of an audience, to listen closely to others, and to rapidly determine what to say and how to say it in order to smooth the way for the development of a favored policy innovation.[3]

As the promoters of innovation, entrepreneurs will typically have to speak in the language of "problems" and "solutions." In presenting an idea to others, it makes sense for a policy entrepreneur to carefully explain the nature of the problem as he or she sees it and, having done this, suggest the kind of innovation that might address that problem. Listening to others' reactions to that narrative might provide valuable clues to the entrepreneur about ways to refine both the innovation itself and the way to present it. Critically, however, we should not conclude that the entrepreneur's linear narrative that links a "solution" to a "problem" is somehow indicative of the process by which he or she came to discern that a given innovation is worth promoting. Such a conclusion could be interpreted to mean that innovations spring fully conceived from the heads of entrepreneurs as responses to obvious problems. This is far from the case. A more appropriate way to think of the entrepreneur is as somebody who approaches the world with sufficient acuity and verve to perceive both the need and potential for change in any given situation. From here, entrepreneurs can go on to engage in the socially embedded processes of problem definition and innovation development.

Problem Framing

Policy entrepreneurs might become aware of specific policy problems in a variety of ways. One possibility is that they come to see that a problem exists primarily through their own observation and reflection upon a given situation. Another possibility is that other people come to them with a problem and looking for advice or support. It is also possible that policy entrepreneurs realize problems in their own jurisdictions from learning of a problem (and a policy innovation devised to address it) that has come to prominence elsewhere. Unavoidably, my use of language here is somewhat deceptive, because at the initial point where a policy entrepreneur becomes aware of a problem the entrepreneur is not actually an entrepreneur and the problem is as yet not actually a public—and, therefore—a policy problem. What we have at this stage is an individual who holds the potential to make a difference and a problem that could conceivably be introduced into the public domain, where it could be treated as a policy problem. It is through bringing a problem to public prominence, in combination with developing and advocating a policy innovation, that an individual assumes the identity of a policy entrepreneur.

No matter how a policy entrepreneur becomes aware of a policy problem, at the moment of first awareness he or she must necessarily view it as a problem in a particular, perhaps idiosyncratic, fashion. This is how all of us must first become aware of a problem and try to make sense of it. As many scholars following Goffman (1974) have observed, we each understand the world through particular interpretative "frames" or "frameworks." These lead us to habitually place more importance on some phenomena than on others; and we are more open to accepting arguments and ideas presented in ways that are consistent with our frames.[4] Given this, recognizing that we each have more-or-less unique ways of viewing the world is an important prerequisite for getting along with others. Furthermore, we can improve our ability to engage in meaningful communication through our efforts to become cognizant of the frames through which others see and come to understand things.[5]

Policy entrepreneurs must be highly reflective if they are to succeed in making others aware of a policy problem and convincing them to interpret that problem in particular ways. Although, initially, policy entrepreneurs will view problems in their own idiosyncratic ways, ultimately they must develop an appreciation for the arbitrariness of the ways in which they see things. Policy entrepreneurs must be able to understand the nature of the frames through which they and others view and come to recognize apparent policy problems. This ability provides the key to problem framing: the conscious effort to bring others to see problems in ways that are consistent with your own positions and policy goals.

Of course problem framing has its limits. When particular ideas and ways of interpreting the world are in ascendance, it is difficult for anyone to change how people perceive particular conditions or events. In addition, where there are multiple groups and individuals whose ways of interpreting and understanding the world are highly divergent, a policy entrepreneur might find it difficult to establish any common ground and to make arguments that multiple groups can simultaneously find agreeable. In such cases, it seems most unlikely that policy entrepreneurs could engage in fruitful problem framing and bring others to accept their narratives of the relationship between the problems they identify and their proposed solutions. At times like this policy entrepreneurs might have to seriously scale back their policy goals. Even under conditions more favorable to problem framing, serious effort will be needed to change how people think about a given situation. Thus, as Kingdon has observed, "Getting people to see new problems, or to see old problems in one way rather than another, is a major conceptual and political accomplishment" (1995, 115). Appropriately judging how to frame a problem and then working hard to do this can greatly improve the odds of a policy entrepreneur successfully introducing a given innovation.

Developing Innovations

In thinking about the development of policy innovations, there is much we can learn by reflecting on how entrepreneurs introduce innovative products in the marketplace. But our understanding can be further informed by Everett Rogers's (1995) influential discussion regarding the development and diffusion of innovations. Rogers defines an innovation as follows:

> An *innovation* is an idea, practice, or object that is perceived as new by an individual or other unit of adoption. It matters little, so far as human behavior is concerned, whether or not an idea is objectively new as measured by the lapse of time since its first use or discovery. . . .
>
> Newness in an innovation need not just involve new knowledge. Someone may have known about an innovation for some time but not yet developed a favorable or unfavorable attitude toward it, nor have adopted or rejected it. "Newness" of an innovation may be expressed in terms of knowledge, persuasion, or a decision to adopt. (1995, 11)

Here, Rogers makes the significant point that knowledge of an innovation is not always sufficient to ensure adoption. This suggests that the "facts"—or the most salient attributes—of an innovation do not always speak for themselves. Before an innovation is adopted potential adopters must realize the value it holds for them. This process by which potential customers are led to accept the value of a new product can be thought of as a key phase in the development of innovations.

Rogers's definition of the term *innovation* has informed, either directly or indirectly, the thinking of the many political scientists and policy scholars who have studied policy innovations. Thus, Lawrence B. Mohr (1969, 112) has stated: "It seems important . . . to separate the idea of invention from the idea of innovation. Invention implies bringing something new into being; innovation implies bringing something new into use." Similarly, in his seminal discussion of the diffusion of policy innovations among the nation's states Jack L. Walker noted: "An innovation will be defined simply as a program or policy which is new to the states adopting it, no matter how old the program may be or how many other states may have adopted it" (1969, 881). Such interpretations of the meaning of innovation have become commonplace. Although drawing this distinction between initial invention and subsequent adoption of an innovation has its merits, the distinction deflects attention from considering those moments of invention and creativity that must accompany efforts to introduce innovations into new settings. In the literature on policy innovation diffusion, therefore, the major focus of inquiry has been the identification of the broad conditions both inside and outside a given jurisdiction that appear to increase the likelihood of adoption. Little attention has been paid to the ways that individuals serve to impart knowledge of innovations and change attitudes toward innovations. Thus we have a literature concerned with policy change where the actual "change agents" are nowhere to be found. Ironically, political scientists analyzing the process of policy innovation and innovation diffusion have written a great deal of the relevant politics out of the story. By paying more attention to the actions of policy entrepreneurs and how they develop innovations, we could improve our understanding of innovation diffusion processes.

Transforming Ideas into Policy Innovations

Policy entrepreneurs seek to have their proposals for policy innovation adopted by decisionmakers in their jurisdictions. The policy entrepreneurs begin with ideas, which may or may not include the knowledge that a given policy innovation is in place elsewhere. They must then promote their ideas to others in ways that build coalitions of supporters who will help create pressure for the desired form of policy change. This suggests that the key thing that policy entrepreneurs must do to successfully transform an idea into a policy innovation is make arguments that others find convincing. Here I use the example of school choice to further elaborate on this matter. As I noted in chapter 1, Milton Friedman advocated the idea of using vouchers and the privatization of the school system in the 1950s. In the 1960s and 1970s efforts were made to experiment with variants of the school choice idea, moving from the knowledge creation to the knowledge utilization phase. However, it has only been since the mid-1980s that many concerted efforts have emerged to introduce this policy innovation at the state and local levels across the United States. Over the years those who have worked with the idea of school choice have adhered to a variety of ideological positions. But no matter what the particular political persuasion of a given policy entrepreneur, to successfully promote a policy innovation like school choice he or she must be able to represent it as an acceptable idea to a range of people with different interests and concerns.

To the extent that past efforts to transform an idea into a policy innovation have succeeded, the task of the policy entrepreneurs is made easier. Hence, policy entrepreneurs will often look for concrete examples when making their arguments to others. In the absence of such examples they must make more conceptual arguments. One possibility here is to try to make arguments that indicate how the proposed policy innovation is consistent with other ideas currently informing public policymaking. Over the past decade or so the buzzwords "deregulation," "privatization," and "reinventing government" have been in ascendance. Given this, we should expect that a school choice policy entrepreneur would try hard to demonstrate how his or her policy innovation represents something of a "natural" addition to this broader policy agenda. In taking this action, the policy entrepreneur seeks to bring other people around to seeing that the innovation is to be welcomed and that it is akin to other popular policy initiatives. To do this successfully policy entrepreneurs must be highly attuned to the prevalent policy rhetoric in their jurisdictions.[6]

In making their arguments for a particular policy innovation policy entrepreneurs must often have a specific audience in mind. Just as we might expect them to adjust how they frame a problem for each of several groups of potential supporters, so we might expect them to adjust how they talk about the policy innovation as they move from group to group. But as policy entrepreneurs change how they present their policy innovations, the meanings that people attach to those innovations will also change. For members of business groups who desire improvements in school quality but who oppose more government spending, a policy entrepreneur might emphasize the way that school choice could lead to quality improvements at no extra cost. To do this, the policy entrepreneur has to argue that school choice introduces a degree of competition among schools for students. Given this, the argument would go, the schools would face increased incentives to improve educational quality in ways that are consistent with the hopes and expectations of students and their parents. For people concerned about the isolation of schools from their communities and from parents, a policy entrepreneur might argue that school choice is a policy innovation that will lead to greater parental involvement in schools. Here, the argument might be made that under school choice the administrators and teachers in school can no longer count on having a "captive" clientele. Thus, they will face strong incentives to listen to students and their parents and engage in the community to build good relations and ongoing support.

As a consequence of the efforts that policy entrepreneurs make to win the support of others, aspects of the policy innovations themselves might actually change. In many instances, these changes will be made with the goal of accommodating the desires of specific groups so that they will readily lend their support to the adoption of the policy innovation. Sometimes, these changes will also be introduced to neutralize opposition to the innovation. In the case of school choice, adjustments intended to build support might include having the policy change introduced on a gradual basis. This can help alleviate concerns that the new policy will be too disruptive to the present system. Efforts might also be made to develop systems of accountability that provide a backstop to the simple idea that, under school choice, schools will be made primarily accountable to students and their parents who represent their clientele. The establishment of some government entity designed to provide additional accountability might prove important for ensuring support for the idea.

Language and the Presentation of Ideas

Through considering the efforts that policy entrepreneurs might take as they seek to introduce a policy innovation like school choice, several other matters emerge that are worthy of discussion. School choice means different things to different people. While we can look across a number of states and say that they allow choice among public schools, or they allow charter schools, or they allow voucher systems, we know that adoption of each of these policy innovations has been accompanied by somewhat idiosyncratic politics. Yes, general patterns can be observed across the adopting states, but the general patterns do not explain everything about why decisionmakers came to adopt a given policy innovation. To the extent that the meanings associated with a given innovation differ across jurisdictions, we might say that policy innovations are shaped in important ways during the course of discussion. Sometimes this will result in the actual nature of the innovation coming to differ across jurisdictions; that is to say, at a minimum, the wording of the authorizing laws will differ. But even if the same wording is used, the innovation itself might be thought of in distinctly different ways by the people who support or oppose it.

Recognition that policy entrepreneurs will make changes in the ways that they describe their particular policy innovations leads us to see that this can, in fact, be a risky business. Altering the way that a policy innovation is explained might serve as an important way to capture the support of various groups to help promote policy change. However, it is possible that if policy entrepreneurs are not careful here the policy innovations they introduce will get so transformed during the policymaking process that the final innovations bear no resemblance to the original idea. If, in fact, the process of promoting the policy innovations to others leads to the serious corruption of the initial plans, then the efforts of the policy entrepreneurs will have been in vain. Given this, policy entrepreneurs must be able to recognize what sort of changes serve to enhance their particular policy innovations and what sort serve to detract from them.

In their discussion of the development of policy innovations, Martin A. Levin and Mary Bryna Sanger (1994) have argued that policy entrepreneurs typically do not work with new ideas. Rather, they are masters at "using old stuff in new ways."[7] Given what we know about the nature of policy entrepreneurship and the development of innovations, why might we so often observe this tendency? Rather than argue that this reflects a certain lack of creativity or inventiveness on the part of policy entrepreneurs, this use of apparently familiar ideas might be a smart strategy. There are two distinct, but consistent reasons for this. First, people are much more likely to adopt an innovation if they can identify with the change agent, or if they both "talk the same language." Policy entrepreneurs would like people to think that their policy innovations are nothing out of the ordinary, even when they are. Downplaying differences and drawing lots of analogies to familiar and well-liked features of existing public policies are two ways of supporting this. Second, it is likely that a policy innovation will receive more support if policy entrepreneurs can argue that the innovation represents an effort to build upon, rather than completely overturn, present arrangements. Thus, we might expect policy entrepreneurs to work hard to show that a proposed innovation is consistent with long-established views about what represents appropriate policy in a given area of government activity. In taking these steps, policy entrepreneurs could raise their chances of developing a strong constituency for their policy innovations. "Using old stuff in new ways" often will make a lot of sense.

Devising Strategies and Working the System

Aside from framing problems and developing innovations, like their marketplace counterparts policy entrepreneurs must engage in activities such as devising strategies, working the system, organizing others, and providing leadership. Such activities can be thought of as the core stuff of politics, and political scientists have had much to say about them. Given this, what might we gain by continuing to work with the metaphor of the entrepreneur in the marketplace? Entertaining the thought that similarities exist among individuals who attempt to introduce innovations, regardless of the context, does, I believe, hold value. In so doing, we gain several insights about the politics that surround the introduction of policy innovations.

Developing a Sense of Efficacy

As a prerequisite for making a difference in any aspect of life, people must have at least some expectation that their actions will have the intended effects. Such expectations emerge as a combination of knowledge and self-confidence. We must assume that when policy entrepreneurs take actions to promote their policy innovations, they believe they know what they are doing and that they can make a difference. Thus, we might say that policy entrepreneurs choose to take specific actions based upon their understanding of the nature of the policymaking process and how the actions of individuals can influence what occurs in that process. To achieve an appropriate level of understanding about the policymaking process, policy entrepreneurs must have some theory of power. But theory alone will not suffice; they must also have a rich, empirically based understanding of how ideas come to have influence. Through developing a sound knowledge of the policymaking process and achieving a realistic sense of their own abilities to make differences there, policy entrepreneurs can begin to devise strategies for promoting their preferred policy innovations.

Probably the best way for a policy entrepreneur to develop a sense of efficacy in any system is to start by working to make small changes in the familiar areas. Here, at the early stages of working with the system, it is important to listen to others, watch their actions, and learn how people conduct themselves and how they get things done. To the extent that an entrepreneur works with a system, he or she comes to understand it more; and to the extent that he or she achieves success in working with it, the entrepreneur develops increasing confidence in being able to make a difference. This is how people learn to make their way in the world of politics and policymaking. The cases of elected decisionmakers who jump from having no experience in politics to holding key positions of power are rare. It is more common to find people in politics who began to learn the ropes as representatives on school boards, or on city councils, and who then used their experience and connections as springboards to higher positions. Some policy entrepreneurs might well be "outsiders," in the sense that they hold no position of power in government, but anyone who wants to make a difference to public policy must have a sophisticated sense of how the policymaking process works. This can be achieved through spending time in and around policymaking circles, talking with others, and seeking out advice and support from those with greater experience and knowledge. The more knowledge that a policy entrepreneur has of the policymaking process and how it works, the greater the likelihood that he or she will feel efficacious and achieve a clear sense of the best actions to take to promote a given policy innovation.

Paying Attention to Venue and Timing

Policy entrepreneurs must pay close attention to matters of venue and timing. Compared with the marketplace, in the realm of politics constraints on the possible venue for action are likely to be much more binding. There is no point in seeking policy change in a jurisdiction where the relevant decisionmakers lack the power to actually make those changes. Therefore, the nature of the system and where the power resides to make particular policy changes will establish the number of venues where a policy entrepreneur can choose to promote a given policy innovation. This might be thought of as a technical constraint on site selection. Another key constraint is the typical human habit of being suspicious toward "outsiders." This habit manifests itself with fervor in politics. So, a policy entrepreneur seeking to introduce a policy innovation within a particular district, town, city, or state will usually have to be well connected to the locality of interest, and most likely actually live in it.

Recognizing these constraints, policy entrepreneurs promoting school choice as a policy innovation, for example, might have a choice of just two venues to work in. One such venue could be the local level, where policy entrepreneurs might attempt to have a particular school district adopt a choice plan. The other possible venue could be the state level, where the constitutional responsibility falls for providing public education. In the case of an innovation like school choice, if a policy entrepreneur cannot achieve success at the local level, it is possible to switch the venue to the state level and promote school choice there. Then again, a policy entrepreneur could just as readily begin by promoting school choice at the state level and, having achieved limited or no success there, switch to trying to make changes at the local level. Nonetheless, the choice of venue is likely to be quite limited for any policy entrepreneur, regardless of the nature of the policy innovation.

Aside from constraints on venue, policy entrepreneurs will also face constraints on the times when they can introduce their policy innovations. Kingdon (1995) has discussed this at length, arguing that policy entrepreneurs must attempt to exploit "windows of opportunity" when pursuing policy change. According to Kingdon, when such opportunities for introducing policy innovations are not immediately apparent, policy entrepreneurs can attempt to "soften up" members of the policymaking community, raising their awareness of the innovation and its merit. Because policy entrepreneurs often need to fit their making of proposals around election, legislative, and budget cycles, it is important that they work hard to create the kind of support for their ideas that can be readily mobilized to take advantage of opportunities when they arise. Policy entrepreneurs also need to think about how they can force opportunities for introducing their policy innovations. Having a good sense of timing is important. But having foresight matters too, knowing how long it will take to build a group of supporters and to refine the proposed innovation so that opportunities can be readily seized. Keeping an eye on policy developments and fashions in the broader political economy can also be useful for policy entrepreneurs. Like their counterparts in the marketplace, by paying attention to what is happening well beyond their immediate locale, policy entrepreneurs can achieve a better understanding of how what they are doing fits with developments elsewhere. This can help them as they continue to refine their policy innovations and their arguments, preparing for those moments when a majority of decisionmakers appear ready to give such proposals serious attention.

Choosing Partners

Of necessity, policy entrepreneurship involves working closely with others. Since the policymaking process is complex and many people are involved in the making of any policy change, policy entrepreneurs must find other people to work with in pursuit of policy goals. In politics, the ways that people come to think about and feel toward a policy proposal will often be closely informed by their attitudes toward the people associated with it. For this reason, a lot is at stake when a policy entrepreneur makes a decision about whom to work with to build support for a policy innovation.

To attract the attention of decisionmakers, policy entrepreneurs must be able to demonstrate that their proposed policy innovations enjoy broad interest and support. Policy entrepreneurs must also be able to somehow convey their seriousness and their integrity to decisionmakers. Choosing the right partners matters. Working to gain the support of established interest groups can be important because they have readily activated sets of contacts that can be used to advantage in policy debates. Established interest groups also have access to resources, which can be especially important for policy entrepreneurs who are passionate about particular policy ideas but who lack the financial means to promote them effectively. Because of their preoccupations, some established interest groups might fall into the category of "natural allies" and they may be relatively easy for the policy entrepreneur to work with. However, if the support of some of these natural allies could, in fact, do harm to the reputation of the policy entrepreneur and his or her proposed innovation, then it would make sense to avoid them. Sometimes, also, to signal broad-based support for a policy innovation, the policy entrepreneur might need to forge working relationships with individuals and groups who might not appear to be natural allies. While this is an important strategy, it can also be risky because it might lead the policy entrepreneur to transform the policy innovation to the point where some natural allies find it less acceptable. Just as important, the policy entrepreneur needs to be concerned that seeking the support of too many diverse groups might lead some people to question how much he or she is actually working with them, and can be trusted. Given limited time and resources, policy entrepreneurs must think carefully about what kind of partnerships make strategic sense before building their rapport with various individuals and groups.

Robert Eyestone (1978, 94) suggests that policy entrepreneurs should usually work in teams, with some members of the team working inside the government and others outside. In this way the outsiders can bring fresh perspectives and ideas to bear on policymaking, while the insiders can draw upon their experience and resources when it comes time to draft legislation and build support for it. This is an insightful perspective on the nature of policy entrepreneurship, and teamwork is likely to be an integral part of any successful effort to introduce a policy innovation. However, to focus on the differences between "insiders" and "outsiders" and how these differences are bridged might lead us to ignore the importance of building partnerships across groups of insiders and groups of outsiders. Clearly policy entrepreneurs, whatever their position, must have close linkages to formal decisionmakers, but they cannot typically rely upon these alone to ensure the adoption of their policy innovations. Working with individuals and groups outside of government and building various partnerships can send important signals to decisionmakers about the nature of the support that lies behind any given proposal for a policy innovation. Thus, all choices concerning whom to work with as partners are important.

Maintaining a Sense of Perspective

In working to promote policy change, policy entrepreneurs will often know of many strategic actions that could advance their efforts. But this does not mean that there is value to be gained from using every available strategy. Rather, a crucial aspect of being strategic involves determining which actions are most fitting, given the particular situation. In addition, it is vital to know when to maintain a low profile and when to make a concerted effort to promote a policy innovation. There may be times when having a clear sense of perspective will lead a policy entrepreneur to decide that compromise is better than making a forceful, but unsuccessful, bid for a more comprehensive adoption of a policy innovation. Often, maintaining good relations and at least getting a policy innovation accepted in some form might leave the door open for achieving more favorable policy outcomes later. As with other elements of strategic behavior, policy entrepreneurs can learn these things both from their own experience and from listening to the "war stories" and advice of others. In this way, policy entrepreneurs might be expected to come, with time, to recognize the people, organizations, and structures that are most important to work with, and where it might make sense to work against them. Policy entrepreneurs might also save a lot of time and energy by taking care to learn how they can use current policy settings to their advantage. It is not uncommon for policy innovations to be adopted formally after they have, in fact, been adopted informally for a time. This was the case with airline deregulation in the 1970s (Derthick and Quirk, 1985). Likewise, the adoption of school choice plans in some states has also followed the informal introduction of more limited plans at the school district level.[8]

These comments suggest one reason why many policy think tanks have emerged over the past few decades in Washington, D.C., and in state capitals. The argument could be made that these organizations represent an understanding on the part of "career" policy entrepreneurs that staying close to the seat of decisionmaking power and maintaining a sense of perspective can, over the longer term, produce many gains, in terms of having ideas for policy innovations accepted and adopted. Often, the leaders of policy think tanks claim that their primary interest lies in changing the terms of policy conversations (Ricci 1993; Smith 1991). To do this effectively, think tanks must work to keep good relations with other people in and around government. But this requires having the good judgment to know when to lobby hard for policy change and when to assume a lower profile. Through developing a sound understanding of how policymaking occurs and who is who among the influential players, members of think tanks can come to recognize when various strategies are most likely to be effective.

Organizing Others and Providing Leadership

There are limits to what individuals can achieve on their own. This is why, to bring their innovations to market, entrepreneurs find it necessary to organize others and provide leadership. Three activities seem particularly important in this regard: choosing production functions, establishing a nexus of contracts, and establishing an organizational culture. Among political scientists, claims about the important role played by entrepreneurs in the public sector typically focus on their efforts to organize others. Hence Elinor Ostrom (1965) explored the role that business actors in California played as "public entrepreneurs" to develop a policy innovation—that is, a workable, coordinated approach to water management in the Los Angeles area. In refining and extending the work of Mancur Olson (1965) on collective action problems, Robert H. Salisbury (1969) argued that interest group formation and the provision of selective incentives for group members would require the initiative of "entrepreneur/organizers." James Q. Wilson (1973) elaborated on the work of Salisbury and others and discussed the different ways that "policy entrepreneurs" might go about organizing others, given particular policy goals. Following these seminal works, many references have been made to the actions of variously described "political entrepreneurs," "public entrepreneurs," and "policy entrepreneurs" and their efforts to organize others and initiate collective action. Here, I use our knowledge of how entrepreneurs in the marketplace organize others to further explore the actions of policy entrepreneurs seeking to introduce policy innovations.

Determining a Production Function

When economists model the activities of firms, the production function serves as their fundamental building block. This is a formula characterizing the relationship between inputs and outputs. When thinking about the activities of policy entrepreneurs, the notion of the production function can be useful. Policy entrepreneurs seek to generate a specific type of output: sufficient argumentation and political pressure to lead decisionmakers to adopt a given policy innovation. In other words, we might say that policy entrepreneurship involves making a case for the adoption of a policy innovation. To produce this output, to make this case, policy entrepreneurs must organize inputs in appropriate ways. Like attorneys attempting to make a case on behalf of a particular party in a court of law, policy entrepreneurs need to think of ways to marshal and generate arguments, evidence, witnesses, and supporters. How policy entrepreneurs choose to combine these inputs to achieve the desired output could be portrayed in terms of a production function. It seems reasonable to expect that such production functions will differ with respect to the preferences of the relevant decisionmakers, the nature of the policy innovations being advocated, and the type of inputs to which the policy entrepreneur has access.

A key point to recognize here is that efforts to promote a particular policy innovation are typically nonrepeating. The "production" of effort to achieve a desired policy change represents a unique combination of actions, undertaken at a given time and place. This marks out the production of a policy innovation from the production of an innovation in the marketplace, where the expectation of the entrepreneur is that the good or service will, once it has caught on, be produced many times over. This obvious distinction between the development and production of innovations in the marketplace and the policymaking process does not, however, significantly limit the extent to which we can draw parallels between the actions of entrepreneurs in the two realms. In both instances, the entrepreneur must think carefully about the organization of inputs and how this can best be achieved. The difference, of course, is that the entrepreneur in the marketplace has the opportunity to continually refine the production process, whereas the policy entrepreneur does not have this luxury.

Consider the case of a policy entrepreneur seeking to introduce school choice as a policy innovation. If the policy entrepreneur holds a position of formal power, such as heading the education committee in one of the houses of a state legislature, then making a case for school choice may be relatively easy. The considerable political effort made to secure a position of this sort will have generated a stock of experience, knowledge, and contacts that the policy entrepreneur could draw upon when seeking support for a given policy proposal. Therefore, while the policy entrepreneur must still take great care in crafting arguments and gathering evidence, he or she has a clear sense of the audience and how to make a convincing case. The "production function" for this policy entrepreneur promoting school choice is quite distinct from the production functions of those who work as policy analysts in state think tanks. For these people, aside from working at the development of the innovation, a large amount of effort has to go into establishing credibility and demonstrating that the proposal has wide support. Even so, while these policy entrepreneurs clearly have to work more to make the case for school choice than someone in a formal position of power, they face fewer difficulties than a private citizen who becomes interested in promoting the idea of school choice as a policy innovation.

If we assume that policy entrepreneurs in different positions in and around government will face distinct problems when it comes to making a case for a particular policy innovation, then we should expect that no given production function will dominate all others. But the uniqueness of the conditions faced by any given policy entrepreneur need not preclude the possibility of using previously developed knowledge and contacts to advantage. Undoubtedly, policy entrepreneurs can learn from observing the actions of others and from taking the time to reflect upon the effectiveness of their own previous activities. It would be inappropriate, however, for policy entrepreneurs to assume that what has worked for others or what has worked for them in the past will necessarily work well again. By definition, an innovation is something new being introduced to a given situation. That novelty alone requires that at least some level of creativity be exercised in thinking about how to work with available inputs to make the case for adoption of the innovation.

Creating Organizational Forms

Like their market counterparts, policy entrepreneurs must find ways to organize others with the goal of developing and producing innovations. Once they have achieved a sense of what would constitute an appropriate production function, policy entrepreneurs must establish something akin to a "nexus of contracts" that will facilitate the generation of the arguments and political pressure required to successfully promote their policy innovations to decisionmakers. In the world of politics and policymaking, however, would be entrepreneurs face a distinct disadvantage compared with entrepreneurs operating in the marketplace. The problem for the policy entrepreneur involves attempting to organize others in an environment where no recourse exists for establishing binding contracts and where the use of cash incentives for participation is routinely frowned on and often forbidden. Even where policy entrepreneurs might be able to make—or at least promise to make—campaign contributions to decisionmakers prepared to support their policy proposals, they still must justify their proposals using sound argumentation. Government is not a cash register where those who make the biggest contributions are rewarded with public policies set to their liking. Of course, money talks. But if the people with resources have only crass things to say, or their proposals obviously serve only to advance their own narrow interests to the detriment of others, then they are unlikely to have the sort of influence that a simple calculation of relative wealth would lead us to expect. We should not conclude that policy entrepreneurship involves coming up with proposals for policy innovation and simply finding ways to couple them with large campaign contributions.

How might we expect policy entrepreneurs to organize others? Three primary approaches are available. The first involves working closely with decisionmakers, and this is the approach that an "insider" is most likely to take. The second approach involves working to develop coalitions of ready-made political organizations and interest groups. The third involves attempting to establish an interest group for the specific purpose of creating pressure for policy change. Under any given set of circumstances, a policy entrepreneur might seek to combine one or more of these approaches. The type of organizational form that a policy entrepreneur works to establish will depend greatly upon the anticipated timeframe and degree of political coordination required to secure adoption of the preferred policy innovation.

Consider first the case of a policy entrepreneur who is a member of a state legislature. To secure adoption of his or her preferred policy innovation, this policy entrepreneur must make convincing arguments to colleagues. Introducing the policy innovation in a separate bill or as part of a broader bill—such as a budget bill or education bill—might be readily organized. The task for the policy entrepreneur then involves lobbying colleagues for their support. In this case, organizing others represents a short-term effort to make the sort of arguments that other members of the legislature will find acceptable, and the policy entrepreneur will most likely follow norms of accepted behavior in the legislature. Thus, the effort to secure the policy innovation might involve logrolling, where the policy entrepreneur agrees to support others in their policy goals in return for obtaining their support for his or her policy goal. Inevitably, any effort to secure policy change must involve some amount of legislative action of this sort. But this does not mean that the legislator who introduces a policy innovation is always a policy entrepreneur. There may be times when a legislator takes such action on behalf of others who have been carefully organized by a policy entrepreneur who is working in a "behind-the-scenes" or "outsider" capacity.

Next consider a policy entrepreneur outside the legislature who is attempting to create the conditions under which a majority of the legislature will decide to adopt his or her preferred policy innovation. In this case, the policy entrepreneur must work to develop credibility both for himself or herself and for the policy innovation being promoted. An important way to do this is to develop a coalition of supporters for the innovation. But how can this be achieved? One possibility is to begin by attempting to win the enthusiasm and support of the leaders of previously established organizations and interest groups. For example, a policy entrepreneur seeking to promote the idea of school choice might attempt to construct a coalition of "natural allies." Such organizations may include business groups who seek improvements in education quality, civic groups who care about education issues, church groups in urban areas who seek improvements in the lives of families in their communities, and parents who currently send their children to private schools to avoid the local public schools. By spending time lobbying the leaders of organizations of this sort, a policy entrepreneur might eventually win their endorsement both of himself or herself as a policy advocate and of the policy innovation being promoted. After gaining the support of these leaders, the policy entrepreneur might then request their support in lobbying elected and appointed officials and other actors in and around government circles to secure support for the policy innovation. Just as important, taking this approach, a policy entrepreneur may gain access to the long-established channels of political mobilization contained within these groups. By working to achieve the support of perhaps just a handful of influential political leaders, it might be possible for a policy entrepreneur to spearhead a credible campaign for policy change. Achieving success in this way reduces the extent to which the policy entrepreneur needs to be greatly concerned with collective action problems. Targeting group leaders means that, for all intents and purposes, the policy entrepreneur can think of the organization of interests as a small-group situation, where concerns about trust and reciprocity can be fairly readily managed, at least relative to other scenarios.

To this point, in discussing organizational forms I have emphasized instances in which policy entrepreneurs seek primarily to tap the goodwill of others to help them pursue their policy goals. This is equivalent to saying that so long as various individuals and groups recognize a common interest in the pursuit of some policy goal or public good, then they will join forces to pursue it. However, Mancur Olson (1965) demonstrated that voluntary collective action in pursuit of a public good is likely to occur only when the number of actors involved is small, and individual contributions to the collective effort are readily monitored. When the number of those who could potentially benefit from collective action grows large, it becomes individually rational for actors to not contribute. Rational individuals would be better off devoting their time and energy elsewhere knowing that if the efforts of others result in the provision of the desired public good, they will get to share in it anyway. In light of this, Olson argued that large "latent" groups of individuals with common interests in the provision of a public good would only organize into actual interest groups and lobby government if members were supplied with "selective incentives" to participate. When such benefits are offered, lobbying in pursuit of public goods for all group members becomes a "by-product" of the provision of the relevant private goods. In the years after Olson presented this theory, several scholars suggested that the initiation of the provision of selective incentives would require the actions of specific individuals. Subsequently it has become common to talk of group organizers as "political entrepreneurs."

In some instances, policy entrepreneurs seeking to introduce a given policy innovation might be expected to establish a lobbying organization by offering selective incentives for membership. In particular, this could be used as a strategy when policy entrepreneurs recognize the need to broaden "the scope of conflict" (Schattschneider 1960) and, thus, generate evidence of widespread support for their preferred policy changes. The efforts made in the 1990s to establish private voucher programs in many cities in the United States could be interpreted as examples of just this sort of effort. For the most part, these programs have been established using money from corporations or philanthropic foundations. They have usually targeted poor families with children attending inner city public schools. The programs provide for a certain number of "scholarships" that give families money to cover some of the costs of taking their children from public schools and sending them to private schools. Typically these programs have generated considerable interest, and applications have far outnumbered available scholarships.

In establishing private voucher programs, policy entrepreneurs offer selective incentives to parents to reveal their dissatisfaction with the public schools their children are currently attending. The parents who receive scholarships and partially pay to send their children to private schools constitute new allies for the policy entrepreneurs who wish to secure the adoption of broader school choice plans. After all, these parents now pay more for education than they did before, and they might legitimately ask why they have to pay to get the sort of quality education that should be provided as a matter of course by their local public schools. Private voucher programs serve as a means of addressing the collective action problem. Thus, policy entrepreneurs can "recruit" scholarship recipients into a coalition designed to lobby for the introduction of school choice as a policy innovation. With these programs in place, policy entrepreneurs can also make readily verified claims about the amount of support they enjoy for their policy positions. For the purpose of this discussion, the emergence of private voucher programs represents an example of how policy entrepreneurs will devise imaginative ways to create organizational forms that support their efforts to introduce policy innovations. I provide an extended discussion of the development of private voucher programs in chapter 10.

Organizational Culture and Belief Systems

Since policy entrepreneurs typically do not have anything they can offer others in the form of immediate tangible benefits as incentives for organizational involvement, they are destined to work in that twilight zone of social organization consisting of informal understandings, personal commitment, and trust relationships. Given this, they must treat the establishment of informal group commitment as a vital organizing device. Based on what we know about how entrepreneurs establish and maintain positive corporate cultures in firms, it is possible to develop some expectations about how policy entrepreneurs might create organizational cultures and belief systems among supporters of a given policy innovation. The most important thing that policy entrepreneurs can do to establish a cohesive group is develop and maintain a focus on the particular policy goal and promote a climate of cooperation. Keeping the focus on the policy goal reduces the possibility for people in the group to draw distinctions among each other based on background, previous activities, and different reasons for supporting the policy innovation. By promoting a climate of cooperation, policy entrepreneurs are more likely to keep individual members from leaving the group. Policy entrepreneurs can promote cooperation through leadership by example. Taking time to regularly meet and talk with others, and finding ways to demonstrate a level of personal sacrifice for the goals of the group, can be helpful. Policy entrepreneurs must find ways to signal that they are sincerely committed to the accomplishment of the policy goals, that they value the contributions of others, and that they care about the questions and concerns that others raise with them. Taking the time to make personal contacts with group members and to create opportunities for face-to-face meetings among members can be beneficial. Policy entrepreneurs might also attempt to keep the coalition together by providing newsletters or other forms of communication that, at least at some level, remind supporters that their involvement matters.

Other methods of establishing a cohesive group are open to policy entrepreneurs. I note here two others that appear important. The first involves attempting to win the support and involvement of well-known individuals who have a record of successes in other relevant areas of public or private activity. The involvement of such people can be used to indicate that the organization is serious and that serious people are now prepared to put their weight behind it. The second method involves finding ways to demonstrate that the organization is going to remain in place until the desired policy change is achieved. In the case of promoting school choice as a policy innovation, policy entrepreneurs might show supporters the set of target policy changes they seek, and the steps needed to achieve them. The emerging efforts of school choice policy entrepreneurs to establish private voucher programs could also be seen as a way to signal a longer term commitment to securing broader policy change. The private voucher programs can be portrayed as representing "prefigurative forms" (Rowbotham 1981) of the future of schooling. For the purposes of maintaining supporters for broader school choice initiatives these programs provide a vivid representation of the end goal. The programs also demonstrate that the policy entrepreneurs are capable of turning ideas into action, and this can be important for maintaining the commitment of supporters.

For policy entrepreneurs, the development of organizational culture and belief systems among supporters represents the primary means of generating group cohesion and a commitment to achieving policy change. But this does not mean that we should expect to find uniformity among the actions of policy entrepreneurs in this regard. Contextual factors and matters of timing will influence many aspects of the ways that policy entrepreneurs seek to organize others and provide leadership.

Recognizing that policy entrepreneurs must be creative individuals, always attempting to refine their case for the adoption of their favored policy innovations, we come to see that many diverse ways of working with others might be sufficient to promote policy change. As in the marketplace, so in politics we should expect to see a range of organizational forms being used to promote various policy positions. These forms will not be dictated simply by the nature of the tasks they have been established to perform. Most often, we should expect to see policy entrepreneurs developing organizational arrangements that make the best use of the resources they have at their disposal. This suggests that even the most rudimentary efforts at organizing others might be sufficient at times to secure the desired policy changes. At other times, policy entrepreneurs may have to engage in protracted and intensive efforts to organize and lead others in ways that could support successful lobbying for policy change. Those who are most socially perceptive and socially connected are more likely to have a clear sense of what they need to do and how to do it. Such policy entrepreneurs might be able to readily "economize" on the costs of organizing others.

Reprise: A Theory of Policy Entrepreneurship

In the past, political scientists have often used the term "policy entrepreneur" to describe certain actors in the policymaking process. Usually the term has been used as a loose metaphor. But whenever this term is employed, an assertion is implicitly made: in the policymaking process we find individuals who represent direct counterparts to entrepreneurs in the marketplace. Although made implicitly, this represents a fairly strong assertion. To what extent might we draw parallels between the actions of entrepreneurs in markets and the actions of particular individuals in the policymaking process? This chapter provided a series of responses to that question. Here, I summarize the key points. Together, they constitute a theory of policy entrepreneurship, a set of assertions or expectations about policy entrepreneurs, from which testable hypotheses might be derived.

Policy entrepreneurs can be identified by their efforts to introduce policy innovations and, thereby, secure policy change. Policy entrepreneurs are not interested in preserving the status quo in policy settings. Their motivations for introducing policy innovations might be quite diverse. However, given their goal of promoting significant policy change, their actions should be expected to follow certain patterns. Just as it is possible to identify entrepreneurs in the market process (although this is by no means an easy task), so it is possible to identify policy entrepreneurs in the policymaking process.

Policy entrepreneurs must be *creative* and *insightful*, able to see how proposing particular policy innovations could alter the nature of policy debates. They must engage in efforts to carefully frame issues so that their ideas for policy change are viewed as appropriate solutions to given problems. In many ways, policy entrepreneurs can be thought of as equivalent to the revolutionary scientists discussed by Thomas S. Kuhn (1970). That is to say, they are not content to accept conventional wisdom. They "question the question" (Krugman 1993) and thus reveal the problems associated with current policy settings, just as those who depart from "normal science" suggest the possibility of new paradigms.

Policy entrepreneurs must be *socially perceptive*, able to see problems and issues from a range of perspectives, so that they can propose policy innovations that hold broad appeal. In achieving some sense of distance from any given social setting, policy entrepreneurs are often able to see things in ways that are unconventional. Yet, they must be able to communicate with others in ways that do not betray this outsider sensibility.

Policy entrepreneurs must be *able to mix in a variety of social and political settings*, so that they can readily acquire valuable information and use their contacts to advantage in pursuit of policy change. In a sense, we might think of policy entrepreneurs as having the ability to engage in the arbitrage of ideas and practices. That is to say, policy entrepreneurs are able to make positive connections between groups of people who previously may have had—or at least *perceived* themselves to have had—little in common with each other.

Policy entrepreneurs must be *able to argue persuasively*. Often, this will mean making different arguments to different groups while keeping their overall story consistent. The greater a policy entrepreneur's social perceptiveness and social connectedness, the greater the likelihood that he or she can make arguments that appeal to a broad range of people.

Policy entrepreneurs must be *strategic team builders*, able to determine the type of coalition best able to support their pursuit of policy change. Just as critical as the ability to work with others is the ability to carefully determine the extent to which others must be involved in an effort to secure policy change. This is where good judgment is vital. Just as we see entrepreneurs in the marketplace creating distinctive forms of firm-like arrangement, so it is that policy entrepreneurs must assemble appropriate coalitional forms for pursuing their desired ends. The choices made here will have as much to do with the goal being sought as with the nature of the policy and political context in which the policy entrepreneur is located. Knowing how to adapt coalitional forms to changing contexts is also vital.

Policy entrepreneurs must be *prepared to lead by example*, where necessary creating "prefigurative forms" of the policy innovations they seek to introduce. It is critical for policy entrepreneurs that others find their ideas and their visions of the future believable. Often, this means that policy entrepreneurs must be able to find ways to "put their money where their mouth is," clearly signaling their personal commitment to their arguments and the political movements they attempt to create.

Undoubtedly, concerns might be raised regarding this characterization of policy entrepreneurs. I note and briefly consider two serious issues here. First, from this discussion, we could come to the conclusion that, to be effective, policy entrepreneurs must be superhuman in their capabilities. Partly, this concern emerges because by definition the theory places emphasis on individuals, rather than on groups or on broader political and social processes, as agents of policy change. Can one individual do all this alone? Although anecdotal evidence abounds of individuals who apparently made crucial efforts toward securing policy change, clearly the answer is no. Simply because of the complex and highly social nature of the policymaking process, no single individual can ever spontaneously generate policy change. But rather than negating the legitimacy of a theory of policy entrepreneurship, acknowledging this point actually adds further weight to the theory. Entrepreneurs, be they in the marketplace or in the policymaking process, cannot affect change without successfully securing the interest and support of others. Every theory of entrepreneurship emphasizes the social nature of the enterprise. The theory of policy entrepreneurship presented here is no different. By noting the ways that policy entrepreneurs must work with others, this theory explains why particular instances of policy change are associated with specific individuals, even when clearly they were not the sole force prompting those changes. Policy entrepreneurs promote the adoption of policy innovations through their efforts to coordinate others. In seeking to identify such individuals—the policy entrepreneurs—and the strategies they use to support their goals of policy innovation and change, we can gain important insights into the nature of the policymaking process.

Another concern that might be raised about this theory is that it does not portray the entrepreneur as a risk taker. Following Joseph Schumpeter (1934) and others, I reject the claim, originally made by Richard Cantillon (1755), that risk bearing is the defining characteristic of the entrepreneur. To the extent that a policy entrepreneur decides to promote a given policy idea, he or she always runs the risk of incurring some cost in the form of better opportunities forgone. But opportunity costs are endemic. Policy entrepreneurs take risks; so do others in the policymaking process. More defining than their ability to take or to bear risks is the ability of policy entrepreneurs to persuade others of the merit of their ideas and the value of taking actions to support the transformation of those ideas into policy innovations. This will often involve persuading elected officials that what might on first consideration appear a risky proposal is, in fact, a policy idea worth promoting. Thus, over and above risk taking, policy entrepreneurs identify themselves through their ability to generate creative ideas, make persuasive arguments, and forge strategic alliances with others.

Outlook

This theoretical exploration of policy entrepreneurship is intended as a starting point for additional theory development and for the launching of various empirical explorations and analyses of policy entrepreneurship. In the next chapter, I introduce my approach to conducting an empirically based study of policy entrepreneurship, and in the subsequent four chapters, I present different aspects of the way that policy entrepreneurs have raised the idea of school choice as a policy innovation in the United States. These following chapters are not, of course, purely empirical. Taking general theory and using it to guide how we interpret events and actions always requires accommodating the particulars of time and place. Further, empirical findings often hold implications for the general theory used for initial guidance. Given this, these chapters can be viewed as empirically driven but very much theoretically engaged. Based on these chapters, I believe it is reasonable to claim that policy entrepreneurs serve as important sources of policy change. But this does not mean I subscribe to some sort of monocausal view of policy change. As recognized in chapter 2, other explanations of policy change have been developed in the past, and they have provided important insights into the nature of the policymaking process. For this reason, having worked through this theory development and my empirical studies, in chapter 11, the final chapter, I return to the established literature on policy change. There, I consider how what I have said about the behavior of policy entrepreneurs relates to what other scholars have said about the antecedents of policy change.

Notes

1. Not surprisingly, many alternative approaches have been developed to portray opportunities for entrepreneurship. But any given approach, though

illuminating some matters, will always have its limits. For example, the product life cycle is often treated as a heuristic for thinking about opportunities for entrepreneurship (Porter 1980). Under this model, it is assumed that most products go through a cycle represented by four stages: introduction, growth, maturity, and decline. The expectation is that opportunities for entrepreneurship are found at the early stages of the cycle and that as the product reaches maturity, the possibilities for realizing profits decline, so that only a few firms end up delivering the product. While it is elegant, I am not convinced that the product cycle model gives us any particular insights into the milieu of the entrepreneur that we cannot attain through considering pace of change and industry concentration. Furthermore, the product life cycle model invites us to focus on individual, preexisting products. But in doing this, we might miss out on seeing how context matters for prompting ideas for innovation. (Likewise, the potential for new growth in a forest cannot be assessed by focusing exclusively on particular trees or even particular species of tree found there at present.)

2. This must be seen as a difference only in emphasis, however. After all, it was Wilson who, in his discussion of the politics of regulation and regulatory change, noted that, among other things, "we must be struck at every turn by the importance of ideas" (1980, 393).

3. In accord with what I have said here, Deborah Stone has noted that "policy politics involves strategically portraying issues so that they fit one causal idea or another. The different sides in an issue act as if they are trying to find the 'true' cause, but they are always struggling to influence which idea is selected to guide policy" (1997, 197). For policy entrepreneurs, this statement implies the need to combine finely honed communication skills with the political astuteness to assess the strategic importance of the words and actions of others. The policy entrepreneur seeking to promote a policy innovation must develop "causal stories" that link problems and solutions in ways that convincingly portray a given policy innovation as necessary and appropriate.

4. For discussions see, for instance, essays collected in Kahneman, Slovic, and Tversky (1982), Nisbett and Ross (1980), and Quattrone and Tversky (1988). Bryan Jones (1994) provides an excellent exploration of the ways that people in the policy realm conceptualize and interpret problems.

5. According to Donald A. Schön and Martin Rein (1994), differences in our interpretative frames constitute the source of policy controversies.

> To contribute to the reframing of policy dilemmas, policy makers must be able to reflect on the action frames held by their antagonists. Even to recognize the existence of such dilemmas, policy makers must be able to reflect on their own action frames: they must overcome the blindness induced by their own ways of framing the policy situation in order to see that multiple policy frames represent a nexus of legitimate values in conflict. (1994, 187)

> 6. Kingdon (1995, 173) refers to this as coupling solutions to problems. An excellent example of the constant solution adapting to the changing mosaic of problems and politics is the case of urban mass transit. When a federal program for mass transit was first proposed, it was sold primarily as a straight-forward traffic management tool. . . . When the traffic and conjestion issues played themselves out in the problem stream, advocates of mass transit looked for the next prominent problem to which to attach their solution. Along came the environmental movement. . . . The environment movement faded, and what was the next big push? You guessed it: energy.

7. This claim resonates with the following statement made by John Kingdon: "Wholly new ideas do not suddenly appear. Instead, people recombine familiar elements into a new structure or a new proposal. This is why it is possible to note, 'There is no new thing under the sun,' at the very same time change and innovation are being observed" ([1984] 1995, 124).

8. See, for example, Daniels (n.d.) for a discussion of this type of approach with the introduction of charter schools in Pennsylvania.

SIX

Empirical Studies of Policy Entrepreneurship

In the previous chapters of this book, my primary concern has been to argue why the concept of the policy entrepreneur is an important one for scholars interested in explaining policy change. In the course of making this argument, I have developed a theory that serves to generate expectations about the activities of policy entrepreneurs. The theory is grounded on one main contention. That is, if we are to legitimately claim that certain individuals in the policymaking process are policy entrepreneurs, then we must be able to demonstrate that they really are counterparts to entrepreneurs in the marketplace. Such argument and theory construction can take us some distance toward making claims for the merit of a concept. But ultimately we need to test our theoretically derived intuitions against what we observe in practice. This, of course, raises additional difficulties. In particular, when turning to empirical investigation we need to be as reflective as possible about our theorizing. The world out there does not speak to us in unmediated ways. What we observe in practice, and how we interpret it, is heavily informed by what we bring to given situations. Therefore, when the concept of the policy entrepreneur is most salient to us, we are likely to produce interpretations of processes and events that are both distinctive and biased. Thinking primarily in terms of party politics or interest group behavior would similarly prompt distinct interpretations of the policymaking process. Given this, depending on our theoretical preoccupations, our perceptions and judgments of processes and events will often be divergent. Yet, as social scientists, what we would most like to achieve is consensus about the nature and relative importance of various factors that shape politics and society. For this reason, I do not seek to add yet another item to a discordant ensemble of theories of policymaking and policy change. Instead, I want to make the claim—and make it as plausibly as possible—that policy entrepreneurs can and do make significant contributions to the creation of policy change. One way to make such a claim is to admit that other factors matter as well, and to then assess the contribution of policy entrepreneurs, taking into account the most important of those other factors. This is the approach taken in the empirical work documented in this and the following four chapters.

I designed the present study to explore whether the presence and actions of policy entrepreneurs have prompted state legislative consideration and adoption of proposals for school choice. The study explicitly controls for the effects of other factors that could prompt such policy change. Thus, the units of analysis for much of this empirical work are not the policy entrepreneurs themselves, but the forty-eight contiguous United States. The dependent variables of interest are legislative consideration and adoption of school choice proposals; policy entrepreneurs are treated as one of several independent variables that could affect those dependent variables.

This research strategy represents a fairly stark departure from the strategies that other researchers have previously used when studying policy entrepreneurship. In particular, my approach is quite different from that found in the small but important literature in which researchers have used a range of case study and biographical techniques to document the behaviors of policy entrepreneurs and their apparent effects on policy development and change. An especially good example of this type of work is Thomas K. McCraw's (1984) Pulitzer Prize-winning historical study of Charles Francis Adams, Louis D. Brandeis, James M. Landis, and Alfred E. Kahn, and the contributions they made to United States regulatory policy. McCraw weaves together biography, economic history, and discussion of political strategy to explain how the insights and actions of these four individuals served to inform public policy choices. Another case study of exceptional merit is provided by Paula J. King (1988), who studied the role played by policy entrepreneurs in the development of Minnesota's pioneering school choice law of 1987. King spent several years documenting and analyzing the behaviors supporting the rise of the school choice idea in Minnesota as it took place. At the time King began her study legislation was being discussed, but had not yet been adopted. King's study is ambitious in scope and ethnographic in detail, exploring the political psychology of several Minnesota policy entrepreneurs, the group dynamics of the team that worked to promote school choice to key decisionmakers, and how private and public worlds became intertwined for those who passionately sought policy change.[1] Other works in this genre include Robert A. Caro's (1974) biography of Robert Moses, New York's long-serving bureaucrat and visionary of public infrastructure; the contributions to Jameson W. Doig and Erwin C. Hargrove's (1987) volume describing alternative styles of entrepreneurial leadership in government; and Donald F. Kettl's (1986) study of monetary policy decisionmaking on the Federal Reserve Board. All of the works mentioned here present deep, captivating studies of complex individuals and their political machinations.[2] In contrast to these works, my own empirical study necessarily appears thinner in terms of description and the elaboration of human interest stories. Unfortunately, this is the price that is often paid for attempting to make statistically supported general statements about particular aspects of politics and society.

Because they differ in the purposes they serve, all research designs contain features that could be subject to harsh criticism when judged against the merits of other approaches. Case studies, biographies, and histories are vital for helping us gain insights into processes and events that we know little about. Without the attention to detail and the striving for theory construction that exemplifies the best contributions of this sort, our knowledge of many aspects of society and politics would be greatly impoverished. However, research work of this sort rarely lends itself to the drawing out of generalized insights. Only through the accumulation of many such studies of the same phenomena can we begin to discern patterns and speculate about general linkages between events and their causes. In contrast, the appeal of quantitative studies lies in the way that they facilitate simultaneous testing of various hypotheses concerning causal relationships. In such studies well-defined categories are the means of research. As Grant McCracken (1988, 16) notes, qualitative research approaches are often undertaken with the goal of figuring out what features of the social and political world are worthy of precise categorization and further analysis, and quantitative analyses of any relevance cannot be done until this initial spadework has been completed. In light of these considerations, it is obvious that my empirical investigation of policy entrepreneurship would be distinctly different had I not been able to benefit from the many insights of scholars before me who have taken the time to wrestle with specific cases and draw provocative insights from them. This present work, this effort at theory construction and testing so as to make generalizable claims about policy entrepreneurship and policy change, is decidedly of the second generation sort. I see it as a logical next step to take from the work of others and hope that it will encourage others to think seriously about policy entrepreneurship and policy change. In turn, perhaps this will stimulate further theoretical and empirical investigations using a range of research strategies, as new questions and new preoccupations emerge among scholars interested in the nature of the policymaking process.

The Research Design

I collected the bulk of my evidence concerning the presence and actions of state-level school choice policy entrepreneurs in the middle of 1993, using a mail survey of education policy experts in each of the forty-eight contiguous United States. At this time, thirty-eight state legislatures had considered various school choice plans, thirteen had adopted open-enrollment plans, two had adopted both open-enrollment and charter school plans, and Wisconsin had adopted the Milwaukee parental choice plan. The survey was accompanied by a brief cover letter containing an explanation of the project, a working definition of the term "policy entrepreneur," and a brief summary of my understanding of the school-choice-related activities that had occurred so far in the relevant states.[3] The definitional sections of the cover letters are excerpted and reproduced in Figure 6-1. The ten-page survey contained eleven multipart questions. Survey recipients were asked to note the names and the years when policy entrepreneurs first advocated school choice in their states. In asking this question, I made sure to note: "I care about *proposals* made by the policy entrepreneurs regardless of their success." Recipients were asked to note specific events and national influences that might have motivated the policy entrepreneurs to advocate school choice in their state. They were then asked a series of questions concerning how the policy entrepreneurs raised the issue of school choice. Here, I listed a variety of strategies, some of which I knew had been used by school choice policy entrepreneurs in particular states. The respondents were also asked whether the policy entrepreneurs had developed various types of coalitions, and again they were provided with examples of concerned citizen,

I am working on a belief that the increasing state-level interest in school choice over recent years is a direct result of the actions of individuals who I term *school choice policy entrepreneurs*. Policy entrepreneurs seek dynamic policy change. They pursue this through redefining policy problems and by carefully working with others in and around government to build support for their ideas.

Currently, I am aware of several people who have been active at the state level and who seem to fit my definition of policy entrepreneurs. Joe Nathan and Ted Kolderie appear to have played a key role in gaining legislative consideration and approval of school choice in Minnesota. Charles Glenn and Polly Williams seem, respectively, to have been key school choice policy entrepreneurs in Massachusetts and Wisconsin. Frequently, these policy entrepreneurs have not worked alone, but they do appear to have provided an impetus that was critical for raising the issue of school choice to a level where it received legislative consideration.

For the purpose of my study, I define school choice policies as those that allow for one or more of the following: intra-district enrollment options, inter-district (or state-wide) enrollment options, publicly and privately funded voucher schemes, and charter schools.

Figure 6-1. ***Defining School Choice Policy Entrepreneurs for the Survey Recipients***

business, and broad-based groups that I knew had been developed to support a campaign for school choice in some states. Questions were then asked about the effectiveness of the policy entrepreneurs in developing and maintaining good relations with key groups and individuals in their states, and how effectively they presented their messages. Finally, a variety of strategies were listed, and respondents were asked how important these were for the school choice policy entrepreneurs that they had identified. These strategies included collecting evidence to demonstrate the merits of school choice, networking with others in and outside their states, engaging in problem framing, and working to create perceptions that the state school system was in crisis. In addition to these questions that pertained directly to the activities of the policy entrepreneurs, survey recipients were asked about the positions of other state-level actors and groups toward the school choice idea. This group of survey questions was developed and refined using a select number of face-to-face and telephone conversations with potential recipients. I also talked about the survey and the material it contained with several people having expert knowledge of the school choice movement in the states.[4] The complete text of the survey questionnaire is contained in the appendix.

This survey questionnaire made significant demands for expert knowledge and judgment on the part of the recipients. It was designed to collect facts rather than attitudes. In determining the group of individuals who should receive the survey, I did not try to obtain a representative sample of education policy experts from each state. I sought, instead, to obtain the best information I could from the most appropriate sources. For all states I requested the chief state school officer to nominate the best person in his or her organization to answer my questionnaire. I also sent copies of the questionnaire to the governor's advisor on education policy in each state and representatives of the state affiliates of the American Federation of Teachers or the National Education Association, or both. Where I could locate them, I also sent questionnaires to academics in each state with a reputation for knowledge of the state school finance system, members of policy think tanks known to have interests in education reform, and members of the grass-roots organization Citizens for Educational Freedom.[5] Using this approach I sent questionnaires to about five well-informed people in each state. A total of 243 individuals received surveys. After mailing the initial set of surveys, I engaged in extensive follow-up of the recipients, both through telephone calls and additional mailings. As a result, I obtained 117 completed questionnaires. The responses included at least two from almost every state. In some states the response rate appears to have been lower simply because school choice was not an issue of any interest to people there. Of the returned questionnaires, 33 (28 percent) came from state education department officials, 12 (10 percent) came from governors' education advisors, 27 (23 percent) came from representatives of state teachers' unions, 16 (13 percent) came from academics, 17 (15 percent) came from members of policy think tanks, and 12 (11 percent) came from state spokesmen for Citizens for Educational Freedom. The respondents were all well-informed participants in the education policy community in their states and they provided sophisticated responses to the survey questions. Often, they augmented their responses with copies of documents that they believed might be relevant to my study. I have occasionally been asked why I did not survey the chairs of education committees in each state house. Actually, I was not interested in knowing about legislative actors and action per se, but in the presence and actions of policy entrepreneurs. In the spirit of John W. Kingdon (1995, 122), I began this research assuming that policy entrepreneurs "could be in or out of government, in elected or appointed positions, in interest groups or research organizations." Indeed, this is exactly what I found.

The School Choice Policy Entrepreneurs

In twenty-six states my survey respondents identified individuals who they considered matched my description of school choice policy entrepreneurs. The states are listed in Table 6-1. In fourteen (53 percent) of these states, all the respondents named the same individuals or representatives of the same group as being policy entrepreneurs; and in six states (23 percent) over two-thirds of the respondents named the same individuals or representatives. For the remaining six states, I had to draw upon further information to make a determination regarding the key school choice policy entrepreneur. Additional information was derived from telephone conversations with some of the survey respondents and also discussions with representatives of the U.S. Department of Education, the Heritage Foundation, and the Carnegie Foundation who had also been monitoring school choice activities in the states. Overall, there was a considerable amount of consensus among the survey respondents about who constituted school choice policy entrepreneurs. When we reflect upon the importance to policy entrepreneurs of networking in and around state governments so as to bring their ideas into good currency, this consensus makes good sense. Or, as Paul E. Peterson (1981, 137) has said in his review and defense of reputational methods of locating powerful people in communities that were used, for example, by Floyd Hunter (1953), "Reputation in a social system cannot be constructed out of nothing; there must be something in an individual's past that leads informed observers to concede him a political status of high rank."

Of the policy entrepreneurs identified, 7 (26 percent) were state legislators, 6 (23 percent) were members of policy think tanks, 5 (19 percent) were members or former members of the teaching profession, 3 (12 percent) were governors, 3 (12 percent) represented business interests, and 2 (8 percent) were representatives of grass-roots groups.[6] To give a better sense of the type of individuals who have served as school choice policy entrepreneurs, I next provide brief portraits of five individuals identified by the survey respondents. As with my portraits of three school choice entrepreneurs in chapter 2, these portraits draw upon information from

Table 6-1. ***States Where School Choice Policy Entrepreneurs Were Identified***

Alabama	Minnesota
Arkansas	Mississippi
California	Nebraska
Colorado	New Hampshire
Connecticut	New York
Delaware	North Carolina
Illinois	Oregon
Indiana	Pennsylvania
Louisiana	South Carolina
Maine	Texas
Maryland	Vermont
Massachusetts	Washington
Michigan	Wisconsin

a variety of sources, including publications, follow-up interviews that I conducted with my survey respondents, and interviews I conducted with some of the policy entrepreneurs directly.

Governor Bill Clinton in Arkansas

As the governor of Arkansas, Bill Clinton took a close interest in education issues.[7] Aside from promoting policy change in his own state, in 1986 and 1987 he served as the chairman of the Education Commission of the States and as the chairman of the National Governors' Association. It was during this time that Bill Clinton became alert to the concept of school choice. For a time Joe Nathan of Minnesota worked with him as an advisor to the National Governors' Association. The idea of allowing students in Arkansas to cross public school district lines in pursuit of a better education struck Clinton as a good idea. There had been considerable concern among some parents that their children, with aspirations to attend college, were not being appropriately prepared by their local schools. The local impetus for school choice came out of this. Because he had been a solid advocate of public education for a number of years, it was quite easy for Clinton to propose a more radical measure like the introduction of choice among public schools in Arkansas.

In developing his proposal for a policy change, Clinton worked closely with several members of the state legislature. He also made sure to obtain the help of Joe Nathan, who visited the state to give expert testimony before the House Education Committee. Anticipating a negative reaction from the teachers' unions in the state, Governor Clinton helped to craft fifteen different bills related to education issues that were considered in the 1989 legislative session. All the bills were dealt with one by one, but this bombardment of proposals forced union lobbyists to deal with a range of issues, thus reducing their ability to launch a concentrated campaign against the school choice legislation. In Arkansas, school choice was both considered for the first time and adopted in the 1989 legislative session, making this state one of the earliest to adopt this policy innovation. There is good reason to believe that the early efforts of Bill Clinton laid the foundation for these subsequent developments. As one survey respondent wrote in 1993: "In this state [school choice] sprang from one source like Minerva [*sic*] from the head of Zeus. . . . In our case, it was Clinton." Another survey respondent said in a follow-up interview: "School choice would never have been done in Arkansas if Clinton had not proposed it. I don't think there was anyone else as informed about it or as enthusiastic about it as he." However, it is clear that Clinton worked closely with members of the legislature and with members of the Arkansas Business Coalition to establish support for this policy innovation. Interest in Arkansas concerning school choice has continued since 1989. In 1995, the state legislature adopted a charter schools law, and a private voucher program is operating in Little Rock. Of course, as president of the United States, Bill Clinton has continued to promote public school choice. As one measure of this, in the years from 1995 through 1999 the federal government's annual commitment to providing start-up money for charter schools increased from $6 million to over $100 million.

The Commit CEOs in Indiana

In the late 1980s business groups across the country became very interested in education issues, especially in thinking about how firms and corporations could help to improve the quality of public schooling. The Business Roundtable held several national forums on this matter and distributed pamphlets to businesses suggesting ways that they could form partnerships with local schools. In Indiana the CEOs of some of the largest corporations in the state, such as Lincoln National Corporation, the Cummins Engine Company, and Eli Lilly and Company, took this call for action seriously. Andre Lacy, the president and CEO of Lacy Diversified Industries, served as the initial coordinator of the business effort in Indiana. Over several months in late 1989 and the start of 1990 he convened a series of discussions. But during these discussions it became clear that there were some stark differences in philosophy and courses of action desired by the CEOs. Some took the view that education is difficult to reform rapidly and that, given its complexity, working from within the system, becoming partners with schools was an appropriate strategy. Others took the view that no meaningful change would occur without external pressure being applied to the school system. This latter group favored fundamental, top-down reform initiatives. Out of these discussions and disagreements, two organizations were formed: Community Leaders Applied for Superior Schools (CLASS) and Commit. CLASS proposed to work with the present school system. By contrast, according to Lacy, "Commit came about more from businessmen clearly frustrated with educators' inability to even recognize they have a problem."[8] While CLASS pursued local partnering initiatives with schools, the Commit CEOs stayed focused on the big picture. However, some key weaknesses in the strategy of the Commit CEOs served to severely limit the impact they had in the state. Over subsequent years, the actions of Commit did seem to change the nature of the education debate in the state and draw significant attention to the issue of school choice. But in terms of actual policy change their efforts were ineffective.

In the middle of 1990, the Commit CEOs contracted with the Hudson Institute to devise a plan for school reform in the state. The principal investigator on the project was Carol D'Amico, who, along with other advisors, created a plan of action and subsequently drafted legislation to support it. School choice, through the use of publicly funded vouchers, was a centerpiece of this proposal for reform that also emphasized school-based management and tougher standards for school leavers. The plan was intellectually coherent, and no effort was made within it to make the sort of compromises that might have won it a broad base of support. The Commit CEOs took the view that, equipped with this plan and the draft legislation, they could rapidly achieve the goal of root-and-branch education reform in the state. One observer said to me: "I think you had some of them who really believe . . . that the mere fact of walking to the state legislature with this phalanx of corporate firepower, locked arm in arm would cause the legislature to say, 'Oh, my goodness, of course, yes!' and pass the bill. . . . They were so used to their own business, writing edicts and having them obeyed. . . ."

To the surprise of many, the bill was considered and adopted in 1991 by the Indiana Senate Education Committee. But it died in the Senate Finance Committee, because it quickly created controversy and it became clear that Commit would have to expend huge amounts of political capital to come even close to gaining majority support for the bill on the senate floor, and that support in the Indiana House would be even more difficult to obtain. During the controversy over the bill, the Commit CEOs came in for a great deal of criticism and personal attack from opponents, who were led by the state teachers' unions. Following this some of the fire went out of Commit. The organization again had a bill introduced in 1993, but this time the proposals were significantly watered down. In a bid to win support from the teachers' unions, emphasis was placed on standards, and, remarkably, school choice was dropped from the proposal. As it turned out, the teachers' unions ended up not supporting this bill either, and again it died in committee. On reflection, the biggest problem with the Commit strategy was that no effort was made by the organization to forge a coalition with natural allies, such as families from the inner cities and parents of children in private schools. Subsequently, some efforts were made to do this, but, by the middle of 1994, the energies of Commit, and the commitment to it by the corporate CEOs had all but evaporated. The organization officially folded in 1996. Today, school choice issues continue to be promoted in the state by Carol D'Amico and her colleagues at the Hudson Institute and by personnel in the Indiana Chamber of Commerce. They have tried unsuccessfully to have a charter school law adopted in the state.

Despite the demise of Commit, school choice issues have remained on the political agenda in Indiana throughout the 1990s. Commit has been responsible for this both directly and indirectly. When the Indiana CEOs were discussing reform approaches early in 1990, J. Patrick Rooney, the chairman of the Golden Rule Insurance Company, kept his distance, looking on with some amusement at the efforts of his peers as they struggled, and ultimately failed, to find a united voice. Rooney opted to work to improve public schooling by circumventing it completely. Thus, in August 1991 Rooney set up a private voucher system, under the rubric of the Choice Charitable Trust, to assist poor families in Indianapolis in sending their children to private schools of their choice. This initiative has now been widely emulated throughout the nation, and I discuss it in more detail in chapter 10. Eventually Rooney might have launched his private voucher plan regardless of the actions of the Commit CEOs. But the actions of Commit made school choice a salient issue in Indiana, establishing the conditions under which a creative individual like Rooney could come to appreciate the value of taking a completely new approach to promoting it.[9]

Jackie Ducote in Louisiana

Jackie Ducote is, by her own telling, "an education reform junkie." She has also been a long-serving and, ultimately, relatively successful advocate of various school choice initiatives in Louisiana. Ducote first became involved in education issues in the 1970s when her son was in elementary school. At that time, she formed a coalition of inner city parents in Baton Rouge to push for improvements in the public education provided there. After working for a number of years as an analyst in the Public Affairs Research Council of Louisiana, Ducote left in 1978 to become chief education lobbyist for the Louisiana Association of Business and Industry (LABI), a post she held until 1996. According to Ducote, the business community in Louisiana took the lead in education reform long before it was fashionable for business groups to do so. Ducote's views on education and educational reform were strongly influenced by those of her former boss, Ed Steimel, at the LABI. Even in the 1970s Steimel was arguing that competition was a vital force that could serve to transform and improve public education. Throughout the 1980s the LABI helped to secure enactment of over fifty education reform laws in Louisiana. But, despite all this activity, education quality indicators in the state hardly budged. Thus, in 1987 Jackie Ducote wrote a report for the LABI titled "Ten Years of Public Education 'Reform' in Louisiana: A Long Journey to Nowhere." According to Ducote, most of the reforms enacted during this time had subsequently been watered down, taken to court by the teachers' unions, or not properly funded. From this experience, Ducote drew the following lesson, contained in an op-ed piece she had published in *The Wall Street Journal* in 1990:

> Piecemeal attempts to change the present system haven't worked and won't work because the present system is a monopoly. It has a captive clientele and guaranteed funding regardless of results. Thus, it has no incentive to change, and parents and students have no leverage. They can't take their business elsewhere unless they are willing and able to pay twice for it.

In her role at the LABI, Jackie Ducote not only developed ideas for educational reform in Louisiana, but she worked energetically to create strong political support for them. Along with writing frequent newspaper articles, she secured public opinion polling on education issues in Louisiana and she compiled information on school choice policy developments in other states. Ducote also worked to develop draft voucher legislation, commissioning the advice of such experts as Professor John Coons of the University of California, Berkeley. In 1990 she created a coalition to support school choice initiatives in Louisiana called "The Right to Learn Committee." To raise funds for the coalition, Ducote organized a series of fundraising breakfasts and brought to the state keynote speakers and school choice advocates such as Wisconsin Representative Polly Williams and Governor Pete du Pont of Delaware. She also attempted to forge alliances with community leaders and black ministers in the state. In a conversation Jackie Ducote told me, "Plan A is to change the system using your traditional approach. Plan B is to totally change the nature of the system to a choice system." Toward the end of the 1980s Ducote increasingly came to see that Plan B, though difficult to pursue, was the one worth seeking.

All this effort has generated some payoffs, but they have been slow in coming. A proposal for school choice was considered by the legislature for the first time in 1990, and proposals were considered again in subsequent years. Most of these proposals involved making vouchers available to families to send their children to any public or private school of their choosing. Yet it was not until 1995, when the state legislature adopted a charter school law, that some form of school choice was introduced in Louisiana. Jackie Ducote was an important member of the coalition that pushed for adoption of the charter school law, although by that time other important and powerful figures in Louisiana politics had begun to take a keen interest in the school choice issue. Today, Ducote is president of the Public Affairs Research Council of Louisiana, the think tank she originally worked for in the 1970s. She continues to work there on school choice and voucher issues.

Charles Glenn in Massachusetts

The school choice idea gained currency in Massachusetts long before it caught on as a reform option in other states. This enduring interest in school choice can be attributed in very large part to the efforts of Charles Glenn. From 1970 until the early 1990s, Charles Glenn served as the director of the Massachusetts Department of Education's Bureau of Equal Educational Opportunity. In that position Glenn did much to promote the use of magnet schools across the state, and he was instrumental in helping to establish the highly acclaimed intradistrict "controlled choice" program in Cambridge that began operation in 1981. According to Glenn, school choice can be used as a means to achieve greater equity in public education. In Glenn's view, providing parents with choice options and giving them sufficient information to make considered choices can be extremely empowering. The ability of parents to move their children freely across a range of schools can then spur poorly performing schools to improve the education opportunities they offer. This can be good for all students, even if only a handful of them actually exercise their choices.

Charles Glenn's effort to introduce a statewide school choice law began in late 1988. Earlier that year, Massachusetts Senate President William M. Bulger had sponsored legislation to introduce a pilot interdistrict transfer program for the cities of Boston and Worcester. This legislation was vetoed by the governor, Michael Dukakis, who, along with other opponents of the legislation, believed that it would result in a mass exodus of white students from Boston's schools. Following this initial skirmish over school choice issues, Charles Glenn drafted a proposal for a much broader school choice program. According to Glenn, the energy behind this effort owed "a tremendous amount" to adoption of the statewide school choice plan by the Minnesota legislature in 1987. What is perhaps most important to note about the rise of school choice in Massachusetts is that it was accompanied by little public support. At the time that the legislation was being developed, Glenn said that "being a one-man band on this means I don't have any unwelcome allies." Yet, this can be a risky strategy to pursue, and, as it turns out, while the Massachusetts legislature considered the school choice plan in 1989, the plan received insufficient support to be adopted into law.[10]

Statewide school choice legislation was finally adopted by the Massachusetts legislature in 1991. This legislation permits students to make interdistrict transfers, so long as the receiving district agrees to the transfer. A parental information center on schools in choice districts was subsequently established. In a further move to increase opportunities for school choice in the state, in 1993 Massachusetts adopted a charter school law. This effort was promoted primarily by the governor's office, and much of the work of promoting the idea was done by the Pioneer Institute, a conservative Boston think tank. So, although Charles Glenn was a critical player in raising the issue of school choice in Massachusetts, and at the national level, as well, he was not heavily involved in the cut-and-thrust of political maneuvering that eventually led to legislative adoption of choice initiatives. Indeed, in the early 1990s Charles Glenn left the Massachusetts Department of Education; since then he has held a professorship in the School of Education at Boston University. This appears to be a natural progression for someone who, while holding his government position, wrote articles, book chapters, and a book manuscript, *The Myth of the Common School* (University of Massachusetts Press, 1988). In his position at Boston University Glenn has continued to be active in contributing to the national dialogue on school choice issues. Currently, he is chairman of the school's Department of Administration, Training, and Policy Studies, where he has recently completed an international study of the treatment of immigrant children by education systems.

David Kirkpatrick in Pennsylvania

Throughout the 1990s Pennsylvania has been the site of some significant legislative battles over school choice. During this time the cast of key elected officials championing school choice has often changed. But David Kirkpatrick has borne the torch for school choice since the early 1970s, and he has played a vital—though often behind-the-scenes—role in raising support for the idea in Pennsylvania. Kirkpatrick's long career has seen him working as a high school educator in the 1960s, president of the Pennsylvania State Education Association from 1969 through 1971, and consultant or staff member in many areas of Pennsylvania state government, including the Office of the Governor and the Pennsylvania Department of Education. Kirkpatrick refined his skills as a political organizer when, in 1980, he founded the Pennsylvania Rural Coalition. Under his chairmanship, the coalition grew to include more than 100 organizations and a newsletter was developed for regular distribution to members. Kirkpatrick has also worked to develop an impressive record of commentaries and other publications concerning school choice. In 1990 Loyola University Press published his historically grounded argument for the idea, *Choice in Schooling: A Case for Tuition Vouchers*.

His combination of practical organizational experience and intellectual depth placed David Kirkpatrick in a strong position to develop a coalition to support the adoption of school choice in Pennsylvania. In 1991, along with Don Eberly, president of the Commonwealth Foundation for Public Policy Alternatives, Kirkpatrick established the REACH Alliance.[11] REACH was designed to promote school choice, especially a public voucher program, through bringing together the resources of a range of organizations and using them to directly lobby state politicians. The Pennsylvania Catholic Conference was a crucial member of the organization, regularly making donations to its budget. Very quickly the organization achieved remarkable influence. This occurred primarily because the school choice idea caught the eye of Senator Hank Salvatore, a Republican from Philadelphia. In November 1991 Salvatore led a successful campaign to achieve state senate adoption of a statewide voucher plan. David Kirkpatrick worked closely with the senator to draft the legislation, which, following intense opposition from teachers' unions and other groups, failed to gain adoption by the Pennsylvania House. The struggle over school choice in Pennsylvania in 1991 was described at the time by *Education Week* as "one of the most acrimonious lobbying campaigns in the state's history." Following this defeat, REACH continued to grow as an organization, keeping the idea of school choice alive in Pennsylvania through the wide distribution of a newsletter, recruitment of members, and the establishment of a political action committee for funding candidates for the state legislature. Kirkpatrick targeted business groups, private school groups, and taxpayer groups as potential members of this coalition for school choice. REACH also sponsored conferences on school choice in Pennsylvania: these conferences brought together school choice activists from around the country to share their views and experiences. Although it is difficult to document, it seems clear that these various activities undertaken by David Kirkpatrick and his associates have significantly changed the nature of education reform debates in Pennsylvania. Various school choice proposals have been considered by the legislature throughout the 1990s.

According to Kirkpatrick, the major impetus for school choice initiatives in Pennsylvania is now coming from the office of Governor Tom Ridge. Ridge made school choice and vouchers a centerpiece of his election campaign in 1994. His 1995 proposal for the nation's first statewide voucher program came up short of winning majority support in the legislature despite considerable lobbying effort on the part of Kirkpatrick and the REACH Alliance. But through the subsequent careful efforts of the governor and his staff in the Pennsylvania Department of Education to generate grass-roots support for charter schools, in 1997 Pennsylvania adopted a charter school law, which is facilitating some level of school choice in the state.[12] Meanwhile, Representative Dwight Evans, a Philadelphia Democrat and a candidate for mayor of Philadelphia in 1999, has proposed to convert all of Philadelphia's schools into charter schools. He has also been active on the Legislative Commission on Restructuring Pennsylvania's Urban Schools, which has proposed a Milwaukee-like program of "opportunity scholarships" for the city. David Kirkpatrick notes with much satisfaction that it was not so long ago that his friend, Dwight Evans, was an entrenched opponent of school choice. REACH remains operational but it has significantly scaled back its activities, and Kirkpatrick, now in his late sixties, continues to work on reform projects and is a distinguished fellow with the Blum Center for Parental Freedom at Marquette University in Milwaukee, Wisconsin.

General Observations

The policy entrepreneurs discussed here all made important efforts to introduce school choice in their respective states. However, only one of them, Bill Clinton, can be thought of as someone who was able to achieve success while keeping very close control of the idea and how it could be transformed into actual policy change. The more typical pattern we observe is one of individuals operating around the edges of state government, making concerted efforts to draw attention to their ideas for policy change. Four of the five policy entrepreneurs noted here have not held elected positions in which they could muster political forces to achieve their policy goals. Instead, over the course of campaigns to bring school choice to their states, the limelight often shifted from these individuals to others who held prominent political positions. Nonetheless, it seems fair to conclude that the initial actions of these policy entrepreneurs made important differences in the nature of public debate about education and education reform in their states. At the very least, they began political movements that then took on lives of their own. Even when that happened, usually these policy entrepreneurs continued to play active roles in the movements they created.

The Validity of the Research Design

My method of identifying policy entrepreneurs represents a departure from previous approaches, which typically have started by noting a policy change and have then traced backward to find and discuss a policy entrepreneur.[13] In the 1960s, a heated debate emerged among political scientists who were interested in examining decisionmaking and identifying the presence of power elites in various jurisdictions. During that debate, Peter Bachrach and Morton S. Baratz (1962) argued that despite the significant differences in their approaches to studying community power, both Floyd Hunter (1953) and Robert A. Dahl (1961) had committed errors because they both used "an approach and assumptions which predetermine their conclusions." In particular, while using distinct methods to identify key decisionmakers, both Hunter and Dahl emphasized the importance of decisions and ignored the possibility that group power can also keep particular issues off decisionmaking agendas. We might state this another way: According to their critics, Hunter and Dahl committed errors because they selected their cases for analysis based on the dependent variable. Hunter and Dahl focused only on cell A in Table 6-2. If I had followed a research strategy of this sort, I would have limited my study of policy entrepreneurship to only those states where state legislatures had considered or adopted school choice plans. But I did not do this. I sent surveys to key members and observers of the education policymaking communities in each of the forty-eight contiguous states, regardless of whether school choice had been a legislative agenda item. Equally important, information from the states, when aggregated, yields entries in all of the cells in the table: A, B, C, and D. Since I could not have obtained data with this structure by following an approach similar to that of either Hunter or Dahl, it is clear that I did not commit the errors they are purported to have made. That said, other questions about the validity of the research design still remain to be addressed. In what follows, I consider two questions. First, were the people named in the survey really school choice policy entrepreneurs? Second, were the survey responses contaminated because school choice had (or had not) been considered and adopted by the relevant state legislature?

The Identity of the Policy Entrepreneurs

Several pieces of evidence confirm that the survey respondents provided accurate information about the identity of the school choice policy entrepreneurs. First, the respondents were all close observers of education policy issues in their states. They identified entrepreneurs in states where the legislatures had considered and adopted school choice as well as in states where there had been no legislative action. Even when state legislatures had considered or adopted school choice, the respondents did not

Table 6-2. ***Legislative Activity and the Identification of Policy Entrepreneurs***

Independent Variable: Policy Entrepreneur Present	*Dependent Variable: Legislative Activity*	
	Yes	No
Yes	A	B
No	C	D

always identify policy entrepreneurs. It is to the credit of the respondents to this survey that they were able to distinguish among legislative bill sponsors, for whom proposing a policy change is relatively easy, and policy entrepreneurs, who work carefully to create the political conditions that support policy change.

Second, the research design permitted cross-validation of responses. This showed that respondents who view the policymaking process from distinct perspectives agreed on who constituted school choice policy entrepreneurs in their states and what actions they engaged in. Furthermore, early in this research project, people with considerable knowledge of school choice issues who had been monitoring developments in all the states were consulted.[14] Their views on who could be thought of as school choice policy entrepreneurs were remarkably consistent with those of my survey respondents.

Third, the respondents provided specific information about the actions of the policy entrepreneurs they named. The survey questions about the activities of the policy entrepreneurs forced the respondents to think carefully about the people they identified and why it was reasonable for them to nominate these people as policy entrepreneurs.

Finally, during the period spent on this project, over half of the policy entrepreneurs named by the survey respondents have been cited in articles and other relevant publications on school choice. Also, I occasionally made direct contact, either intentionally or by chance meetings at conferences, with many of the policy entrepreneurs named by the survey respondents. These people have proven to be experts on school choice issues and have spoken at length about the strategies they have used to promote school choice.

Legislative Activity as a Cue to Identifying Policy Entrepreneurs

Were the survey responses contaminated because school choice had (or had not) been considered and adopted by the relevant state legislature? The critical base conditions to be measured here are the presence and actions of school choice policy entrepreneurs. Here, I consider whether any apparent influence of policy entrepreneurs on legislative deliberation of school choice was driven by measurement problems. The conceptual issue is straightforward. The investigation involved establishing, across a range of research sites, the nature of the base conditions that may influence the likelihood of an event occurring—either legislative consideration or legislative adoption of school choice. An ideal investigation would involve choosing the base conditions to record and then measuring them *prior to* the event of interest taking place. However, in this investigation the ideal conditions did not pertain. At the time of measurement, in some sites the event had occurred. Lacking control over the timing of the event, we must be concerned that occurrence or nonoccurrence before measurement of the base conditions affected the measurement procedures. This concern is heightened here because measurement of the base conditions relied on the perceptions of informants, and it is easy to imagine instances where perceptions might have been influenced by prior occurrence or nonoccurrence of the event of interest.

Details of the research design suggest that occurrence of the event might not have unduly influenced the perceptions of the informants. First, policy entrepreneurs have to begin working closely with people in and around government to build support for their policy ideas long before legislative consideration occurs. As a result, knowledge of the presence of policy entrepreneurs and common perceptions of their abilities will typically have been established in policy circles some time in advance of legislative deliberation. Second, given their knowledge of education policy issues in their states, many of the survey respondents would have first heard of, and made assessments of, the school choice policy entrepreneurs in the period before legislative deliberation began. Therefore, it seems unlikely that the respondents' perceptions would be influenced by the outcomes of legislative activity alone.

Data derived from the survey itself also provide some reassurance on the matter of potential measurement problems. Of the thirty-eight states where the legislatures considered school choice in the period from 1987 through 1992, policy entrepreneurs were identified in twenty-two states (58 percent). Of the ten states that did not consider school choice, policy entrepreneurs were identified in four (40 percent). Although this difference is in the direction suggesting bias from measurement error, it is not statistically significant. Next, consider the relationship between legislative adoption of school choice and the identification of policy entrepreneurs. Of the fifteen states where school choice was adopted in the period from 1987 through 1992, policy entrepreneurs were identified in eleven (73 percent). Of the thirty-three states that did not adopt school choice in the period, policy entrepreneurs were identified in fifteen (46 percent). This difference is statistically significant at the 0.10 level. However, to argue that legislative activity on school choice drove the identification of school choice policy entrepreneurs by the survey respondents, it would be necessary to explain why the reported percentages fall so far from their hypothesized values. But the differences in these figures can readily be explained by the argument that policy entrepreneurs promote legislative interest in school choice.

Finally, consider evidence for the argument that legislative adoption of school choice might have biased the survey respondents' assessments of the abilities of the policy entrepreneurs. I developed an activity score for each policy entrepreneur based on the respondents' perceptions of their abilities in several activities: problem framing, team leadership, networking around the state government, and networking outside the state. This measure added responses to fourteen 5-point scale questions. Where no entrepreneurs were identified, I coded the variable zero. In theory, the effectiveness score could range up to 70. The actual scores ranged from 21 to 63, with a mean of 41 (n = 26).

To test the validity of my research design, I divided states where policy entrepreneurs were identified into two categories: states with policy entrepreneurs who received activity scores above the mean, and those where the activity scores were below the mean. In the fourteen states where policy entrepreneurs were identified but the legislature did not adopt school choice, three (21 percent) had policy entrepreneurs who received above average activity scores. In the twelve states where policy entrepreneurs were identified and the legislature adopted school choice, eight (67 percent) had policy entrepreneurs who received above average scores. This difference is statistically significant at the 0.05 level. This finding could be interpreted to mean that the activity scores assigned to the policy entrepreneurs were influenced by whether or not school choice had been adopted. But to insist on this interpretation requires explaining sizable differences between the hypothesized and the observed relationships. By contrast, it is quite reasonable to argue that the greater likelihood of legislative adoption of school choice was driven by the skillfulness of the policy entrepreneurs.

In sum, the method used to determine the presence of policy entrepreneurs and their actions extracted the best available information from the best informed people throughout states in a systematic fashion. While, in theory, better identification procedures could be devised, for the purpose of data collection practical approaches must be found. When compared with previous approaches, this research design represents a significant advance in the identification of this class of political actors. It provides a starting point from which more sophisticated explorations of policy entrepreneurship may evolve.

Four Studies of Policy Entrepreneurship and School Choice: A Preview

In this chapter I have provided an overview of the research strategy used to gather information on state-level policy entrepreneurs. In the next part of the book I use this information to conduct a series of analyses of the ways that the actions of policy entrepreneurs can serve to influence policymaking and policy change. In chapter 7 I use event history analysis to explore the extent to which the presence and actions of policy entrepreneurs increased the likelihood of legislative consideration and adoption of school choice. In chapter 8 I continue using event history analysis, but this time with the purpose of exploring how policy networks serve as resources for policy entrepreneurs. In chapter 9 I explore how policy argumentation can serve to support coalition building and, ultimately, policy change. This chapter uses interviews with a subset of the school choice policy entrepreneurs to explore empirically the practice of policy advocacy. In chapter 10 I consider how policy entrepreneurs use evidence to support their arguments for policy change. Here, I combine survey-based information with more recently gathered information to examine how efforts to develop local-level private voucher plans have stimulated further state-level interest in school choice initiatives.

Notes

1. Much of the work in this dissertation has subsequently been published in Roberts and King (1996), although the latter work should not be seen as a substitute for the dissertation itself.

2. Another body of work that has been important for developing notions

of policy entrepreneurship has used the development of particular policies as the units of analysis. These works have also provided rich descriptions of individual actions and strategy. Such works include, but are by no means limited to, Eyestone (1978), Cobb and Elder (1983), Derthick and Quirk (1985), Kingdon (1995), and Nelson (1984).

3. I based this summary information on material contained in information sheets provided by the Education Commission of the States, the appendix to the Carnegie Foundation's (1992) report on school choice, and annual reports of school choice activity in the states produced by the Heritage Foundation (1992, 1993).

4. These individuals included Jack Klenk from the U.S. Department of Education, Professor John Witte from the University of Wisconsin, Madison, and John Brandl from Minnesota, who as both an academic and a legislator had played an important role in securing school choice in that state (see Brandl 1989, 1998).

5. Through newsletters and conferences Citizens for Educational Freedom keeps members informed of school choice activities occurring across the nation.

6. No state agency officials were identified by survey respondents as school choice policy entrepreneurs in this study. Of course state agency officials could serve as policy entrepreneurs. In many instances of policymaking, including those where innovations are being introduced, state agency officials undoubtedly develop and promote policy ideas, and could thus be seen as policy entrepreneurs. John W. Kingdon (1995) provides examples of policy entrepreneurs located within the government bureaucracy, as do Derthick and Quirk (1985).

7. Bill Clinton was governor of Arkansas over two terms: 1978–1980 and 1982–1992.

8. Quoted in Weisman (1991).

9. In addition to promoting private voucher programs, J. Patrick Rooney has acted as a policy entrepreneur for greater consumer choice in the field of health insurance. Some call Rooney the father of medical savings accounts (MSAs), which allow employees to purchase health insurance policies with large deductibles and contribute to a savings account for medical expenses. The concept was invented by economists at the Dallas-based National Center for Policy Analysis in the 1980s. However, Rooney is credited with pushing for 1996 U.S. congressional legislation that, under a pilot program, gives tax-favored status to MSAs established by small employers. Since Rooney's insurance company, Golden Rule, targets individuals, it stands to gain handsomely from expansion of MSAs. See Geisel (1997).

10. These quotes come from Snider (1988).

11. REACH stands for "Road to Educational Achievement Through Choice."

12. This effort is documented in a paper by Timothy Daniels, a policy specialist in the Pennsylvania Department of Education. See Daniels (n.d.).

13. Such studies include Derthick and Quirk (1985), Schiller (1995), and Weissert (1991).

14. These people were members of the U.S. Department of Education's Office of Intergovernmental and Interagency Affairs, the Heritage Foundation, and the Carnegie Foundation.

SEVEN

Policy Entrepreneurs and State Adoption of School Choice

When called upon to identify individuals acting as policy entrepreneurs, well-informed participants in and around government can often do so. In the previous chapter I noted the way that members of the education policy community in twenty-six of the forty-eight contiguous states of the United States identified state-level policy entrepreneurs who had actively promoted the idea of school choice, with the goal of seeking policy change. But do policy entrepreneurs actually contribute to policy change? The portraits of five policy entrepreneurs presented in chapter 6 revealed that often, despite their ambitions, policy entrepreneurs do not achieve the kind of outcomes they would like. This suggests that some skepticism is in order when we think about the contributions that policy entrepreneurs actually make in the end. Might it be that they are simply surfing waves created by others? Since my focus is on policy entrepreneurs acting in states nested within a broader national system, it seems reasonable to wonder whether broader national trends have been driving state policy changes relating to school choice, rather than the actions of state-level characters. Those trends seem all the more likely in this case, given the increasing national-level attention that has been given to education issues and school choice ideas beginning in the 1980s. In this era, Presidents Ronald Reagan, George Bush, and Bill Clinton all expressed at least some level of interest in school choice as a policy idea, and their sentiments doubtless received careful hearings by sympathetic state-level politicians.

Taking a skeptical approach to thinking about the causal relationship between policy entrepreneurship and policy change is important for theory construction. Considering the possibility that other factors might also be at play can lead us to see both the limits and, potentially, additional strengths of the theory of policy entrepreneurship. In this chapter, I discuss the approach that I used to test the impact that policy entrepreneurs had on legislative consideration and adoption of proposals for school choice from 1987 through 1992. Looking back from the present time, we see that these years represented the early phase of a movement that has subsequently flourished. It turns out that, given the myriad legislative efforts that have since been used to introduce school choice in the states, the five years from 1987 to 1992 were marked by a relative level of consistency across states in the school choice proposals that were made. Yet, as I will demonstrate in chapter 10, state-level activities at that time also sowed the seeds from which many of those subsequent initiatives grew.

To explore the linkage between policy entrepreneurship and state policy change, I work within the policy innovation diffusion framework. This framework has frequently been employed by scholars of state politics seeking to identify the antecedents of policy change in individual states. Using this approach, it is possible to test for the impact of policy entrepreneurs while controlling for a variety of other possible causes of state legislative consideration and adoption of school choice. Thus, for example, it is possible to isolate the effects of school choice policy entrepreneurs from the effects of broader national debate and dialogue. The results of this quantitative study support the claim that the presence and actions of policy entrepreneurs have significant impacts on legislative activity. This finding is critical for supporting my argument that the concept of the policy entrepreneur is an important one for scholars interested in explaining policy change. In addition to that, the analysis and results presented in this chapter suggest that placing policy entrepreneurs at center stage can very much help to explain why we might observe innovative policy ideas spreading from state to state. In other words, my use of the policy innovation diffusion framework allows me to draw conclusions that might influence the way we think about not only the impact of policy entrepreneurs on policy change but innovation diffusion processes as well. I pay additional attention to this matter in chapter 8, where I explore the importance of policy networks for policy entrepreneurs.

The Policy Innovation Diffusion Framework

Following Jack L. Walker (1969), for the purpose of this empirical study I define a policy innovation as a policy that is new to the state adopting it. To assess the impact of policy entrepreneurs on policy innovation, I present a quantitative analysis of state legislative consideration and adoption of school choice. My analytical strategy involves developing event history analysis models and testing them on data collected in my survey of state education policy experts, augmented with published data on state school systems, state politics, and the diffusion of the school choice idea. As noted in chapter 1, among policymakers school choice started receiving serious attention in the United States in the late 1980s. From 1987 through 1992, legislatures in thirty-eight states considered the school choice idea. Of these, fifteen adopted some type of school choice. I explore why some states but not others considered and adopted school choice during this period, and what difference was made by the presence and actions of policy entrepreneurs.

In the development of techniques to analyze state policy variation, two major quantitative approaches have emerged. Following Thomas R. Dye (1966), one approach has focused on internal state determinants of policy settings and policy innovation. Following Walker (1969), the other approach has focused on the diffusion of innovations across states. Frances Stokes Berry and William D. Berry (1990, 1992) have incorporated internal and regional influences into a unified theory of state policy innovation. Paralleling this quantitative work, other researchers have produced case studies of the policymaking process and the role individuals play in promoting policy ideas.[1]

I use the quantitative approach introduced by Berry and Berry (1990) but augment it with insights from the case study work on policymaking. I do this by paying attention to the presence and actions of policy entrepreneurs and by distinguishing legislative *consideration* of a policy innovation from legislative *adoption*. Legislative adoption of a policy innovation often comes only at the *end* of political struggles. Separating initial legislative consideration of a policy from adoption allows us to examine how the forces influencing policy innovation manifest themselves at different stages in the policymaking process.

Event History Analysis: An Overview

To test the impact of policy entrepreneurs on state legislative deliberation of school choice, I developed a taxonomy of event history analysis models. These models predict the likelihood of an event occurring at a specific time. The technical term for this likelihood is the "hazard rate." I use event history models here to capture the essence of the processes that led to state legislative consideration and adoption of school choice. To motivate this part of my discussion, I define the event of interest as initial state legislative consideration of school choice. School choice can be broadly construed to mean a range of open-enrollment, public voucher, or charter school approaches, but here the focus is restricted to proposals for some form of statewide open enrollment. Legislative consideration and adoption of location-specific voucher-style plans and state charter school plans is excluded from the analysis. Legislative consideration could consist of any action ranging from select committee consideration of the policy to a full legislative vote on the policy.[2]

To analyze patterns of policy consideration, I examined the yearly action of state legislatures from 1987 to 1992.[3] From determining the year each state legislature initially considered school choice, I developed a data set where the cases consist of state-years. For each state-year, I included a dichotomous (0,1) consideration variable. I set this variable equal to 0 for every year before consideration and 1 for the year of consideration. After the year of consideration no more state-years are observed for the state.[4]

The states included in the data set for any given year constitute the "risk set" for that year. For legislative consideration of school choice in 1987, all forty-eight contiguous states appear in the risk set.[5] In some states the legislature meets in alternate years only. When the legislature did not meet the state was excluded from the risk set. Since Alaska and Hawaii are not included in the analysis, and the legislature in Kentucky meets only on even years, for 1987 the risk set contained forty-seven states. Of these, one, Minnesota, considered school choice. So the consideration hazard rate for 1987 is 1/47, or 0.02. Having considered school choice, Minnesota drops out of the risk set for subsequent years. Since six state legislatures meet only on odd years, for 1988 the risk set contained forty-one states (i.e., 48−6−1). Working with the data in this way, the consideration hazard rate, h, can be calculated for each year, j, given that the event has not occurred before. I present the consideration results in the top panel of table 7-1: I present the adoption risk sets and hazard rates in the lower panel of the table.

The year-to-year profile of the consideration hazard rate, h_j, presented in table 7-1, shows the expected likelihood that any state legislature will consider school choice in year j, given that it has not considered it before. In studies using event history analysis, interest usually centers on differences in hazard rates, h_{ij}, across members, i, of a population. Thus the hazard rate is treated as the dependent variable, and event history data sets can then be augmented to include data representing potentially important explanatory variables. Some of these explanatory variables may vary with time, while others may remain constant over the period of interest. Estimation of the models is done using logit regression analysis.

The Dependent Variables: State Legislative Consideration and Adoption of School Choice

In using event history models to analyze state legislative deliberations of school choice, I specified the events of interest as (1) initial legislative consideration and (2) legislative adoption. These events may or may not occur in a given period. The research problem then involves considering for any state what determines the hazard rate associated with the event during a specified period.[6] My method of modeling consideration and adoption of school choice collapses some real-world variance among both the school choice proposals made to state legislators and the school choice policies that states have adopted. How much we should ignore specific details depends critically on the primary research goal. If interest lies in exploring the nature of policy reinvention and how policies change as they diffuse, then state-to-state differences in the scope of the policy proposals and actual legislation should be scrutinized.[7] If, in contrast, interest lies in exploring why policy ideas get on legislative agendas in the first place, as in this study, then it is reasonable to ignore state-to-state variance among the innovations. For the purpose of this study, the school choice proposals included are similar enough that they can be modeled as the same policy innovation.[8]

Table 7-1. ***Calculating Year-to-Year Hazard Rates for State Legislative Consideration and Adoption of School Choice***

Year, j	*States where the legislature* considered *school choice*		*Risk set*[a]	*Hazard rate,* h_j
1987	MN	1	47	0.02
1988	NJ	1	41	0.02
1989	AZ, AR, CA, CO, IA MA, MS, MO, NE, NV NM, NY, NC, OK, WI	15	45	0.33
1990	AL, ID, IL, LA, MI NH, OH, OR, UT, WA	10	27	0.37
1991	IN, PA, SC	3	20	0.15
1992	DE, FL, KS, KY, MD TN, VA, WV	8	15	0.53

Year, j	*States where the legislature both* considered *and* adopted *school choice*		*Risk set (states where school choice was* considered*)*[b]	*Hazard rate,* h_j
1987	MN	1	1	1.00
1988		0	1	0.00
1989	AR, IA, NE	3	16	0.19
1990	CO, ID, IL, OH, WA	5	23	0.22
1991	AL, MA, MI, OR	4	21	0.19
1992	CA, UT	2	25	0.08

Notes: [a] The risk set changes from year to year as a function both of the event occurring in states (thus removing them from the risk set) and the fact that seven state legislatures meet biennially. A policy proposal cannot be considered in such years.

[b] The risk set here is much smaller for each year because only states where the legislature *considered* school choice are categorized as "at risk" of ***adoption*** of school choice. It should also be noted that *consideration* of school choice is treated as a repeated event in the analysis of legislative ***adoption***.

Key: AL = Alabama, AR = Arkansas, AZ = Arizona, CA = California, CO = Colorado, DE = Delaware, FL = Florida, IA = Iowa, ID =Idaho, IL = Illinois, IN = Indiana, KS = Kansas, KY = Kentucky, LA = Louisiana, MA = Massachusetts, MD = Maryland, MI = Michigan, MN = Minnesota, MO = Missouri, MS = Mississippi, NC = North Carolina, OK = Oklahoma, NE = Nebraska, NH = New Hampshire, NJ = New Jersey, NM = New Mexico, NV = Nevada, NY = New York, OH = Ohio, OR = Oregon, PA = Pennsylvania, SC = South Carolina, TN = Tennessee, UT = Utah, VA = Virginia, WA = Washington, WI = Wisconsin, WV = West Virginia.

Modeling School Choice Policy Entrepreneurs

Based upon the responses to the survey of members of state education policy communities, I constructed two variables relating to the policy entrepreneurs that were identified. The first simply notes whether a policy entrepreneur was identified as present in a state; the second concerns the activities of the policy entrepreneurs.

Entrepreneur Present in State

I asked survey respondents to name the most important school choice policy entrepreneurs in their states and to record the year in which they first advocated school choice. In twenty-six states, my survey respondents identified individuals whom they considered as matching my description of school choice policy entrepreneurs. Using this survey information I constructed presence and activities variables. The presence variable is coded 1 for all state-years beginning with the year in which the policy entrepreneurs were identified as present and active. (The assumption is made that the policy entrepreneurs remained present and active until initial legislative consideration and adoption occurred.) The variable is coded zero where a policy entrepreneur was not present.[9]

Having identified school choice policy entrepreneurs, I then asked my survey respondents to assess how important various strategies (such as issue framing, networking, and collecting evidence) were to the policy entrepreneurs they had mentioned. I also asked them to rate how effective the policy entrepreneurs were in inspiring and leading like-minded people, presenting their message, and developing and maintaining good relations with others in and around government. From this information I developed a variable relating to the activities of policy entrepreneurs.

Activity Score

The activity score measures the survey respondents' perceptions of the abilities of the policy entrepreneurs in several activities: problem framing, team leadership, and use of policy networks. This measure added responses to fourteen 5-point scale questions. Where no entrepreneurs were identified, I coded the variable zero. In theory the effectiveness score could range up to 70. The actual scores ranged from 21 to 63, with a mean of 41 (n = 26).[10] In the postscript to this chapter I discuss the construction of this variable in more detail.

Rival Explanations of the Rise of School Choice

How might we account for the rise of the school choice idea among states if we had never heard of policy entrepreneurs? To fairly test the impact of policy entrepreneurs on legislative consideration and adoption of school choice ideas, I controlled for the impact of other factors that could influence state education policies.

School System Characteristics

Percentage of Education Funding Provided by the State. In their discussion of issues and strategies in systemic reform of public schools, Susan H. Fuhrman and Diane Masell (1992, 5) pointed out that the higher the ratio of state funding to local funding, the higher the chances of the state legislature being prepared to consider a systemic reform like school choice. Following this logic, I expected the relative level of state spending on schools to raise the likelihood of state legislative consideration and adoption of school choice.[11]

Relative Change in Student Test Scores. I included this variable as a measure of the quality of school outcomes. Educational outcomes are difficult to measure, and any indicator is subject to criticism. However, student scores in standardized tests, like the Scholastic Aptitude Test (SAT) and the American College Testing (ACT) programs, provide an indication of the comparative effectiveness of the schools in and across states. I expected that the greater the decline in the average test scores in a state relative to the change at the national level over a given period, the greater the probability that members of the education policy elite would perceive a problem with the school system. This would raise their likelihood of turning to reforms like school choice. In working with these test scores, I started with the approach Kevin B. Smith and Kenneth J. Meier (1995) used to develop their standardized education index (SEI). For any given year, this is constructed using a state's mean SAT or ACT score expressed as a percentage of the highest score possible. This approach allows a standard score to be given to each state, even when the majority of graduating high school seniors in some states prefer to take the SAT, while elsewhere the ACT is favored.[12] To get a better measure of the trend in state school performance, I calculated the improvement (or decline) in this score relative to the national mean over five-year intervals. The resulting measure was lagged by one year.

Percentage of Private Schools in the State. I included the percentage of schools in each state that are private as a measure of the extent to which people can and have chosen to opt out of the public schools in the state. In the spirit of Albert O. Hirschman (1970), this measure serves as a proxy of demand for alternative public education in a state. This demand, and the interests developed around established private schools, could serve to increase general interest in school choice approaches. Further, following the intuitions of John E. Chubb and Terry M. Moe (1990), we might view the presence of private schools as serving to remind policymakers that viable institutional alternatives can be created that look distinctly different from "the one best system" (Tyack 1974). I expected that the greater the percentage of private schools in a state, the higher the likelihood that school choice ideas would be considered.[13]

Previous Adoption of Other Education Reforms. Another potential measure of "demand" for school choice in a state is provided by evidence concerning adoption of other reforms. Since the early 1980s, many states have attempted to improve their public school systems by introducing a range of different reforms. I expected that state legislatures with a propensity to adopt any kind of school reform might be more open to the prospect of adopting a school choice proposal. So, this variable is a count of the number of reforms that each state adopted in the 1980s. Up to five other reforms were counted for inclusion in this variable, which ranges in value from 0 to 5.[14]

State Politics

Elements of state politics were also expected to influence the hazard rates for legislative consideration and adoption of school choice. The following explanatory variables were included in the event history models: state house election year, Republican control of the legislature, Republican governor, and opposition of teachers' unions.[15]

State House Election Year. I expected that consideration and adoption of school choice would be more likely to occur in years other than state house election years. First, the legislative agenda is typically narrower in an election year because legislators spend more time on campaign issues. Second, school choice can create significant political battles, and risk-averse politicians are more likely to avoid controversial legislation in an election year. Therefore, I expected the likelihood of consideration and adoption of school choice to be lower in election years. The variable is dichotomous and is coded 1 for house election years and 0 otherwise.[16]

Republican Control of the Legislature and Republican Governor. School choice is often—but certainly not always—associated with the advocates of limited government and greater use of market forces in the allocation of government services (Friedman 1962; Wolf 1979; Savas 1987; Wilson 1989b; Chubb and Moe 1990). Further, school choice is a policy approach championed more by the New Right and the Republican Party than by the Democratic Party (Green 1987, 268–269; Himmelstein 1990, ch. 3). Therefore, I expected consideration and adoption of school choice to be more likely in states where Republicans ruled the legislature and where there was a Republican governor. These variables are both dichotomous. For each year they are coded 1 for Republican control and 0 otherwise.[17]

Opposition of Teachers' Unions. State teachers' unions are renowned for their lobbying abilities and influence on education policy. Furthermore, state teachers' unions have almost always opposed school choice. In my survey I asked recipients to judge the degree of opposition shown to school choice by the teachers' unions in their state. From this information, I built a simple dichotomous variable, where 1 = strongly opposed and 0 = somewhat opposed. (I discuss the construction of this variable in more detail in the postscript to this chapter.) I chose this measure rather than a measure of union membership for two reasons. First, not all state teachers' unions publish membership statistics, making it difficult to construct a measure of union strength. Second, local union strength is probably not as important as the attitudes of the union leadership. In battles over education policies, state teachers' unions often draw on personnel and financial resources from national union organizations. How much this external power is called upon will typically be a function of the attitudes of the state teachers' union leaders, which is precisely what my measure was designed to capture. I expected that the stronger the opposition of teachers' unions to school choice, the lower the probability that state legislatures would consider or adopt the idea.

Innovation Diffusion

Neighbors Considering or Neighbors Adopting. Various scholars have suggested that policy innovations diffuse across states on a regional basis, although little has been said about the mechanisms of idea transfer. To model the potential impact of geographic innovation diffusion of the school choice idea I developed two independent variables. For each state, the first variable shows in each of the years from 1987 to 1992 the proportion of its neighbors whose legislatures had considered school choice before the relevant year. The second variable does the same thing for adoption of school choice. The variables are proportions ranging from 0 through 1.

In developing these variables I followed Berry and Berry (1990, 1992), who sought to build variables that captured the essence of Walker's (1969) regional influences innovation diffusion hypothesis. Of the conventional explanatory variables listed here, this is the only one that could be thought of as a proxy for the impact of policy entrepreneurs. A positive effect on the probability of consideration of school choice would suggest that ideas are "brokered" from state to state in some manner. As the regional diffusion hypothesis implies, I expected that the hazard rate for consideration and adoption of school choice would increase with increases in the proportion of neighboring states that had considered or adopted school choice.[18]

Maturation Effects

The hazard rate for legislative consideration and adoption of school choice could be affected by time alone. State legislators might see school choice as an idea whose time has come for a variety of reasons. Some of these reasons might have little to do with matters in their states and more to do with national influences, such as federal-level interest in the idea or the national promotion of a key book, like that of Chubb and Moe (1990). Conveniently, my event history analysis models control for time or maturation effects because of the inclusion of dichotomous (0,1) time variables for each year. (For a defense of this approach, see Singer and Willett 1993.) Since the models make this time dependence explicit, other time-varying explanatory variables (like the neighbor-to-neighbor innovation diffusion measures) are not contaminated by picking up otherwise general maturation effects.

Given that the time variables capture maturation effects, we must consider their relationship to the school choice consideration and adoption hazard rates. In many studies of innovation diffusion, plots of the cumulative adoption time path produce an S-shaped distribution (Mahajan and Peterson 1985, 8). The evidence on consideration and adoption of school choice presented in table 7-1 conforms to this pattern. Therefore, I expected that maturation effects would manifest themselves with time control parameters that increase (but at a declining rate) with each year under investigation. I included dichotomous time variables for 1989, 1990, 1991, and 1992 and treated 1987 and 1988 as the baseline.[19]

Event History Analysis: Models and Findings

To test the hypothesis that policy entrepreneurs have a significant impact on state policy innovation, I developed two sets of event history analysis models. The first set of models explores initial legislative consideration of school choice; the second explores legislative adoption, given that the policy is up for consideration. In both cases, I first predicted the hazard rate with baseline models containing only my rival explanatory variables. I then used these models as the basis against which to measure the increase in explanatory power gained by modeling the presence and actions of policy entrepreneurs.[20]

Throughout the analysis, I treat the initial legislative consideration of school choice and adoption of school choice as independent events. In the first test, I seek to isolate the factors that tend to increase the likelihood of initial consideration of school choice by a state legislature. In the second test, I take all the cases of legislative consideration of the policy idea (i.e., all cases include those of initial and of subsequent consideration), and, given that the bill is under consideration, I seek to isolate the factors that tend to raise the likelihood of adoption of school choice by the legislature.

Consideration of School Choice

In the first model tested, C1: Baseline, I found that the consideration hazard rate is affected in a statistically significant way by three of the substantive explanatory variables. These are whether or not it is a state house election year, opposition of teachers' unions, and the proportion of neighboring states where the legislature has considered school choice. The signs of these coefficient estimates accord with the relevant hypotheses. (See the first column of figures in table 7-2.)

The negative and statistically significant coefficient for state house election year indicates that the policy innovation is less likely to be considered in an election year. Similarly, the coefficient for opposition of teachers' unions suggests that union opposition reduced the likelihood

Table 7-2. *Models of Initial State Legislative Consideration of School Choice*

Models:	*C1: Baseline*		*C4: Entrepreneur Present*		*C5: Entrepreneur Score*	
Independent Variables	*Coefficient Estimate*	*Standard Error*	*Coefficient Estimate*	*Standard Error*	*Coefficient Estimate*	*Standard Error*
Policy Entrepreneurs						
Present in State			1.583[a]	0.555		
Activity Score					0.049[a]	0.014
School System Characteristics						
State Spending (% of total)	0.014	0.018	0.023	0.019	0.029	0.020
Relative Change in Test Scores	0.133	0.208	0.324	0.224	0.410[b]	0.235
Private Schools (% of total)	0.100	0.066	0.096	0.070	0.093	0.072
Count of Other Reforms in 1980s	0.007	0.206	−0.027	0.214	−0.068	0.221
State Politics						
State House Election Year	−1.371[b]	0.781	−1.733[b]	0.842	−1.798[b]	0.860
Republican Legislature	0.155	0.721	0.753	0.781	0.881	0.794
Republican Governor	−0.110	0.479	−0.082	0.495	−0.013	0.510
Opposition of Teachers' Unions	−1.500[b]	0.819	−1.579[b]	0.857	−1.461	0.891
Innovation Diffusion						
Legislative Consideration of School Choice in Neighboring States	2.025[b]	1.005	1.877[b]	1.059	1.870[b]	1.094
Time Controls (base = 1987 and 1988)						
1989	2.133[a]	0.896	1.834[b]	0.924	1.808[b]	0.942
1990	2.965[a]	1.136	2.925[a]	1.203	3.051[a]	1.227
1991	0.852	1.164	0.441	1.212	0.690	1.216
1992	3.683[a]	1.376	4.094[b]	1.457	4.580[a]	1.506
Constant Term	−4.103[a]	1.608	−4.736[a]	1.716	−5.316[a]	1.814
Summary Statistics						
Number of Cases	195		195		195	
−2 × Log Likelihood	135.86		124.58		121.97	
Chi2	54 (13*df*)		62 (14*df*)		68 (14*df*)	
Pseudo R^2	0.28		0.33		0.36	

[a] Significant at 0.01, one-tailed test; [b] significant at 0.05, one-tailed test.

of consideration. The positive and statistically significant coefficient estimate for consideration in neighboring states suggests that state legislators are more likely to consider school choice as the number of neighbors that have considered it grows. School system characteristics that could suggest a latent demand for school reform, and for school choice in particular, do not come up statistically significant.

Party control of the legislature and governorship do not appear to be important determinants of consideration of the school choice idea. This might suggest that *how* the idea is presented, rather than to *whom* it is presented, is critical for determining if it will be given serious consideration. However, this model does not allow us to do more than speculate on that possibility.

Although this model supports important hypotheses about the nature of the policy process and the diffusion of policy innovation, it does not speak to our question of how ideas get articulated onto government agendas and what goes on in the policymaking process. To allow it to do this, I first augmented the model by including my variable indicating the presence in states of school choice policy entrepreneurs. I call the revised model C2: Entrepreneur Present and the coefficient estimates for this model are presented alongside those for C1: Baseline in table 7-2.

In model C2: Entrepreneur Present, the coefficient estimates for all the variables included in model C1: Baseline remain much the same as before. The variables indicating a state house election year, opposition of teachers' unions, and the proportion of neighboring states where the legislature has considered school choice remain statistically significant. However, in this model the variable indicating the presence of policy entrepreneurs in states is also statistically significant and has the expected sign. Thus, while controlling for all other relevant variables, the presence in states of school choice policy entrepreneurs raises the likelihood of consideration.[21] Compared with the baseline model, by containing a measure of policy entrepreneurship, this model suggests an explicit link between advocacy of school choice and legislative consideration of the idea.

The information I gathered on state-level school choice policy entrepreneurs allowed me to go beyond modeling their presence to model their actions as well. In my third model of legislative consideration, C3: Entrepreneur Score, I substituted the activity score variable for the presence variable, but retained the other variables. For model C3: Entrepreneur

Score, the coefficient estimates for all the other variables continue to have magnitudes close to those estimated in models C1 and C2.[22]

In model C3: Entrepreneur Score, the election year variable remains statistically significant, as does consideration of school choice in neighboring states. The main differences in this model is that the opposition of the teachers' unions drops just below statistical significance (p = 0.051). Substantively, however, the impact of this variable changes little from in the other two models.

Predicting the Likelihood of Consideration

To assess the impact of policy entrepreneurs relative to the impact of the election year cycle and neighbor-to-neighbor diffusion on consideration of school choice, I use model C3: Entrepreneur Score to make a series of hazard rate predictions. Here I fixed the year to 1990 and all other variables at their mean observed levels in 1990. As I reported in table 7-1, the observed consideration hazard rate for all states in the risk set in 1990 was 0.37. table 7-3 contains the consideration hazard rate predictions.

The presence and activities of policy entrepreneurs are shown to be important for influencing the hazard rate, but in fact the predictions in table 7-3 show that this hazard rate can be influenced strongly by other factors. When no entrepreneur is present and no neighboring states have considered school choice, the model predicts that the hazard rate for consideration will be .05 in a state house election year and .24 in an off year. These hazard rates increase with the number of neighboring states that have considered school choice (see the first column of predicted hazard rates in table 7-3). The predicted consideration hazard rates in the subsequent columns of table 7-3 clearly demonstrate the influence that the presence and activities of policy entrepreneurs can have on the policymaking process. Yet the results suggest that only the most active policy entrepreneurs will have a serious chance of obtaining legislative consideration of school choice in an election year. They also suggest that the extent of diffusion of the school choice idea among neighboring states will influence the chances that the actions of policy entrepreneurs will lead to policy consideration. This is true especially in states where policy entrepreneurs are less adept at problem framing, team leadership, networking around the state government, and networking outside the state (see the second column of predicted hazard rates). I interpret this as showing that policy ideas must pass a credibility test to gain legislative

Table 7-3. ***Model Estimates of the Hazard Rate for Initial State Legislative Consideration of School Choice***

Predicted consideration hazard rate for 1990, given these conditions:	*No entrepreneur present*	*Entrepreneur with minimum observed activity score*	*Entrepreneur with mean observed activity score*	*Entrepreneur with maximum observed activity score*
State house election year, and consideration of school choice by:				
–No neighbor states	0.05	0.12	0.28	0.53
–50% of neighbor states	0.12	0.27	0.50	0.74
–All neighbor states	0.26	0.49	0.72	0.88
No state house election, and consideration of school choice by:				
–No neighbor states	0.24	0.47	0.70	0.87
–50% of neighbor states	0.45	0.69	0.86	0.95
–All neighbor states	0.67	0.85	0.94	0.98

Note: The hazard rate predictions in this table are made for 1990 using the coefficient estimates generated by model C3. The observed consideration hazard rate in 1990 was 0.37 (see Table 7-1). To obtain the hazard rate predictions presented here, all predictor variables were set at their mean observed levels for the forty-eight states for 1990, with the exception of the predictors of interest set out here. The order of magnitude of the predicted hazard rates differs for each year, but the relative sizes of the hazard rates under the different sets of circumstances indicated in this table remain fairly stable from year to year.

consideration. A skilled policy entrepreneur who has developed good relations with key political actors can imbue a policy idea like school choice with credibility. Furthermore, the credibility of the policy entrepreneur's claims about the idea is enhanced when neighboring states have taken the idea seriously.

Adoption of School Choice

I next tested a set of models of state legislative adoption of school choice. Having found that policy entrepreneurs play an important role in promoting ideas that get onto legislative agendas, I wanted to test for the impact of policy entrepreneurs on policy change. For this analysis, I switched to using the adoption data set that contains only the state-year records in which the legislature considered school choice.[23] Although the legislatures in only thirty-eight states initially considered school choice from 1987 through 1992, eighteen of those legislatures reconsidered it at least once during the period. So, the adoption data set, while small, is large enough to facilitate statistical analysis paralleling the analysis performed on the consideration data set.[24]

The first model I report is A1: Baseline in table 7-4. This model includes the same predictor variables as C1: Baseline in table 7-2, with one exception. Here, I substituted the *neighbors adopting* for the *neighbors considering* measure of state-to-state innovation diffusion. The coefficient estimates for the first adoption model are presented in the first column of figures in table 7-4. Some aspects of these results are of interest. First, the strength of opposition expressed by the teachers' unions remains significant: the stronger the opposition of the teachers' union to school choice, the lower the probability that the policy will be adopted. None of the coefficient estimates for the other state politics variables are statistically significant.

The coefficient estimate for the measure of state-to-state innovation diffusion is also not statistically significant in this model. Although legislative *consideration* of the school choice idea has diffused across the states partially as a result of neighbor-to-neighbor transmission, different factors appear to drive the *adoption* stage of the policymaking process.

With legislative adoption of school choice, the results for model A1: Baseline suggest that one characteristic of the state school system is important. This model gives considerable support to the expectation that decreasing student performance relative to the performance of students in other states (when measured by relative changes in the test scores over a five-year period) works in favor of the adoption of school choice. It appears that legislators will be more supportive of radical education reform if they have evidence of problems with the current system.[25]

In sum, in this first model it seems that legislative adoption, in contrast to legislative consideration of school choice, is driven more by issue-specific policy concerns and not by what has happened in neighboring states nor by the electoral cycle.

My primary purpose in developing and testing model A1: Baseline was to use it as a comparator against which to assess a model incorporating my measure of the presence of policy entrepreneurs. Model A2: Entrepreneur Present adds the policy entrepreneur variable, while retaining the variables included in A1. The measure of the presence of policy

Table 7-4. ***Models of State Legislative Adoption of School Choice***

Models:	*A1: Baseline*		*A2: Entrepreneur Present*		*A3: Entrepreneur Score*	
Independent Variables	*Coefficient Estimate*	*Standard Error*	*Coefficient Estimate*	*Standard Error*	*Coefficient Estimate*	*Standard Error*
Policy Entrepreneurs						
Present in State			1.860[b]	1.032		
Activity Score					0.051[b]	0.025
School System Characteristics						
State Spending (% of total)	0.016	0.022	0.014	0.025	0.017	0.025
Relative Change in Test Scores	−2.092[a]	0.807	−1.793[b]	0.839	−1.612[b]	0.861
Private Schools (% of total)	−0.163	0.112	−0.158	0.116	−0.165	0.119
Count of Other Reforms in 1980s	−0.220	0.360	−0.198	0.366	−0.273	0.379
State Politics						
State House Election Year	2.355	2.187	1.831	2.635	1.764	2.511
Republican Legislature	−0.630	1.133	−0.066	1.249	−0.100	1.254
Republican Governor	−0.189	0.750	−0.106	0.800	−0.085	0.813
Opposition of Teachers' Unions	−1.660[b]	0.950	−2.396[b]	1.119	−2.546[b]	1.174
Innovation Diffusion						
Legislative Adoption of School Choice in Neighboring States	−0.056	1.529	0.362	1.760	0.103	1.771
Time Controls (base = 1987 and 1988)						
1989	−3.166	2.451	−3.888	2.889	−3.618	3.559
1990	−5.139	3.460	−4.947	4.014	−4.291	4.452
1991	−3.171	2.513	−3.843	2.951	−3.140	3.583
1992	−7.365[b]	3.625	−7.222[b]	4.154	−6.200	4.592
Constant Term	5.274	3.212	4.585	3.596	4.141	4.197
Summary Statistics						
Number of Cases	64		64		64	
−2 × Log Likelihood	51.97		48.14		46.71	
Chi2	18 (13*df*)		22 (14*df*)		23 (14*df*)	
Pseudo R^2	0.25		0.31		0.33	

[a] Significant at 0.01, one-tailed test; [b] significant at 0.05, one-tailed test.

entrepreneurs has a positive and statistically significant coefficient estimate. Further, the coefficient estimates for all the other variables change little from the estimates obtained for them in A1 (see table 7-4).[26]

In my third model of legislative adoption of school choice, A3: Entrepreneur Score, I substituted the activity score variable for the presence variable, but retained all the other variables. This variable allowed me to explicitly model the abilities of the policy entrepreneurs, as measured in terms of team leadership, problem framing, and networking (both in and outside their states). The coefficient estimates for the other variables in the model remain little changed from those obtained in models A1 and A2 (see table 7-4).[27]

These results suggest that the presence and the actions of policy entrepreneurs can increase the likelihood of state legislative adoption of school choice. With the results from the consideration models, they provide an empirical basis for asserting that policy entrepreneurs help to promote ideas and get them onto government agendas. However, policy entrepreneurs can do more than get people talking: they can also raise the chances of legislatures adopting a policy innovation. Next I explore the magnitude of the impact policy entrepreneurs have on the adoption hazard rate.

Predicting the Likelihood of Adoption

I used the coefficient estimates obtained in model A3: Entrepreneur Score in table 7-4 to make a series of adoption hazard rate predictions. Here I fixed the year to 1990 and all other variables at their mean observed levels in 1990: that is, I followed the same procedure that I used for predicting the consideration hazard rates shown in table 7-3. The observed adoption hazard rate for all states in the risk set in 1990 was 0.22 (see table 7-1). I compared the impact of policy entrepreneurs with that of the two other statistically significant variables—changes in student test scores over the past five years (relative to changes at the national level) and teachers' union opposition to school choice. I present the results of my adoption hazard rate predictions in table 7-5.

These predictions suggest that legislatures in states with strong teachers' union opposition to the school choice idea are less likely to adopt school choice than their counterparts in other states. The predicted hazard rates in the first column show that with no entrepreneur present, and assuming that test score performance in the state tracks the national average, strong opposition from state teachers' unions can drop

Table 7-5. ***Model Estimates of the Hazard Rate for State Legislative Adoption of School Choice***

Predicted adoption hazard rate for 1990, given these conditions:	*No entrepreneur present*	*Entrepreneur with minimum observed activity score*	*Entrepreneur with mean observed activity score*	*Entrepreneur with maximum observed activity score*
State teachers' unions strongly oppose school choice and, relative to the national average, state test score gains over the past five years have been:				
–1 s.d. above the mean	0.01	0.04	0.10	0.26
–At the mean	0.03	0.09	0.21	0.44
–1 s.d. below the mean	0.07	0.18	0.37	0.64
State teachers' unions do not strongly oppose school choice and, relative to the national average, state test score gains over the past five years have been:				
–1 s.d. above the mean	0.16	0.34	0.59	0.81
–at the mean	0.29	0.54	0.76	0.91
–1 s.d. below the mean	0.48	0.73	0.88	0.96

Note: The hazard rate predictions in this table are made for 1990 using the coefficient estimates generated by model A3. The observed adoption hazard rate in 1990 was 0.22 (see table 7-1). To obtain the hazard rate predictions presented here, all predictor variables were set at their mean observed levels for the forty-eight states for 1990, with the exception of the predictors of interest set out here. The order of magnitude of the predicted hazard rates differs for each year, but the relative sizes of the hazard rates under the different sets of circumstances indicated in this table remain fairly stable from year to year.

the predicted adoption hazard rate from 0.29 to 0.03. These predicted adoption hazard rates also show that perceptions of decline in the performance of state schools (as measured by relative changes in student test scores) can make a significant difference in the likelihood that school choice will be adopted. Given weaker union opposition to the idea and evidence of relative declines in student performance on standardized tests, state legislatures would have an adoption hazard rate of 0.48 even if no policy entrepreneur was present.

Other predictions presented in table 7–5 show that the presence and actions of policy entrepreneurs can significantly increase the hazard rate for adoption of school choice. But the context in which the policy entrepreneur operates also matters. The predictions suggest that policy entrepreneurs—even highly active ones—will have great difficulty securing legislative adoption of their policy ideas when union opposition is strong and changes in test scores are tracking the national average.

In sum, the predicted hazard rates in Table 7-5 show that the actions of the policy entrepreneurs will not always be enough to ensure adoption of policy innovations. There are clear, and theoretically valid, limits to the impact of policy entrepreneurship. These results show why state-level school choice policy entrepreneurs have frequently gained legislative consideration of their ideas, but have had difficulty winning adoption of school choice.

Summary

The empirical study presented in this chapter supports the argument that policy entrepreneurs play an important role in setting innovative ideas onto government agendas and securing policy change. Naturally, policy entrepreneurs, like other actors in the policymaking process, must be aware of the constraints imposed by election cycles and interest-group opposition to their proposals. But many possibilities remain for policy entrepreneurs to form relationships and develop arguments that will help them gain adoption of policy innovations. In sum, then, this study takes us a long way toward answering the *So what?* question about policy entrepreneurs and policy change. Nonetheless, questions having to do with exactly *how* policy entrepreneurs manage to make a difference in the policymaking process still need to be addressed. It would be useful to know more about what policy entrepreneurs do, and to have more of a sense of the actions that underlie the activity score used in the present study. In the next chapters I present three studies of entrepreneurial activity. Methodologically, the first of these, my examination of the school choice policy entrepreneurs and their use of policy networks, represents a rather subtle variation on the analysis that I have just presented. Theoretically, however, the study is useful for clarifying the ways that policy networks serve as resources for policy entrepreneurs. Subsequent chapters look more closely at how policy entrepreneurs build support for their ideas and the uses they make of evidence when arguing for policy change.

Postscript: Relevant Survey Questions

To develop the activity score, I built four scales each relating to four separate (but related) activities. These were problem framing, team leadership, networking around the state government, and networking outside the state.

Questions and Scores

Problem Framing Score. This scale measures the ability of the policy entrepreneurs to reframe issues. It is based on responses to the following questions:

> How important were each of the following strategies for the school choice policy entrepreneurs in your state? (1) Finding out the attitudes to school choice of members of the policy elite in your state; (2) Using or developing perceptions of crises to increase interest in and support for alternative ways of organizing the school system; (3) Framing problems with the state school system to make school choice seem an appealing alternative; (4) Presenting the problems with the state school system in a way that led to a realignment of interests into a new coalition supporting school choice.

Answers concerning each activity could range from 1 to 5, where 1 indicated "not important" and 5 indicated "very important."

Team Leadership Score. This scale measures the team-building abilities of the policy entrepreneurs. It is based on responses to the following questions:

> Compared with interest group lobbyists and policy advocates in your state, how effective were the school choice policy entrepreneurs you have identified in terms of the following activities? (1) Inspiring and leading like-minded people.

This answer could range from 1 to 5, where 1 indicated "not effective" and 5 indicated "very effective."

> How important were each of the following strategies for the school choice policy entrepreneurs in your state? (1) Team-building among subordinates and colleagues to inspire commitment to change.

The answer could range from 1 to 5, where 1 indicated "not important" and 5 indicated "very important."

Government Networking Score. This scale measures the ability of the policy entrepreneurs to network with significant actors within the state government. It is based on responses to the following question:

> Compared with interest group lobbyists and policy advocates in your state, how effective were the school choice policy entrepreneurs you have identified in terms of the following activities? Developing and maintaining good relations with: (1) The State Governor; (2) State Legislators; (3) The Chief State School Officer; (4) School Superintendents; (5) Public School Boards.

Answers concerning each activity could range from 1 to 5, where 1 indicated "not effective" and 5 indicated "very effective."

Interstate Networking Score. This scale measures the ability of the policy entrepreneurs to network with people in states other than their own. Like the other scales, this scale is additive, consisting of scores contained in survey responses to the following questions:

> How important were each of the following strategies for the school choice policy entrepreneurs in your state? (1) Collecting evidence from other choice experiments to demonstrate the merits of the idea; (2) Networking with school choice advocates from neighboring states; (3) Networking with school choice advocates from other (i.e., non-neighboring) states.

Answers concerning each activity could range from 1 to 5, where 1 indicated "not important" and 5 indicated "very important."

Activity Score. Because of the high correlation between the four scales presented above (i.e., $r > 0.85$ in all cases), for the purpose of the analysis presented in the body of this chapter I added them all together into one activity score. In theory the effectiveness score could range up to 70. The mean score for the identified entrepreneurs was 41. The minimum observed activity rating was 21. The maximum observed rating was 63.

The Measure of State Teachers' Union Opposition to School Choice

This measure was constructed from responses to the following question:

> When the idea of school choice was first suggested in your state, what were the positions of the following individuals and groups? . . . State Teachers Associations.

The respondents could check responses on a 5-point scale ranging from "strongly opposed" = 1 to "strongly supportive" = 5. There was also space to check "no clear position."

The teachers' unions overwhelmingly opposed the school choice idea. Hence I developed the dichotomous measure used in the analysis, where 1 = "strongly opposed," and 0 = "somewhat opposed." Where there was missing data for states, the dichotomous measure was set to 0.

Notes

1. Examples include Derthick and Quirk (1985), King (1988), Kingdon (1995), Kirst, Meisner, and Rowley (1984), and McCraw (1984).

2. I follow the approach of Singer and Willett (1993) in setting up my event history analyses. Allison (1984), Berry and Berry (1990, 1992), and Yamaguchi (1991) also provide useful explanations of this procedure.

3. I chose 1987 as my starting point since this was the year that the Minnesota legislature adopted a pioneering school choice policy. Berry and Berry (1990, 398) argue that it is reasonable to assume that no state is "at risk" of adopting a given policy until after at least one state has given it serious consideration.

4. This truncation following the occurrence of the event requires us to employ different data sets whenever we want to analyze distinct events.

5. Because I was interested in exploring the process of state-to-state policy diffusion (and possible regional influences), in this research I focused only on the forty-eight contiguous states. For similar approaches see Berry and Berry (1990, 1992), and Walker (1969).

6. Throughout my analysis I modeled initial state consideration and adoption of public policies as nonrepeatable events. This is logically correct. However, legislative consideration and reform of policies are repeatable. The event history analysis approach can be adapted to estimate the hazard rates for repeatable events (see Allison 1984; Yamaguchi 1991; for a practical application see Berry and Berry 1992). But my primary interest is in assessing the impact of policy entrepreneurs on state policy innovation and this can be done using the nonrepeatable events approach.

7. Works by Glick and Hays (1991) on living-will law adoptions and Mooney and Lee (1995) on abortion regulation permissiveness suggest that later adopting states tend to introduce more comprehensive laws. However, more conceptual clarification and further studies across policy domains must be undertaken before we can make confident statements about general patterns.

8. In making this decision I followed the approach of, among others, Walker (1969) and Berry and Berry (1990, 1992).

9. An important question that I do not address here is why school choice policy entrepreneurs emerged in some states and not in others. In a separate analysis, I developed an event history data set to determine whether any contextual factors in each state could be used to predict the timing of the emergence of the policy entrepreneurs. Only the time controls came out statistically significant, suggesting that policy entrepreneurs who were late on the scene were motivated by observing the rising level of activity elsewhere. In contrast to this analysis, by focusing on local governments (and hence being able to work with a much larger data set), Schneider and Teske with Mintrom (1995) isolated a range of theoretically plausible correlates of the emergence of public entrepreneurs in local settings. Replicating that study at the state level was beyond the scope of this project.

10. Given this approach to variable construction, in which the activity score is only positive if a policy entrepreneur is present, we should expect the correlations between these two entrepreneur variables to be high. In fact, for the forty-eight states (i.e., n = 48), the correlation between presence and the activity score is 0.94. Therefore, this pair of variables cannot be placed in the logit regression equations together without incurring typical problems associated with high levels of multicollinearity.

11. This variable is measured annually as a percentage. U.S. Bureau of the Census, *Statistical Abstract of the United States* (Washington, D.C.: U.S. Government Printing Office, Annual).

12. I am grateful to Kevin Smith for kindly sharing with me his multistate, multiyear ACT, SAT, and SEI data.

13. Following the logic of Hirschman (1970, 60), it is also possible to take the view that the presence of a high number of private schools in a state could siphon off the strongest advocates for change to the public schools.

14. The reforms included in the count were curriculum reform, introducing new graduation requirements, introducing high school exit testing, introducing more student testing, and introducing teacher certification testing (Sunderman 1992, table 1).

15. In preliminary analyses, in addition to these state politics variables, I worked with a measure of the Ranney competition index (Bibby and Holbrook 1996, 105) and the Wright, Erikson, and McIver (1985) state ideology scores to determine whether party competition and the ideology of the state

population could help explain the timing of legislative consideration and adoption of school choice. In all cases the results failed to meet any test of statistical significance, suggesting that the politics of school choice needs to be analyzed in ways that, among other things, pay greater attention to the inner workings of the policymaking process.

16. Council of State Governments, *The Book of the States* (Lexington, Ky.: Council of State Governments, 1992).

17. Council of State Governments, *The Book of the States* (Lexington, Ky.: Council of State Governments, 1992); U.S. Bureau of the Census, *Statistical Abstract of the United States* (Washington, D.C.: U.S. Government Printing Office, Annual).

18. I obtained data on state legislative consideration and adoption of school choice from several published sources. I also verified and, where necessary, updated this information within the context of my survey of education policy experts in the states. The published sources were U.S. Department of Education Center for Choice in Education, *Issue Brief: Review of State Choice Legislation* (Washington, D.C.: United States Department of Education, 1992); The Education Commission of the States, Clearing House Notes "Legislative Activities Involving Open Enrollment (Choice)," 1992; Ernest Boyer, *School Choice* (Princeton, N.J.: Carnegie Foundation for the Advancement of Teaching, especially appendix C, 1992); The Heritage Foundation, *School Choice Programs: What's Happening in the States* (Washington, D.C.: Heritage Foundation, 1992, 1993); Richard Fossey, "School Choice Legislation: A Survey of the States," Consortium for Policy Research in Education occasional paper (New Brunswick, N.J.: Consortium for Policy Research in Education, 1992).

19. Among other things, the constant term in my equations subsumes the time controls for those two years. I collapsed these years together because of the small number of observed legislative considerations or adoptions of school choice in those years (for details see table 7-1).

20. The models of consideration and adoption have virtually identical independent variables. In modeling only the process of policy adoption, previous quantitative studies have collapsed important aspects of the policymaking process. Thus the implicit null hypothesis in these works has been that the two processes are the same. Here, I have separated the processes to see if different factors matter at different stages in the policy process. Given the approach of the previous literature, it is not clear that *a priori* we can specify differences in the factors driving the two steps in the policymaking process.

21. A comparison of goodness-of-fit statistics for models C1 and C2 confirms that presence is a statistically significant predictor of consideration. The change in $-2 \times LL = 11.28$, $\Delta df = 1$, $p < 0.005$.

22. Because the activity score measures not only the presence of policy

entrepreneurs but also what different policy entrepreneurs do, the goodness-of-fit of model C3 is even more of an improvement on model C1 than was model C2. The change in $-2 \times LL = 13.89$, $\Delta df = 1$, $p < 0.005$.

23. For justification of this approach, see, for example, Allison (1984, 69) and Yamaguchi (1991, 161–162).

24. Logically, the event of initial consideration must occur before the event of adoption. Further, some of the same factors (for instance, the presence and actions of policy entrepreneurs) appear to influence the hazard rate for both initial consideration of school choice and adoption of school choice. But this does not imply dependence between the two events. To test the reasonableness of this independence claim, in ancillary analyses I adapted Heckman's (1976, 1979) procedure for dealing with censored data to allow the data to be used in the context of event history analysis. To do this I first constructed a data set that allowed for prediction of the legislative consideration hazard rate, where consideration was treated as a repeatable event. The predicted hazard rates were then treated as observations for the cases included in the data set used to estimate the hazard rate for legislative adoption of school choice to be given consideration. Although results for the baseline adoption model showed the consideration equation hazard rate variable to be a predictor of adoption (thus suggesting dependence between the hazard rates for the events), this result was not sustained when the adoption model was augmented to include the measures of the presence and actions of policy entrepreneurs. Here, then, is a case of an extraneous factor (policy entrepreneurship) producing an apparent relationship between independent events. Since the consideration hazard rate variable was highly correlated with the entrepreneur variables, it was left out of the adoption models reported here.

25. For a discussion of the importance of indicators see Kingdon (1995).

26. However, inclusion of the policy entrepreneur variable improves the goodness of fit of A2 compared with A1. The change in $-2 \times LL = 3.83$, $\Delta df = 1$, $p < 0.10$.

27. However, the goodness of fit of model A3 is better than that of the previous models, as a comparison with model A1 demonstrates. The change in $-2 \times LL = 5.26$, $\Delta df = 1$, $p < 0.01$. I also tested a model consisting only of the time controls producing a $-2 \times LL$ score of 66.26. The improvement in goodness of fit going from this to model A1 is not significant (Δ in $-2 \times LL = 14.30$, $\Delta df = 9$, $p < 0.25$). The improvement going from this to model A2 is more apparent (Δ in $-2 \times LL = 18.12$, $\Delta df = 10$, $p < 0.10$). The improvement going from this to model A3 is also apparent (Δ in $-2 \times LL = 19.56$, $\Delta df = 10$, $p < 0.05$).

EIGHT

Policy Networks and the Diffusion of School Choice

In chapter 4 I noted the considerable value that scholars of entrepreneurship attribute to formal and informal business networks as conduits for the timely transmission of ideas and information among participants in particular industries. An entrepreneur with the ability to listen carefully to others and extract new meanings from what is said can greatly benefit from participation in networks. Being well attuned to the industry conversation, an entrepreneur might rapidly latch onto an idea for an innovation that he or she could subsequently bring to market. Knowledge acquired from participation in both formal and informal industry networks can also help entrepreneurs to identify individuals with the skills and knowledge needed to support the development of innovative products. Thus networks can be thought of as repositories of crucial information. Tapping into those networks can help an entrepreneur to both identify opportunities for gain and coordinate those with the know-how and resources to exploit them.

In chapter 5 I suggested that involvement in networks can be vitally important for policy entrepreneurs. But we need to think carefully about the nature of the policy networks that support policy entrepreneurship. Knowledge of policy developments in other jurisdictions, or even in other policy areas within the same jurisdiction, can help policy entrepreneurs generate ideas for policy innovations that they can then seek to articulate onto the legislative agenda. Yet we should expect to find limits to the value of this kind of networking with outsiders. Inevitably, to have some policy impact, a policy entrepreneur must be able to influence the ways that political insiders think about issues and the matters they choose to focus upon. This suggests that policy entrepreneurs need to be connected to multiple policy networks.

My purpose in the present chapter is to test the claim that policy networks serve as valuable resources for policy entrepreneurs. Toward this end, just as in chapter 7, I work within the policy innovation diffusion framework. Using event history analysis models, I explore the extent to which engagement in policy networks improves the likelihood that policy entrepreneurs will realize their policy goals. I do so by modeling the processes that have led to state legislative consideration and adoption of school choice legislation. Crucially, working with event history analysis models allows me to control for rival explanations of the rise of school choice in the states. The results obtained from this quantitative work suggest that policy entrepreneurs do indeed benefit from involvement in policy networks. Those who are most adept at manipulating policy networks are more likely than others to attain their policy goals. But these results also suggest that different types of network involvement matter at different stages in the policymaking process.

Beyond telling us something important about how it is that policy entrepreneurs manage to secure policy change, this study of the relationship between network engagement and legislative change also contributes to our understanding of policy innovation diffusion processes. Over the past three decades, political scientists have made some significant advances in their conceptualization and modeling of diffusion processes. However, previous diffusion studies have given scant attention to modeling the actual *mechanisms* through which policy ideas are communicated from state to state. Jack L. Walker hinted at the work to be done when he stated: "In order to develop explanations of these [innovation diffusion] processes we must go beyond the search for demographic correlates of innovation and develop generalizations that refer to the behavior of the men who actually make the choices in which we are interested" (1969, 887). In subsequent work Walker (1981) revisited this matter, arguing that interactions among members of policy communities are vital for ensuring the diffusion of innovations. But Walker's claims were not accompanied by supporting empirical evidence. I believe that researchers can improve upon past efforts. In the present study, as a by-product of my interest in how policy networks serve to support the efforts of policy entrepreneurs, we gain new insights into the processes of policy innovation diffusion.

The Nature of Policy Networks

A policy network consists of a group of actors who share an interest in some policy area and who are linked by their direct and indirect contacts with one another.[1] Theoretically, the activities of policy networks are critical for promoting the diffusion of policy innovations. Although an innovation can be communicated in a variety of ways, interpersonal contacts have been found to facilitate the exchange of information about new ideas. Rather than relying upon mass-media channels or the outcomes of scientific investigations, most potential adopters base their judgments of an innovation on information from those who have sound knowledge of it and can explain its advantages and disadvantages. Everett M. Rogers elaborates: "This dependence on the experience of near peers suggests that the heart of the diffusion process consists of the modeling and imitation by potential adopters of their network partners who have adopted previously. So diffusion is a very social process" (1995, 18).

Ongoing interactions among network members permit the formation and dissemination of judgments about the character of actors who propose innovations. Consequently, network information about innovations will be tagged with opinions on the reliability and trustworthiness of their proponents. Mark S. Granovetter (1985) refers to this type of communication as "embedded" social action. He suggests that concrete personal relations and structures (or "networks") generate interpersonal trust. Network communications thereby serve to screen proposed innovations based on merit. Lawmakers and others do not wish to support innovations that could produce potentially threatening or embarrassing unintended consequences. In a well-developed network with a robust communication system, actors of poor character and judgment, as well as poorly conceived ideas, can be quickly identified and discredited.

The important role played by social networks in the process of policy formulation has not been entirely missed by social scientists. Beginning with Hugh Heclo's (1978) discussion of "issue networks," a rich literature exploring the nature and role of policy networks has developed. But this literature is somewhat problematic. Although some complex empirical studies have been reported, most investigations of policy networks have been grounded in the case study modality.[2] Clearly, there is a need for scholars to take time to understand the nature of phenomena when first studying them, thus identifying the important questions to ask. But ultimately the research effort needs to proceed beyond that point to develop empirical propositions and test them in a rigorous fashion. To date, researchers have made little effort to assess the comparative impact of activities within policy networks on policy formulation, while controlling for other potential causes of policy change. This is the case even in the more methodologically sophisticated network studies, which identify members of policy networks and the strength of the ties between them, rather than show how the ideas and resources manifest in these networks are marshaled to secure policy change (see, for instance, Laumann, Knoke, and Kim 1985). The political science literature has been silent in terms of clarifying whether and how policy networks facilitate state-to-state diffusion of policy innovations. Consequently, much remains to be learned about how policy ideas gain power and catch on in policymaking circles.

Why this silence on the role of policy networks in the diffusion of policy innovations? The answer appears to be that previous studies of policy innovation diffusion have been preoccupied with demonstrating the *existence* of state-to-state diffusion processes. Typically, proof of diffusion processes has relied upon reports of simple correlations between policy innovations adopted in nearby or neighboring states and adoption of the same innovation in the state of interest.[3] The research effort has gone no further. Thus, diffusion scholars have placed great store on the *as if* assumption that activities in one state influence activities elsewhere without showing exactly how or why this process occurs. Since good social science involves making an ongoing effort to assess the reasonableness of our facilitating assumptions, I suggest that policy diffusion studies should closely consider the underlying forces that produce various diffusion patterns.

Policy Entrepreneurs and Policy Networks

I contend that policy entrepreneurs who are best able to manipulate the resources in policy networks will be the most able to make convincing arguments on behalf of the policy innovations they promote. Of course, many people see policy gaps and even think of solutions. But this does not make them policy entrepreneurs. Policy entrepreneurs are distinguished by their decisions to expend effort to bring new policy ideas into "good currency," to use a term borrowed from Donald A. Schön (1971, 123). How do policy entrepreneurs develop and sell their ideas to others? This is where the role of policy networks becomes paramount. In a federal system like that of the United States, two broad types of policy networks can be found. First, policy entrepreneurs operating at the state level will most often develop their ideas for policy innovation through their conversations and interactions with members of interstate or *external policy networks*. These policy networks are issue specific, and a key function is to convey new information. Connections develop between individuals with a common interest in a given policy innovation. An external network provides a forum in which ideas, war stories, and strategies for selling a policy innovation are discussed.[4] Communicating with individuals in this network helps policy entrepreneurs develop their arguments in support of their ideas. In the case of school choice, this external policy network has consisted of, among others, staff members at the Education Commission of the States, The Heritage Foundation, the U.S. Department of Education; staff members in think tanks such as the Hudson Institute in Indiana and the Manhattan Institute in New York; members of Citizens for Educational Freedom; and politicians, bureaucrats, academics, and policy entrepreneurs across the country.

It is one thing to hear about new ideas and want to have them transformed into policy innovations. Making the innovations happen is much more difficult. In attempting to bring a policy innovation into good currency in their own states, policy entrepreneurs must plan how to sell their ideas to others. They aim first to convince others of the worth of the innovation as a solution to a political problem, and then to mobilize people to help secure adoption of the policy. Policy entrepreneurs need to establish standing for themselves: part of this involves listening to the local policy "conversation" and thinking strategically about how best to contribute to it. The problem for policy entrepreneurs who want to sell their particular ideas—and who, unlike interest-group lobbyists, will not have a ready-made constituency—is to find ways to make it through the political screening process. Establishing standing and grounds for trust are both fundamental for policy entrepreneurs who want their ideas to receive legislative attention. This is where state-level policy networks can provide a critical resource.

Intrastate or *internal policy networks* comprise the second type of policy network operating in a federal system. These networks are generally issue specific and comprise individuals with established connections to the local policymaking community and who, perhaps, have some connections to the broader external policy network relevant to the issue domain they focus upon. For example, an internal policy network might include legislators and their staffs, bureaucrats and personnel in the office of the governor, lobbyists, staff members from the local chamber of commerce or other business groups, representatives of concerned citizen groups, and staff members in local think tanks. Policy entrepreneurs can make good use of internal networks by capitalizing upon the contacts of the network participants.

Beyond ensuring that their policy ideas are technically feasible, policy entrepreneurs must also strive to demonstrate their own credibility and trustworthiness as sellers of their ideas. Just as consumers can be put off from purchasing high-quality merchandise simply because of their treatment by store employees, politicians can respond negatively to policy ideas due to the actions and reputations of the policy entrepreneurs who push the ideas. So, policy entrepreneurs must be sensitive to what people are looking for when developing ways to present their messages. Individuals in the relevant internal network can provide strategically valuable information to policy entrepreneurs.

In sum, scholars have long recognized the importance of interpersonal contacts in the diffusion of innovations. Drawing upon insights from the network analysis literature, I suggest that policy networks comprise a vital resource for policy entrepreneurs who seek to have their ideas for policy innovation placed on legislative agendas. In the rest of this chapter, I present a test of the validity of these contentions by focusing on the use that the school choice policy entrepreneurs made of policy networks as they sought to gain legislative attention for their ideas.

Policy Entrepreneurs and Network Use: An Event History Analysis

To test the hypothesis that policy entrepreneurs and the use they make of policy networks have a significant impact on state policy innovation, I developed event history analysis models. As in chapter 7 I specified two events as being of interest: (1) initial legislative consideration and (2) legislative adoption. These events may or may not occur in a given period. The research problem then involved considering, for any state, what determines the likelihood of occurrence of the event during a specified period. To fairly test the impact of policy entrepreneurs and the use they make of policy networks on legislative consideration and adoption of school choice ideas, I controlled for the impact of other factors that could influence state education policies.

From information provided by survey respondents, the policy entrepreneurs were each assigned scores for their use of external (interstate) and internal (intrastate) policy networks.

Use of External Networks

This score was based on respondents' answers to two questions: "How important were each of the following strategies for the school choice policy entrepreneurs in your state? [1] Networking with school choice advocates from neighboring states. [2] Networking with school choice advocates from other (i.e., non-neighboring) states." Responses could be given on a 5-point scale where 1 = "not important" and 5 = "very important." Where no entrepreneurs were identified, the variable was coded 0. For ease of comparison of the coefficient estimates for external network use and internal network use, total scores were divided by 2. In theory, the score could range from 0.5 to 5. The actual scores ranged from 1 to 5, with a mean of 2.9 (n = 26). I hypothesized that higher scores for external networks increase the likelihood of state legislative consideration and adoption of school choice.

Use of Internal Networks

This score was based on respondents' answers to this question: "How important [was] the following strategy for the school choice policy entrepreneurs in your state? Networking with others in and around government and using these contacts to achieve their policy goals." Responses could be given on a 5-point scale where 1 = "not important" and 5 = "very important." Where no entrepreneurs were identified, the variable was coded zero. The scores ranged from 1 to 5, with a mean of 3.1 (n = 26). I hypothesized that higher scores for use of internal networks also increase the likelihood of state legislative consideration and adoption of school choice.[5]

Rival Explanations of the Rise of School Choice

The control variables used in the models reported here are identical to those used in the models reported in chapter 7. Therefore, in what follows I describe these variables in the briefest of terms. For elaboration on each of these variables and for information on the sources of the data from which they were constructed, readers are referred to the previous chapter. It should be noted that fewer control variables are used in these models than in those reported in chapter 7. The excluded control variables were found to have no significant impacts on policy consideration and adoption in the earlier models. Thus, their exclusion here has no substantive effect on the reported results and allows for a more focused discussion.

School System Characteristics

Percentage of Education Funding Provided by the State. I expected that greater relative levels of state spending on schools increase the likelihood of state legislative consideration and adoption of school choice. This variable is measured annually as a percentage.

Relative Change in Student Test Scores. I expected that greater declines in the average test scores within states relative to the change at the national level over a given period increase the likelihood of state legislative consideration and adoption of school choice. The variable is measured annually.

State Politics

Elements of state politics were also expected to influence the likelihood of legislative consideration and adoption of school choice. However, political debate over school choice has often evolved in surprising ways that would be difficult to predict based on knowledge of partisan control of state legislatures and governorships, degree of party competition, or the ideological makeup of a state's population.

State House Election Year. I expected the likelihood of consideration and adoption of school choice to be lower in election years. The variable is dichotomous and is coded 1 for house election years and 0 otherwise.

Opposition of Teachers' Unions. I expected that strong opposition from the state teachers' unions reduces the likelihood of legislative consideration and adoption of school choice.

Innovation Diffusion

Neighbors Considering or Neighbors Adopting. I expected that high proportions of neighboring states having considered or adopted school choice increase the likelihood of consideration or adoption in the home state.

Maturation Effects

I expected that maturation effects would manifest themselves with time control parameters that increase (but at a declining rate) with each year under investigation. I included dichotomous time variables for 1989, 1990, 1991, and 1992 and treated 1987 and 1988 as the baseline.

Analysis and Results

I performed standard logit regression analysis on two event history data sets: one designed to explore whether, all other things equal, network use raised the likelihood of initial state legislative consideration of school choice; the other to explore whether, all other things equal, network use raised the likelihood of adoption of school choice, given that it had received legislative consideration. Two regressions were performed on each data set. Since these regression models represent variants of models C1–C3 and A1–A3 presented in chapter 7, I refer to the two consideration models presented here as C4 and C5. I refer to the two adoption models as A4 and A5.[6] In each case, the first regression (C4, A4) was used to assess the effects of external network use. The second (C5, A5) was used to explore the effects of internal network use. The results for the initial consideration data set are reported in table 8-1. The results for the adoption data set are reported in table 8-2.

Policy Entrepreneurs and Use of Networks

Use of External Networks. The results of Model C4 support the hypothesis that higher scores for external networks use increase the likelihood of state legislative consideration of school choice. However, the results for Model A4 suggest that external network use does not affect the likelihood of legislative adoption of school choice. I interpret this finding to mean that the use of external networks is most important for supporting the generation of innovative ideas and getting them onto the policy agenda. In contrast, when it comes to adoption of an innovation other factors are more important. Using the results from Model C4, I find that holding all other variables at their mean, in 1990, increasing the use of external networks from the level associated with a score of 1 to that

Table 8-1. *Factors Affecting the Likelihood of Legislative Consideration of School Choice*

Models:	*C4: External Network Use*		*C5: Internal Network Use*	
Independent Variables	*Coefficient Estimate*	*Standard Error*	*Coefficient Estimate*	*Standard Error*
Policy Entrepreneurs				
External Network Use Score	0.628[a]	0.168		
Internal Network Use Score			0.616[a]	0.187
School System Characteristics				
State Spending (% of total)	0.015	0.019	0.014	0.018
Relative Change in Test Scores	0.282	0.209	0.285	0.212
State Politics				
State House Election Year	−1.56[b]	0.794	−1.600[b]	0.789
Opposition of Teachers' Unions	−1.375	0.849	−1.215	0.843
Innovation Diffusion				
Legislative Consideration of School Choice in Neighboring States	1.693[b]	1.019	1.680[b]	1.009
Time Controls				
(base = 1987 and 1988)				
1989	1.858[b]	0.930	1.888[b]	0.922
1990	3.017[a]	1.155	3.005[a]	1.144
1991	0.549	1.196	0.752	1.186
1992	4.188[a]	1.388	4.238[a]	1.389
Constant Term	−3.717[a]	1.479	−4.293[a]	1.511
Summary Statistics				
Number of Cases	195		195	
−2 × Log Likelihood	123.58		127.16	
Chi2	65.89 (10 *df*)		62.32 (10 *df*)	
Pseudo R^2	0.35		0.33	

[a]Significant at 0.01, one-tailed test; [b]significant at 0.05, one-tailed test.

associated with a score of 5 would increase the likelihood of initial legislative consideration of school choice from 0.42 to 0.90.

Use of Internal Networks. The results of Model C5 and Model A5 support the hypothesis that higher scores for internal networks use increase the likelihood of both state legislative consideration and adoption of school

Table 8-2. ***Factors Affecting the Likelihood of Legislative Adoption of School Choice***

Models:	*A4: External Network Use*		*A5: Internal Network Use*	
Independent Variables	*Coefficient Estimate*	*Standard Error*	*Coefficient Estimate*	*Standard Error*
Policy Entrepreneurs				
External Network Use Score	0.374	0.246		
Internal Network Use Score			0.772[b]	0.338
School System Characteristics				
State Spending (% of total)	0.017	0.022	0.016	0.024
Relative Change in Test Scores	−1.496[b]	0.673	−1.388[b]	0.776
State Politics				
State House Election Year	1.799	2.209	2.238	2.539
Opposition of Teachers' Unions	−2.531[a]	1.063	−3.081[a]	1.224
Innovation Diffusion				
Legislative Adoption of School Choice in Neighboring States	0.296	1.564	−0.866	1.785
Time Controls				
(base = 1987 and 1988)				
1989	−2.638	2.199	−2.293	2.445
1990	−3.330	3.161	−2.866	3.532
1991	−2.059	2.203	−1.247	2.475
1992	−5.762	3.411	−4.630	3.809
Constant Term	1.221	2.344	0.616	2.636
Summary Statistics				
Number of Cases	64		64	
−2 × Log Likelihood	52.96		49.18	
Chi2	16.74 (10*df*)		20.53 (10*df*)	
Pseudo R^2	0.24		0.29	

[a]Significant at 0.01, one-tailed test; [b]significant at 0.05, one-tailed test.

choice. Using the results from these models, I find that holding all other variables at their mean, in 1990, increasing the use of internal networks from the level associated with a score of 1 to that associated with a score of 5 would increase the likelihood of initial legislative consideration of school choice from 0.29 to 0.82. The same increase in the use of internal networks would increase the likelihood of legislative adoption of school choice from 0.12 to 0.75.

The Control Variables

Although I am most interested here in the use that policy entrepreneurs make of different policy networks and what this tells us about the role policy networks play in the diffusion of innovations, for completeness I briefly discuss the coefficient estimates obtained for the control variables in the event history analysis models. In all cases, the changes in the coefficient estimates for these control variables were small as I changed the specifications of the models being applied to each data set. Consequently, the coefficients were found to be either significant as predictors of initial legislative consideration in both consideration models (C4, C5) or they were significant in neither. The same held true for the adoption models (A4, A5) in their application to the adoption data set. However, none of the control variable coefficient estimates that were significant for consideration were significant for adoption. Likewise, none of the control variable coefficients that were significant for adoption were significant for consideration. This suggests that the factors determining why a policy innovation gains legislative attention are different from those determining whether the innovation gains adoption. By implication, it appears that the political processes that lead to legislative consideration of a policy idea are distinctive from those that lead to legislative adoption once a policy has gained consideration. This finding supports my claim that external network use is important for purposes of agenda setting but has less relevance when it comes to engaging in battles to achieve state legislative adoption of a policy innovation.

While it is clear that the use policy entrepreneurs make of both external and internal networks affected the likelihood of *legislative consideration* of school choice, it is also clear that the timing of state house elections and the attention given to this policy innovation by legislatures in neighboring states is important. School system characteristics and the opposition of teachers' unions, however, do not appear to be important at this stage in legislative deliberation. The results also show that the actions of policy entrepreneurs are important for securing *legislative adoption* of school choice. But, again, policy entrepreneurship is not all that counts. The performance of the school system, as measured by changes in test scores, and the opposition of teachers' unions are significant factors affecting policy adoption. For our purposes, the most interesting element of the adoption results is that neither legislative activity in neighboring states nor the policy entrepreneurs' external network use have significant impacts. Yet, even though external network use is not important at the adoption stage, the policy entrepreneurs' internal network use is important.

Implications

The results presented here support the contention that policy networks represent repositories and conduits of information that can greatly assist policy entrepreneurs as they generate ideas for policy innovation and pursue policy change. When it comes to placing new ideas on the policy agenda in their states, policy entrepreneurs find it important to make use of both external and internal policy networks. The external networks serve as the source for generating new ideas and for providing the policy entrepreneurs with insights into how approaches used elsewhere could be applied in their own states. However, having a good understanding of the relevant internal state policy networks and how best to use them is also critical. This knowledge allows the policy entrepreneurs to determine appropriate ways to present their proposals so they will gain serious attention. Intuitively, then, it makes sense that both external network and internal network use matter when seeking legislative consideration of a policy innovation.

When it comes to seeking legislative adoption of a policy innovation, the relative importance of internal and external policy networks changes. At this stage in the policy process, the focus of attention moves from the novelty of the innovation to serious questioning of its relevance and viability, given the local context. Hence, the power of interest groups—in this case, the teachers' unions—now becomes important, as do indicators of the need for policy change—in this case, student test scores. Where the idea came from and what is happening in other states is now irrelevant. At the adoption stage, internal policy networks are the most important ones for policy entrepreneurs to use. The greater the knowledge that a policy entrepreneur has of the concerns of members of the relevant internal network, the better the chances that he or she will be able to frame the policy innovation in terms that appeal to the network. This raises the likelihood of legislative adoption of the innovation.

In addition to supporting the argument that policy networks support policy entrepreneurship, this study also demonstrates the important role that policy networks play in facilitating the diffusion of policy innovations. The results of the event history analyses suggest that external or interstate networks serve as important mechanisms for the dissemination of innovative ideas. The results also suggest that successful proposals for policy innovation must be framed in ways that address the concerns of the would-be adopters situated in internal or intrastate networks. Finally, the results are consistent with key arguments found in the general literature on innovation diffusion (see, for example, Rogers 1995).

Cyberspace and the Changing Nature of Policy Networks

In 1993, the year I collected the survey information upon which this study is based, interstate policy networks were sustained primarily through people organizing conferences, circulating newsletters, and engaging in informal contacts resulting from face-to-face meetings or referrals. In the following two years, when I had conversations with various policy entrepreneurs identified by the survey respondents, I was often told of how policy entrepreneurs used the resources of external networks to support their policy goals. Frequently, I would hear how a policy entrepreneur would set up a conference or meeting of members of the education policy community in his or her state and then bring in policy entrepreneurs from elsewhere to give keynote speeches. Activities of this sort would facilitate the passing on of information about school choice ideas and how various groups had worked to secure adoption of school choice laws in their states. Through personal contact and the provision of high-quality information, such meetings could do much, in John W. Kingdon's (1995) term, to "soften up" various state actors, increasing the likelihood that they would eventually look with favor on proposals for this kind of policy change. Today, of course, such conferences and meetings continue to be arranged. But a dramatic change in communication methods has occurred in the space of just a few years. Now, the Internet and e-mail communication have greatly expanded opportunities for policy networking across a multitude of jurisdictions.

For well over a decade Joe Nathan has frequently traveled from state to state, giving talks and testifying before state legislative committees about the merits of school choice and, more recently, the introduction of charter schools. Thus Nathan has often been available to share his knowledge and ideas concerning political strategy with others. But the rapid acceleration in the development of the Internet and in the use people make of e-mail has taken that availability to a whole new level. Currently, Nathan receives from sixty to eighty e-mail messages a day from people who have questions about issues to do with school choice and charter schools.[7] Nathan, like many other school choice policy entrepreneurs, frequently contributes to e-mail discussion groups about these topics. All of this has greatly increased his exposure to others interested in school choice ideas. In so doing, others have learned about the ways that he makes arguments and have seen firsthand how he chooses to refute those that he opposes.

The speed with which individuals across the United States can now obtain high-quality information about policy developments elsewhere, and the ease with which they can contact experts for ideas and advice, is serving to transform policy innovation diffusion processes. So far scholarly documentation of this transformation is all but nonexistent.[8] In a contribution that raises several points of direct relevance to the present discussion, Christopher Swope (1997, 2940) has observed how the Internet is changing the nature of participation in national politics in the United States:

> The cyber-polity is growing to include the typical cast of Capitol Hill characters such as lobbyists, journalists, researchers and congressional staff.
>
> But more and more, it's a diverse crowd of concerned citizens and distant Congress-watchers who are becoming cyber-constituents, firing up their Web browsers and talking politics through their modems.

What is becoming increasingly clear is that the Internet reduces the costs associated with both acquiring politically relevant information and with keeping members of coalitions informed about events and how they can support the attainment of specific policy goals. Yet, as David Hosansky (1997, 2943) notes, the Internet most often serves to support and enhance, rather than supersede, traditional efforts to create and maintain support for policy change. Face-to-face contact still matters greatly for generating and sustaining political support for an idea.

My discussion in this chapter of how policy networks support policy entrepreneurship can also tell us something about the likely scope and limits of cyberspace as a medium for political activity. Without doubt, the Internet has already greatly expanded opportunities for policy entrepreneurs to rapidly acquire information about ideas and policy approaches being tried and tested outside of their own jurisdictions. We might say that the Internet represents a significant tool for allowing policy entrepreneurs to tap into external policy networks. Through this medium, policy entrepreneurs can now more easily learn about approaches and strategies that might inform their own ideas and arguments regarding policy change. That said, in terms of finding ways to introduce their ideas for policy innovation to key individuals in their own jurisdictions (e.g., lawmakers and their advisors), the Internet is likely to be of less help. In fact, according to Jonathan Weisman (1997, 2936), the ability to have instant communication without face-to-face contact has served to reduce the amount of time that lawmakers spend together. In Weisman's view, greater use of the Internet might further erode the personal bonds that lawmakers have traditionally forged during legislative sessions. To the extent that these personal contacts are weakened, it might become all the harder for policy entrepreneurs to use traditional networks in and around government as channels for building support for policy change.[9] My analysis in this chapter shows that use of internal networks is vital for achieving both legislative consideration and adoption of a policy innovation. Given this, as lawmakers make increasing use of cyberspace and other nontraditional forms of communication, to remain effective, policy entrepreneurs will likely have to devise new strategies for achieving influence. Then again, assuming that changes in the actions of lawmakers will change the rules of the game for everyone, it might also be the case that this new development will present a significant opportunity for political outsiders—and that is what policy entrepreneurs often are—to have even more influence on policy development than has ever been the case in the past.

Summary

My primary goal in this chapter has been to present the method that I used to assess how much engagement in policy networks helps policy entrepreneurs to achieve their policy goals. The results I have reported suggest that external policy networks, composed of people across the nation, are important primarily for facilitating agenda setting. Making use of internal policy networks—made up of people in and around state government—is useful not only for agenda setting, but also for supporting adoption of policy innovations. To assess the value to policy entrepreneurs of using policy networks, I worked within the policy innovation diffusion framework. In so doing, I deliberately sought to integrate insights from policy network studies into diffusion studies. Although it represents a by-product of the work needed to fulfill the primary goal of this study, an integration of this sort opens the way for scholars to gain a better understanding of the causal mechanisms that lead to observed patterns of policy diffusion. Such an integration also serves to highlight the important political considerations that accompany the successful transfer of information about innovations in a federal system. Admittedly, much of what I have said and done here is, at best, only suggestive. But it establishes a starting point from which others might go on to inform future diffusion studies with insights from the literature on the nature and workings of policy and social networks.

Engagement in policy networks supports policy entrepreneurship. Yet, to be effective as a policy entrepreneur, many other forms of political engagement must also be undertaken. In the chapter to follow I explore the relationship between policy argumentation and coalition building. As in this chapter, I use an empirical study of the actions of the school choice policy entrepreneurs as a site for both theory testing and additional theory construction.

Notes

1. Terms comparable with "policy networks" include "issue networks" (Heclo 1978), and "policy communities" (Walker 1981). As in the previous literature, I take the view that the boundaries of policy networks are porous. However, this characteristic of networks should not be construed as an impediment to rigorous analysis of how they facilitate policy development and the diffusion of policy innovations. See Granovetter (1973) for a discussion of how strong and weak ties in networks facilitate information exchanges.

2. For reviews of quantitatively based studies of policy networks, see Knoke (1990) and Kenis and Schneider (1991). Case studies of policy networks can be found in Walker (1981); Kirst, Meister, and Rowley (1984); and Peterson (1993).

3. For a methodological critique see Berry 1994.

4. For evidence of this sort of network use, see Walker (1981); Kirst, Meister, and Rowley (1984); and Kaplin and Usdan (1992).

5. For another element of the broader research project on policy entrepreneurship, I conducted in-depth telephone interviews with a purposive

sample of over one-third of the policy entrepreneurs identified by our survey respondents. These interviews included discussions about networking activities. The comments of the policy entrepreneurs on this matter were consistent with the information provided by the survey respondents. Thus, this follow-up work supports the validity of both my approach to identifying the policy entrepreneurs and my approach to measuring their use of policy networks.

6. Given the approach I used to construct the network variables, in which the network scores are positive only if a policy entrepreneur is present, the zero-order correlations between them are extremely high. For the forty-eight states (i.e., n = 48), the pair-wise correlation between presence and the external network use score is 0.92; the pair-wise correlation between presence and the internal network use score is 0.85; and the pair-wise correlation between the two network use scores is 0.88. As Gujarati (1995, 336) notes, zero-order correlations above 0.80 are a sufficient condition for the existence of multicollinearity. To avoid the high standard errors associated with multicollinearity, I placed each of these variables in separate regression models, the results of which I report. Theoretically, this is a justifiable remedial step because the use that entrepreneurs make of networks can only be ascertained if the entrepreneurs have been identified. So, to include any two of the presence or network use measures in the same regression model is redundant.

7. Reported by Joe Nathan in an interview available on the Internet bookstore, Amazon.com.

8. Discussions of the ways that the Internet is transforming political participation are beginning to emerge. For example, Rash (1997) has contributed a discussion and analysis of the role that use of the Internet played in the 1996 general election. Some scholars of international relations have begun to examine the role played by the Internet in the transnational dissemination of ideas for policy and political change. See, for instance, Sassen (1998, ch. 9).

9. Alan Rosenthal (1998, 90–92) argues that, for several years now, state legislative cultures have been undergoing a transformation that has led to the erosion of community and, thus, informal opportunities for face-to-face deliberation. "Preoccupied with their constituencies, their causes, their campaigns, and their careers, today's legislators have little spare time to get very involved with their colleagues." David Hedge (1998) makes a series of observations that support Rosenthal's claim. A pessimistic implication of this is that greater use of cyberspace will further erode ties among legislators. A more optimistic view is that growing use of electronic forms of communication could serve to create "virtual communities" that fill the void caused by increased state legislative careerism, professionalism, and term limits.

NINE

Policy Argumentation, Coalition Building, and School Choice

In the marketplace entrepreneurs must create organizational arrangements that facilitate the development and distribution of innovative products. To do this well they must find ways to convince others that participation in a given venture will be beneficial. Often this requires entrepreneurs to enter into formal contracts with various individuals and firms, some of whom may care little about the entrepreneur's primary goal. Yet even though entrepreneurs can use the promise of specific benefits to secure necessary help, they must still spend time making arguments and promotional pitches to persuade others of the worth of working with them. Like their counterparts in the marketplace, policy entrepreneurs must also seek help from others if they are to successfully introduce policy innovations. But for policy entrepreneurs the "product" to be delivered is policy change, something that—until implemented—remains essentially a set of ideas. Given this, policy entrepreneurs cannot enter into binding contracts or offer tangible inducements to those willing to support them in their political struggles. To organize others with the goal of securing policy change, policy entrepreneurs must rely entirely upon the making of persuasive arguments. Coalition building, then, can be viewed as primarily an act of bringing others to see the merit of a particular set of ideas.

In this chapter I discuss the ways that school choice policy entrepreneurs have created coalitions in pursuit of policy change. The chapter contains three parts. First, I report some general findings from my survey of members of the education policy community in each state. Then I discuss the argumentation and coalition-building efforts used by school choice policy entrepreneurs in Nebraska, Oregon, and Michigan. Finally, I discuss some of the implications this empirical work holds for thinking about the nature of policy entrepreneurship and policy change. While noting some general tendencies in the actions of the school choice policy entrepreneurs, I also note how sharp differences can be found, even in a fairly small group, whose members all have shared policy goals. The evidence in this chapter shows that policy entrepreneurs do not follow some kind of universal approach to coalition building. Perhaps this is to be expected. After all, entrepreneurs in the marketplace establish differing organizational forms depending upon their specific contexts, resources, and objectives. Therefore, we might expect entrepreneurs in the policymaking process to also form somewhat idiosyncratic coalitions of supporters, even in cases where the policy changes sought are identical. These distinctions, these idiosyncrasies, will emerge because of differences among policy entrepreneurs in their strengths and weaknesses and their operating contexts. As both strategic and creative individuals, policy entrepreneurs can be expected to make the most of the resources available to them.

Inevitably, because of differences among the groups and individuals they work with, policy entrepreneurs will now and then forge unexpected alliances, striving to establish organizational forms that are practicable and appropriate, given the operating environment. In light of this, it would seem misguided to go looking in every state for some fixed organizational form identifiable as a *school choice advocacy coalition*.[1] A potentially more fruitful approach—and one that could tell us more about the nature of contemporary politics—involves looking beneath observed relationships, with the goal of understanding why they emerged in the first place. This is the approach I have chosen.

Argumentation and Coalition Building: General Findings

Through my survey of members of the education policy community in each state, I learned of the presence of school choice policy entrepreneurs in twenty-six states. My survey contained a range of questions concerning the policy argumentation and coalition-building efforts of these policy entrepreneurs. The survey responses showed that policy entrepreneurs in twenty-one states produced policy advice for state legislators in which the implementation of school choice was advocated. Such action greatly improved the likelihood that school choice would receive legislative consideration.

Legislative consideration of school choice occurred in nineteen (90 percent) of the twenty-one states in which advice was given to legislators. In contrast, the idea was considered in three (60 percent) of the five states where policy entrepreneurs did not give direct advice ($\chi^2 = 2.9$, $df = 1$, $p < 0.09$). While adoption of school choice occurred in 48 percent of the cases where advice was given, compared with 20 percent of those where advice was not given, this difference is not statistically significant ($\chi^2 = 1.3$, $df = 1$, $p < 0.26$).

In nineteen states policy entrepreneurs wrote newspaper articles or op-ed pieces advocating school choice as a policy innovation, although such action did not appear to affect the likelihood that school choice would be considered or adopted by the state legislature. In addition to taking action of this sort to draw attention to the idea of school choice, policy entrepreneurs in eighteen states were reported either to have attempted to build a coalition or to have used an established education-related coalition to help promote it. Yet the coalition-building activities of school choice entrepreneurs, taken in isolation, do not serve as good predictors of success in gaining legislative consideration or adoption of school choice. As it happens, coalition building was somewhat more prevalent among *un*successful than among successful policy entrepreneurs.

Legislative consideration of school choice occurred in fourteen (78 percent) of the eighteen states in which policy entrepreneurs formed coalitions. In contrast, the idea was considered in all of the eight states where policy entrepreneurs were present but coalitions were not formed ($\chi^2 = 2.1$, $df = 1$, $p < 0.15$). Legislative adoption of school choice occurred in seven (39 percent) of the states with coalitions, compared with four (50 percent) of those where coalitions were not formed ($\chi^2 = 0.3$, $df = 1$, $p < 0.60$). In follow-up interviews with some of the school choice policy entrepreneurs identified in the survey, I found a tendency for coalitions to be used where initial overtures to legislators and the education policy elite had proved unproductive. At first consideration then, the evidence might suggest, "If at first you don't succeed, form a coalition." However, a closer inspection reveals instances where skilled policy entrepreneurs carefully developed coalitions, while also networking extensively in and around the state government and drawing attention to the idea of school choice in the local media. Coalition building might be most appropriately viewed as part of a broader set of efforts that policy entrepreneurs engage in as they pursue policy change. Such action can serve to draw greater attention to an issue, and signal to state legislators that a substantial group of people are committed to keeping the issue alive.

Problem Framing

In seeking support for their ideas policy entrepreneurs often engage in efforts to frame problems in particular ways. As I mentioned in chapter 5, the mechanics of framing involve both the careful choice of language and the careful selection of the aspects of a problem to highlight. These actions are critical because of the socially constructed nature of policy problems and the extent to which skillful presentation of information shapes their meaning. To test the importance of problem framing for the rise of school choice as a policy idea, in the survey I asked: "How important was . . . framing problems with the state school system to make school choice seem an appealing alternative . . . for the school choice policy entrepreneurs in your state?" The respondents could answer using a scale ranging from 1 ("not important") to 5 ("very important"). The mean response was 4, and 69 percent of the entrepreneurs were given a score of either 4 or 5. Framing was clearly an important strategy. The mean level of importance for entrepreneurs who succeeded in gaining legislative adoption of school choice (4.3) is slightly higher than for those who did not (3.7), although this difference is not statistically significant.[2]

Developing Coalitions

In one survey question, I suggested some possible ways that policy entrepreneurs could develop coalitions, and, where possible, I provided specific examples of particular kinds of school choice coalitions operating in the nation's states.[3] I then asked what sort of coalitions had been developed and used by the named school choice policy entrepreneurs in each state. I also asked whether the policy entrepreneurs had used an established education-related coalition to advocate school choice. In the responses, coalitions of concerned citizens were mentioned most often. Such coalitions were created in nine out of the eighteen states where policy entrepreneurs had established coalitions. None of these coalitions were developed from established education-related coalitions. Rather, the policy entrepreneurs involved showed considerable resourcefulness in building grass-roots support. Compared with their counterparts in other states, these policy entrepreneurs made special efforts to present the problems with the school systems in their states in ways that led to a realignment of interests. On a scale ranging from 1 ("not important") to 5 ("very important"), the policy entrepreneurs who had established a coalition of concerned citizens received a mean score of 4 for the importance of making arguments to support coalition building, compared with a mean score of 2.5 for the other policy entrepreneurs identified in the study ($F = 9.65$, $df = 1.24$, $p < 0.01$).[4] Thus, the content and persuasiveness of the arguments made by school choice policy entrepreneurs appear to have significantly affected their ability to build coalitions of supporters.

Among coalition-building efforts, establishing private-business coalitions was another fairly common strategy for the policy entrepreneurs. In six states, such coalitions were used to promote the school choice idea. Typically, these coalitions were built where no such organization had existed before. In only one case was a business coalition for school choice formed out of a coalition that had been previously created to pursue education-related policy change. The primary distinguishing feature of the policy entrepreneurs who established private business coalitions is that they were effective at developing and maintaining good relations with private business groups. On a scale ranging from 1 ("not effective") to 5 ("very effective") in working with businesses, the entrepreneurs who established private-business coalitions received a mean score of 4.3, compared with a mean score of 3.2 for the other entrepreneurs ($F = 5.65$, $df = 1.24$, $p < 0.03$).[5]

Working to Advantage and Building Support

A particular pattern can be detected in the actions of the policy entrepreneurs who established coalitions of concerned citizens and business coalitions. That is, these policy entrepreneurs appear to have based their choices of the types of coalitions they would build on an assessment of their present stock of skills and contacts. They established coalitions that made the best possible use of their talents and relationships. This action is consistent with the view that policy entrepreneurs, like other political actors, must think carefully about how to allocate scarce resources. In interviews with a subset of the school choice policy entrepreneurs I found additional support for this claim. For example, Jackie Ducote in Louisiana noted that the organization she worked for, the Louisiana Association of Business and Industry (LABI), had for many years identified education as a priority area in which to contribute to policy debates. Ducote said that LABI had initially sought legislative action on school choice through lobbying state legislators. However, this had not been particularly fruitful. According to Ducote, she saw a need to expand the coalition beyond its business base. Thus, she observed that, "quite honestly, having a conservative business group leading these efforts is not the ideal." I asked Ducote what groups she believed would be most useful in expanding the coalition, and she replied that her priority was to organize parents in private schools and minorities. Thus, we might conclude that policy entrepreneurs often start their coalition-building efforts by working with a nucleus of supporters whom they know fairly well and whom they believe they can rely upon. From there they seek to expand their support base, beginning with those whom they see as "natural allies" in particular policy battles.

Maintaining the Coalitions

Often coalitions are made up of individuals and groups who, while they may share a policy goal, have a variety of interests and agendas, some of which may be in conflict. Policy entrepreneurs have to be aware of the potential for conflict here as they work with various individuals and groups to maintain their coalitions. Politicians and policy advocates use a variety of techniques to keep their coalitions together, and the literature on collective action has documented some of these strategies.[6] In my survey I listed several common techniques and asked if the policy entrepreneurs used any of them. By far the most important technique that the policy entrepreneurs used involved stressing public policy goals. On a 5-point scale ranging from 1 ("not important") to 5 ("very important"), this technique was given a mean score of 4.1. This result is consistent with the finding that in twenty-one of the twenty-six states where school choice policy entrepreneurs were identified, the entrepreneurs provided policy advice directly to legislators. So not only did the policy entrepreneurs attempt in the first instance to persuade legislators with ideas, but they also attempted to use the power of ideas to win and keep supporters. Eventually, having a stable coalition of supporters could help policy entrepreneurs to demonstrate to legislators that their ideas held popular appeal.

Providing information to coalition members through such devices as newsletters was at least moderately important (i.e., given a score of 3 or more) in eleven out of the nineteen states where coalitions were established. The mean score was 3.3. In telephone conversations, several school choice policy entrepreneurs told me of the importance they placed upon developing a newsletter or just getting out and talking to people. As David Kirkpatrick of Pennsylvania told me: "It's not so much a matter of convincing people. It's a matter . . . of trying to reach everybody. . . . If I go out and speak to a group, I have very great success. Because once people start to think about this it makes a great deal of sense to them."

Talking directly with various groups helped policy entrepreneurs to win their support. In addition, it helped to keep supporters in the coalition. Since time and budget constraints prohibited the policy entrepreneurs from talking with individuals and groups as frequently as they would have liked, newsletters provided a cost-effective way of staying in contact.

None of the school choice policy entrepreneurs identified in the survey relied on the provision of private benefits with a pecuniary aspect to keep their coalitions together. More indirect personal benefits do not appear to have been important either. I asked how important possible professional or personal payoffs from being part of a successful coalition might have been for keeping the coalition together. In this case, the mean score was 2.3. Admittedly, sometimes the potential gains from belonging to a successful coalition did appear to be important. This is confirmed by anecdotal evidence. One policy entrepreneur told me that after he established a strong coalition for school choice, gubernatorial candidates representing a variety of political parties showed interest in identifying with it.

Overwhelmingly, nonpecuniary private benefits were more important for keeping the coalitions together than other possible benefits. A technique that was at least moderately important involved making coalition members feel as though they were part of a team that was trying to accomplish an important job for the state. On the 5-point importance scale, this technique received a mean score of 3.7. Placing stress on friendships was also important. In twelve of the states where coalitions were established this technique was rated at least moderately important.

Summary of General Findings

The evidence presented here reinforces the point that talk and argumentation are the very stuff of politics and coalition building. For this reason, the critical determinants of legislative consideration and adoption of school choice appear to have been the strength of the arguments made by the policy entrepreneurs and the number of influential people to whom those arguments could be presented. Policy entrepreneurs successfully raised the issue of school choice when they framed problems with the state school system in a way that showed legislators why school choice should be taken seriously. An effective way to do this was through providing policy advice directly to legislators. Some policy entrepreneurs worked hard to establish the credibility of this advice through operating out of policy think tanks, or by taking time to ensure that the proposals and the arguments they used to promote them were intellectually coherent.

Coalition building was not always considered a necessary strategy for the school choice policy entrepreneurs. If they could do without developing a coalition, the policy entrepreneurs often did. This makes sense in terms of conserving time and energy: building and maintaining coalitions is demanding work. For those who persevered with coalition building the task was frequently difficult, but it could also be rewarding. The "glue" that held these coalitions together consisted mainly of shared views concerning policy goals and how those goals could be achieved. Simply keeping in touch with coalition members was important for maintaining a collective sense of purpose.

These general findings take us some distance toward understanding how policy entrepreneurs actually go about getting their ideas for policy innovation into the public domain and securing legislative interest. But the primary value of survey-based inquiry lies in its ability to reveal broad tendencies in social and political behavior and to answer *when* and *what* questions. In terms of providing answers to questions of *why* and *how*, such inquiry can never really take us beyond the level of superficiality. Yet, to further develop our understanding of how policy entrepreneurs can prompt policy change, we need to find out why those seeking the introduction of school choice used the strategies that they did and how they implemented them. With this goal in mind I interviewed several school choice entrepreneurs, asking them to reflect upon and explain the approaches they took to making policy arguments and to coalition building.

Argumentation and Coalition Building: Three Cases

Here I report and discuss what I learned from talking with three school choice policy entrepreneurs. The interviews were semistructured in nature. That is, I had a set of questions that I used as prompts, with the goal of learning how the policy entrepreneurs engaged in policy argumentation and coalition building. With the consent of the three individuals the conversations were taped. I have chosen to present these particular cases for two main reasons. First, these policy entrepreneurs were unusually candid and articulate when it came to discussing their actions and the intentions behind them. Second, their individual stories are all quite distinct from one another. State Senator Dennis Baack from Nebraska found that he was able to realize his goal of having school choice adopted by his fellow legislators without building a coalition of supporters outside the legislative process. His comments tell us a great deal about why, as E. E. Schattschneider noted, "Conflicts are frequently won or lost by the success that the contestants have in getting the audience involved in the fight or in excluding it, as the case may be" (1960, 4). Steve Buckstein, president of the Cascade Policy Institute, a libertarian think tank in Portland, Oregon, discussed his attempts in 1990 to build a coalition of supporters for a state ballot initiative creating school choice. Buckstein's comments illustrate the potential dangers to policy entrepreneurs of seeking to build coalitions among people who, while agreeing on one specific policy issue, might vehemently disagree on others. Finally, Paul DeWeese of Michigan explained the procedures he used to build TEACH Michigan, a grass-roots coalition that has supported a range of school choice approaches. DeWeese's comments serve to underscore some of the points made by William H. Riker (1986) and Bryan D. Jones (1994) in their discussions of the manipulation of issue dimensions and the packaging of issues. I do not present the stories of the three school choice policy entrepreneurs because they are representative. Clearly, the motives and actions of each of these policy entrepreneurs were distinct, and they were each operating in unique contexts. But listening to particular policy entrepreneurs reflect upon their own activities is a good way to gain fresh insights into the actual practice of policy entrepreneurship.

State Senator Dennis Baack in Nebraska

When the state legislature in Minnesota was deliberating the idea of school choice, State Senator Dennis Baack of Nebraska followed developments closely. For some years he had been interested in school choice as a policy innovation. In his view the one-to-one assignment of students to public schools made no sense when compared with the choices that people faced for selecting preschools and the choices that students could make about the colleges they would attend. Once Minnesota had adopted a school choice law, Baack decided it was time to prepare for a policy change in Nebraska as well. During his years in the legislature Baack had learned a lot about the nature of politics and, especially, education politics in his state. Earlier in his career he had worked with the Nebraska School Boards Association, and during that time he had come to understand the ways that it, and the Nebraska State Education Association, went about organizing their political activities. Baack anticipated that if he introduced a school choice bill in the legislature that it would take him four or five years to actually achieve policy change. "I figured it would take that much groundwork and working my way through the process to actually pass it." In fact, Baack greatly overestimated the necessary timeframe. He introduced his school choice bill in early 1989 and, by the end of May of that year, it had been adopted by his legislative colleagues and signed into law by Governor Kay A. Orr. "I was very surprised . . . my colleagues were very, very accepting of the idea." This overestimation of the time he needed to devote to this bill was probably the only miscalculation that Baack made as he worked on the school choice issue. Mostly he acted as a shrewd strategist. For example, Baack did not attempt to extend choice to include attendance at private schools because he knew that this would be declared unconstitutional in Nebraska. And he took great care to think of ways to accommodate the concerns of others without compromising his own policy goals. As a result, passage of school choice into law in Nebraska took a smooth course; in the end few people treated the idea with hostility. Even the teachers' union supported it.

In talking with Baack, I asked him what efforts he made toward coalition building before he introduced the bill. He responded:

> One of the things that I did . . . was that I wrote [the school choice bill] very quietly. And, actually, I did not tell many people that I was going to even introduce it. I actually didn't even let most of my colleagues know that I was going to introduce it until the day that I actually did. I felt it was one of those very dramatic kinds of changes that if I tried to involve a lot of organized school people, like administra-

> tors, or teachers, that there was no way I would ever get to first base with it. . . . So I didn't actually seek out allies. I simply introduced the bill. I did find some allies, though, after I introduced the bill.

Dennis Baack introduced the bill to the legislature's Education Committee after the Nebraska School Boards Association and the Nebraska State Education Association had held their annual meetings. Because those meetings had been held, he knew that these organizations would not have time to debate the bill among their members and thus they would not be able to launch concerted efforts to oppose it. As a result, the bill quickly met with approval by the Education Committee. It then went to the floor of the legislature, where it received thirty-seven votes of support and zero votes of opposition. This, however, was not the end of the matter. In Nebraska, bills have to go through three rounds of debate before the final vote is counted. To maintain support for the bill, Baack then took a number of steps to address the concerns of potential opponents, especially school board and teacher groups.

> I anticipated that both of those groups would probably really come out very strongly against it. And, I think, once I introduced it, one of the first things I did was make arrangements to sit down with . . . the leaders of both of those groups, and explain my thinking, and let them know exactly what I was trying to do with the bill, and I think that was very helpful from the very beginning. Because they had a very good concept going in, where I was going with it.

Dennis Baack also stated that "one of the things I said right from the very beginning was, 'if you can give me concepts that make this better, I'm more than willing to amend those in, or you can amend them into my bill. If it makes it better, I'm willing to do it.'"

Senator Baack wanted a significant change from the status quo in the level of choice, but teachers and administrators preferred moderate changes, if any at all. To win support for his proposal in the second and third rounds of debate, he agreed to add new dimensions to the bill, which were acceptable to all parties. This allowed him to win over his potential opponents and not have to compromise on his own policy goals. For example, one amendment that all parties agreed to was a provision that restricted students from competing in high school athletics for a full year if they chose to move to another school district. Teachers insisted that such a rule was essential for maintaining academic standards. Baack's willingness to accommodate the concerns of teachers about what they perceived as an important issue boosted their valuation of the bill relative to the status quo.[7] This strategy worked extremely well. In fact, the Nebraska State Education Association turned out to be a strong supporter of the bill. Baack said "they went on record supporting it, and I guess they've been trying to explain themselves to the national organization ever since."

In the subsequent rounds of debate in the state legislature Baack's school choice bill continued to receive support. However, by the final round, he was beginning to count votes, and by then some opposition to the bill had developed. This came primarily from rural school districts, where it was feared that school choice would lead to small schools being closed. But, to address this concern, Baack proposed that the school choice program be phased in over a period of several years: in the first year only 10 percent of students would be allowed to leave a district. This percentage was set to rise by 10 percent a year for two more years, and then there would be no cap. Actually no district ever reached the point where the cap could be invoked, but the phase-in concession helped to ward off potential opposition. In addition, and independently of Baack's actions, as the school choice issue in Nebraska began to receive broad publicity, staff members from the White House in Washington began making some calls to the state, reminding the governor and several members of the state legislature that President Bush was a school choice supporter. Baack believes that this might have kept opposition to the bill in abeyance—and strengthened the resolve of Governor Orr, a strong Republican, to sign the bill into law.

Steve Buckstein in Oregon

For many years now, the issue of school choice has gained considerable attention in Oregon. In 1990 the idea received limited attention in the state legislature. In 1991 the state adopted a fairly restrictive school choice law, as part of the much broader "Oregon Education Act for the 21st Century." Subsequently there has been continuing debate in the state over the introduction of charter schools. A charter school law was adopted, finally, in June 1999. In addition, various individuals in Oregon have developed plans to establish private voucher programs. The genesis of this statewide interest in school choice issues in Oregon can be attributed in large part to the ideas and actions of Steve Buckstein, president of the Cascade Policy Institute in Portland. Buckstein, a philosophical libertarian, and several friends had decided in 1989 to make school choice a ballot initiative in the 1990 election. The mechanism for achieving school choice was to be a tax credit for families who chose to send their children to private schools. But once it was on the ballot, the initiative was defeated by a ratio of two to one.

Buckstein says: "We knew that it was an uphill battle and we knew that there was a high probability that the measure would lose at the polls. But somebody had to do it. . . . And we felt it was time to start that discussion, and the best way to do it was putting an initiative on the ballot."

I asked Steve Buckstein why he did not choose to use the legislative approach to obtaining a school choice law. In response, he observed: "I'm sure that we could have gotten one legislator to introduce something, but we didn't feel it would go much further than that. And so we did have the ability, we believed, to gather signatures and put an initiative on the ballot, which we were sure would generate a lot of public discussion. Which happened."

In Buckstein's view, the state teachers' union, the Oregon Education Association, would have made sure that any school choice legislation would be blocked or seriously watered down. So, running a ballot initiative seemed a way to draw attention to the school choice idea without having to compromise on aspects of the proposal. Buckstein readily admits that, on looking back, the initiative probably could have been written in a way that would have attracted more support. Part of the difficulty he faced was figuring out the sort of language to include in the initiative that would, on the one hand, be politically viable and, on the other, be consistent with his position as a libertarian.

> At that point, probably our perfect, *practically* perfect choice scheme, would have been taking whatever amount of money was spent per child in Oregon at that time. I think it was in the range of $5,000. And basically giving that to every child in one form or another to go to any school of their choice. What we settled on was a $2,500 tax credit, basically half of . . . what was being spent per child in the public schools. Basically, on practical political grounds, that is, you could make a case that this would save the public schools money if a lot of kids left. . . . So it wouldn't take too many leaving, and taking just half

> the money with them, before the public school would be better off financially.

Buckstein said he did not try to make too much use of the argument that school choice was a way to address serious problems in Oregon's public schools. In fact, Buckstein said that he would still have promoted the idea of school choice if the present public school system was providing every child with a great education, simply because "people shouldn't be forced by government to do anything, within a broad range." So he wanted to emphasize the value of choice on its own merits. Buckstein also felt that when you try to promote school choice by denigrating the present system, you still lose "because if you're saying that there are all these problems, who should fix them but experts? And we were certainly not experts."

To get an initiative on the ballot in Oregon, over 89,000 signatures must be collected. Just to run a viable signature drive, Steve Buckstein knew that he would have to court some allies. He says: "The groups that we found that really wanted school choice, and didn't want the current system to deal with it, were the home-schooling people, the religious right, and probably that was it. . . . Even people that had their kids in private schools, just for educational reasons, did not like the idea of weakening the public school system."

As it turns out, school choice is one of just a few issues upon which libertarians like Buckstein and members of the Christian Right agree. The Oregon Citizen's Alliance (OCA), which is the most prominent group in the Christian Right in the state, has been very vocal in its advocacy of conservative positions. The points of disagreement between libertarians and members of the OCA include such issues as gay rights, abortion rights, and the advocacy of prayer in public schools. Libertarians believe that government should keep out of people's private lives; the Christian Right believes that government should play a significant role in regulating the social sphere according to a set of moral principles. But with respect to school choice, an alliance between political libertarians and the Christian Right seemed natural:

> Our view was that we didn't want to create a system that had any control over curriculum, for example, we thought that diversity and competition would lead to the best curriculum. . . . So we had no problem with writing an initiative that was silent on most of those issues. And

> they [the Christian Right] liked it because they knew what they wanted . . . for their kids to get an education.

In addition to attracting support from the Christian Right and from parents of children in private schools, Steve Buckstein attempted to obtain support from the leaders of the Catholic Church and from black community leaders from the United Front and the Rainbow Coalition in Portland. However, representatives of the Catholic Church took the view that the ballot initiative would be very unpopular and, in being seen to support it, they could damage their good relations with various members of the state legislature. For their part, black community leaders did not see school choice as the right mechanism for addressing problems with urban schools. They believed that the public schools their children were attending would not improve just because of competition and a few children leaving. (Incidentally, however, Buckstein found that even though the black leadership opposed the initiative, people sent out to collect signatures for the initiative in the black community found support for the initiative to be very high.)

Steve Buckstein said that he ended up developing a coalition that had a mailing list with 8,000 names on it, and these people gave money or expressed interest in the campaign for school choice. In total, 130,000 people signed the petition to get the initiative on the November 1990 ballot. Once school choice was on the ballot, the coalition that Buckstein developed began to fund television advertisements and deliver flyers in support of it. But at this stage in the campaign, differences between the goals of the political libertarians and the members of the OCA began to interact in ways that did damage to the school choice initiative. Buckstein picks up the story:

> In that same election there were two measures on the ballot to restrict abortion. One of which [the OCA] put on the ballot and one of which a more moderate group put on the ballot. And the OCA was going door to door during the campaign, putting out our literature for school choice and their literature against abortion. And we told them, in the strongest possible terms, that we thought that was a bad political decision. And we're sure it lost us more votes than it gained, because we'd have calls to our office just incensed. . . . They said that they would never vote for school choice because of the antiabortion literature that they were receiving at the same time.

This story demonstrates the difficulty that a policy entrepreneur can face in choosing coalition partners. Of course, in terms of distributing political literature, the OCA lent the coalition an important helping hand. But citizens do not always make the kind of rational separation of issues that would have saved this situation. As T. S. Eliot observed, and as savvy advertising people have long known: "There is a logic of the imagination as well as a logic of concepts."[8] Often this can be used by politicians to great advantage, as when issues are redefined in ways that lead former adversaries to believe that they share common interests.[9] But the very same logic of the imagination that might give advantage to a politician who introduces a new dimension into a debate can also prove deadly. When done unwittingly, as when school choice was "packaged" with the emotion-charged abortion issue, introducing a new dimension into a debate can quickly turn allies into adversaries. Even so, it is not entirely clear that this situation could have been avoided without creating other kinds of conflicts in the coalition. This suggests that making careful choices about coalition partners is vital. As one politician campaigning in Oregon for election to the U.S. Congress in 1994 said of the OCA, "People who want to help you—it's not necessarily smart to spit in their face. . . . But it may reach a point where I might just ask them to stay out of my race."[10]

I asked Buckstein to comment on developments in his state following the demise of the ballot initiative. Among other things, he said: "[People in] the public school system are talking about public school choice. In my view, to deflect any discussion of private school choice. They say they're all in favor of working out ways to let kids choose public schools. But, in reality, there has not been much done about it."

Steve Buckstein's efforts in Oregon were successful to the extent that they drew attention to the issue of school choice and to his particular vision of how school choice plans should work. At present the state offers some public school choice, and the concept has continued to attract serious attention over the past few years. Still, the question remains whether school choice might have gained broader acceptance in the state if the development of the coalition in 1990 had been more carefully orchestrated.

Paul DeWeese in Michigan

As noted in chapter 2, Paul DeWeese, an emergency room physician, has played an important role in bringing prominence to the idea of school choice in Michigan. His major contribution has been to develop a broad-based coalition called TEACH Michigan to support the adoption of school choice. Initially, DeWeese saw the development of a coalition of this sort as vital for securing a change to the Michigan constitution to allow state money to fund private schools, including religious schools. A ballot initiative of this sort is yet to occur, but other school choice policies have been adopted in the state, and the presence of TEACH Michigan has affected debate over those policies. In conversations with DeWeese, I asked him about the strategies that he used to develop this coalition.

Before organizing TEACH Michigan, Paul DeWeese had talked to many people. The most important people he approached were those he anticipated to be his opponents: representatives of the teachers' unions and various other stakeholders in the public education system. "I targeted people that I thought might be the opposition, because I wanted to find out what they were thinking, what their arguments were." DeWeese found that opponents of school choice "have always . . . tried to cloak themselves in the kind of mom, apple pie, and the American flag kind of thing. And . . . they accuse people who raise these kinds of things [e.g., school choice] as being racist, or elitist, or underminers of public education."

Based on what he learned from his opponents, DeWeese aimed to build a coalition of actors who could be used to counteract these arguments. First, he wanted support from the corporate community because he saw it as having a sort of independent credibility. He also knew that the corporate community had the financial resources needed to underwrite his efforts. Second, he sought the support of others with political credibility, such as local mayors, who had important symbolic positions. Third, he reached out to ethnic minorities and to leaders in the black community, such as the Association of Black Pastors in Detroit. Finally, he worked with organizations representing the interests of private schools.

DeWeese presented his ideas to these groups with specially tailored messages. For the Michigan corporate community, he emphasized competitiveness and economic development arguments:

> We talked . . . a lot about the fact that Ford . . . and Chrysler and General Motors became more competitive, they delivered a better quality product because people could choose a German automobile, or a British, or a Toyota. And they understood that intuitively. . . . So I could

> talk to them about choice. But the other thing the business community did seem to be very concerned about [was] . . . the fact that we have many people who are falling through the cracks in the system. And my argument was that if different schools could be created that would reach out in creative and sensitive ways to children . . . more of those children would stay in school . . . and they would become taxpaying, productive workers. . . .

For the private school groups, DeWeese placed the emphasis elsewhere: "All these private school parents were paying taxes and then they were paying tuition on top of that . . . the economic argument there was that these parents are tax-paying citizens and they ought not be treated as second-class citizens."

By contrast, the appeal he gave to black community leaders revolved around improving the quality of inner city schools. When asked why he used these different arguments for different groups, DeWeese replied: "People tend to come to these issues, they look at them and say, 'Well, why would I be supportive of this?' And unless you can engage them at where they are at in their own lives, in terms of something that would interest them and have an incentive for them to be interested . . . they tend to lose interest, you know, they're not going to be supportive."

Using appropriate "subthemes" was an important part of Paul DeWeese's coalition-building strategy.[11] However, telling target groups what they want to hear is not enough to build a viable coalition. DeWeese noted the difficulty of using multiple appeals to sell the same proposal: if it is not done carefully, such a strategy can be perceived as manipulative doublespeak. Rather than hiding the fact that he was using different themes with different groups, he worked hard to get potential coalition members to tolerate parts of his proposal that they did not like. DeWeese described to me his strategy for addressing these concerns: "So what I would come back and say is 'Look, we need *this* in there in order to get what *you* believe in. And this is going to help immunize us from the attacks that we're going to get.'" He continued,

> If they can see that the whole thrust of what you're doing . . . is beneficial, then they are willing to accept parts and whole subsections that they wouldn't approve of in and of themselves. But they understand

> that there is compromise. . . . If, by and large, what you're getting is a significant improvement over what you have right now, then . . . they will be willing to embrace it.

Often in politics, when individuals or groups significantly differ on how to change the status quo, it is best if they also differ on how they weigh the issues at stake. When this happens, each individual or group can potentially gain on the issues that they care relatively more about, and this can offset the concessions on other issues that they would rather not make. It seems that Paul DeWeese well understood this logrolling approach to coalition building. His use of multiple subthemes may be viewed as an attempt to induce coalition partners to weigh most heavily the gains they could receive from his proposal. These gains could then presumably overwhelm whatever concessions the partners were asked to make to other coalition members. Potential coalition partners must see the *overall* policy package as superior to the status quo, and DeWeese appears to have recognized that he would have to generate such an assessment.

With all the juggling of different positions that Paul DeWeese needed to engage in so as to build TEACH Michigan, we might wonder whether his own preferences for school choice were ever compromised. On this matter, DeWeese stated: "I don't think I've ever found myself actually promoting a concept that I don't believe in. But I have emphasized themes that I think are relevant to the audience that are not as immediately relevant to me, I guess." By playing up issues that he personally did not consider centrally important, DeWeese was able to extract more gains on those that were more important to him and to groups who share his assessment.

Through his efforts at coalition building Paul DeWeese created a strong and coherent political force to support school choice initiatives in Michigan. Once TEACH Michigan was established, DeWeese said that it became an important resource, allowing him and other proponents of school choice to gain insights into how various groups in the community were thinking about the issues. The coalition also served as a powerful means by which DeWeese and other supporters of school choice in Michigan—including Governor John Engler and a number of legislators and senators—could convince other elected officials that their ideas enjoyed strong grass-roots and business support.

Summary of the Cases

The policy entrepreneurs discussed here each held specific views concerning the sort of policy changes they wanted to secure. They all recognized, however, that they would have to assert their ideas for policy change in the public domain and that inevitably they would face strong opposition from supporters of the status quo. The actions of the three policy entrepreneurs, however, each represent different approaches to dealing with opposition. Dennis Baack in Nebraska decided to introduce his policy proposal at a time when opportunities for the rallying of oppositional forces were restricted. He also took great care to explain his position to potential opponents and let them know that he was willing to make changes to his school choice bill that would address their concerns. Steve Buckstein in Oregon attempted to avoid the need to compromise with opponents by circumventing the legislative process altogether. His desire to avoid compromises allowed him to propose a form of school choice reflective of his own philosophical position. But all political action involves making concessions of one sort or another, and Buckstein came to realize that. Paul DeWeese talked with opponents before building his coalition, and this helped him to determine whom he wanted to approach to join TEACH Michigan. DeWeese recognized that coalition building involves making compromises, but he worked carefully at developing his arguments so that compromise with any particular group became a two-way street.

These three cases suggest that to achieve success, policy entrepreneurs must have a solid grasp of the policy preferences and worldviews of both potential allies and potential opponents before they start promoting their ideas for policy innovation. Therefore, policy argumentation and coalition building can be greatly supported by networking efforts in and around government circles. The ability to think about a given policy proposal from the perspective of multiple groups, combined with the social dexterity needed to engage those groups in productive dialogue, can greatly increase the chances that a policy entrepreneur will achieve success.

Good arguments for particular policy ideas cannot be developed in isolation from the social and political context in which they will be introduced. This suggests that good arguments for policy change are not based on pure logic, but rather on a logic deliberately intended to exploit the frames of reference of the intended audiences. Pierre Bourdieu (1977, 109–113) terms argument of this sort, *economic* logic (that is, it *economizes* on the use of logic). We might say that policy entrepreneurs use economic logic as they strive to create arguments displaying a minimal, common-sense coherence. When Paul DeWeese used the car industry analogy to support his argument that school choice would create competition among schools and that this in turn would lead to higher quality schooling, he was using economic logic. It does not take much reflection to see just how limited and, in many ways, utterly flawed an argument is that compares car production with what goes on in schools. In terms of "logic's logic" (Bourdieu), an argument implying that schooling and car production are equivalent social and economic activities simply cannot be sustained.[12] But in terms of economic logic, using no more logic than is required by the needs of practice, the argument works well. DeWeese used it to advantage.

Implications

For entrepreneurs in the marketplace, success can be measured by the speed and magnitude by which demand for an innovative product grows over time. Having other people see how that product could be beneficial for them in their lives is critical for ensuring its acceptance. With time, new groups of purchasers might come to see how the product could benefit them. It might happen that eventually the product is used in ways that the entrepreneur never initially imagined. This has surely been the case for computer software developer Bill Gates of Microsoft. Over the past decade, increasing numbers of people in all walks of life have come to use Windows® software to support a vast range of activities. However, it is important to note that during this process of increasing market penetration of Windows® software, the product itself has been adjusted in various—typically incremental—ways to make it more acceptable to a broader range of users.

In this chapter, I have discussed the ways that school choice policy entrepreneurs have made use of argumentation and coalition building to create support for policy change. Parallels can be drawn between the actions of these individuals and those of entrepreneurs in the marketplace. In seeking to build support for school choice as a policy innovation, the policy entrepreneurs had to bring other people around to seeing the benefit of changing policy in a particular direction. The policy entrepreneurs worked hard at how they framed problems and they made considered efforts to reach out to the people who they believed would find their ideas acceptable. Just as innovations in the marketplace can change as they are developed, so we see how policy entrepreneurs were prepared to make adjustments to their policy proposals to capture the support of particular groups.

A key difference between the market and the policymaking process is that in the latter support for a policy innovation must be created even as it remains nothing but a set of ideas. The equivalent situation in the marketplace would be for entrepreneurs to canvass support for a new product, while making the proviso that it will only be delivered if sufficient numbers of people say that they will buy it. Clearly, if entrepreneurs in the marketplace had to work under these conditions, many innovations would never see the light of day. People often need to have actual access to a product before they can decide how much they like it. Because policy entrepreneurs must engage in this sort of conceptual selling of policy innovations, it is almost inevitable that they will have to make compromises to their proposals in seeking the support of other parties. This process can be full of traps for the unwitting. After all, the more open the policy entrepreneur is to making compromises, the greater the danger that the nature of the policy innovation will change so much that when it is finally adopted, it will bear little resemblance to the original. In light of this, policy entrepreneurs must have the good judgment to know when to make compromises as they choose coalition partners, and when to attempt to secure policy change without the support of any particular group. Rarely can issues like this be cleanly determined before a campaign for policy change is launched. Policy entrepreneurs must therefore have very good interpersonal skills in order to work successfully with others in ways that rapidly defuse potential conflicts. This is a tall order, but we do find policy entrepreneurs managing situations in this way, and in so doing they are able to improve the chances that their policy innovations will be adopted. In addition, through careful coalition building, it seems likely that policy entrepreneurs can occasionally build sufficient momentum to ensure that policy implementation occurs rapidly and meets with popular support.

In the present study, I lack sufficient longitudinal evidence to examine whether any relationship exists between the skill with which policy entrepreneurs build support for policy change and the extensiveness of subsequent policy implementation. Both the market analogy and studies of innovation diffusion and contagion effects strongly suggest that there should be some sort of positive relationship here. In the case of adoption of charter school laws during the 1990s, there have been considerable differences across states in the number of such schools permitted by the legislation. Often the limits imposed on the number of schools allowed by law have served as a barometer of the political will supporting this policy change. In Michigan, where the coalition supporting a charter schools law was very strong, a permissive law was adopted that placed no limits on the number of such schools that could be started.[13] A few years after the adoption of that law, it is obvious that much of the political momentum for the policy change in Michigan has served to energize the rapid growth of charter schools. And the advent of a thriving charter schools sector has subsequently encouraged the development in Michigan of much of the infrastructure necessary for supporting full privatization of public schooling. Obviously, there remains much to be researched concerning how the introduction of certain policy innovations can build momentum for broader forms of policy change.[14] Thinking in terms of policy entrepreneurship can be greatly illuminating when studying the development of political momentum for policy change and the antecedents of changes in broader policy settings.

Summary

In the literature on policymaking and policy change, scholars have often sought to explain why some policy ideas gain currency and acceptance while others do not. Here I have discussed how policy entrepreneurs used policy argumentation and coalition building to support their efforts to introduce school choice. Policy entrepreneurs can determine how to appropriately frame problems and present their ideas by taking the time to learn how others around them think about public policy issues. This suggests that there is no such thing as a universal way of acting that will beat all other approaches when it comes to engaging in policy entrepreneurship. The world of politics and policymaking is messy and multifaceted. Particular arguments and strategies used successfully in one time and place cannot be expected to necessarily yield success elsewhere.

Of course argumentation in and of itself has its limits. There are times when people want concrete evidence that proposals for policy innovation really will work as intended. In the next chapter, I discuss how policy entrepreneurs have augmented their efforts at policy argumentation and coalition building with the development of private voucher plans in cities across the United States. Before turning to that study, now is a useful time to reiterate that in highlighting any one strategy in these empirical studies, I do not mean to suggest that policy entrepreneurs could secure policy change by using it to the exclusion of all others. Maybe with good luck that could happen now and then. But policy entrepreneurship requires the use of multiple strategies in concert. I have treated these strategies separately in these empirical studies simply because that is the best way to sharpen the analytical focus and thus learn more about how specific activities contribute to broader efforts.

Notes

1. But this is precisely what Paul A. Sabatier (1988), the originator of the Advocacy Coalition Framework, would have us do. In much of their work, Sabatier and his colleagues make the claim that advocacy coalitions embody universal and immutable patterns of political behavior. Thus, for example, Sabatier (1993, 27) surmises: "On major controversies within a policy subsystem where core beliefs are in dispute, the lineup of allies and opponents tends to be rather stable over periods of a decade or so."

2. For the one-way ANOVA test of the differences in the means, $F = 2.10$, $df = 1.24$, $p < 0.16$. Perhaps because it was such a popular strategy among the school choice policy entrepreneurs, the use of problem framing had no effect on the likelihood of legislative consideration of the idea.

3. See question 8 of the survey, reproduced in the Appendix to this book.

4. An analysis of the responses to my question on the initial positions of various individuals and groups did not indicate that private school associations, parent groups, and the news media in the relevant states—groups we might expect to help build a coalition of concerned citizens—had any greater predisposition to support school choice than their counterparts in other states. Therefore, the choice of strategy on the part of the policy entrepreneurs appears to be independent of initial conditions in their states. (See question 6 in the survey questionnaire reproduced in the Appendix.)

5. A question of causation arises here. Were the policy entrepreneurs considered very effective at developing and maintaining relations with private business groups because they established a private business coalition, or did they choose to develop this sort of coalition because they had the appropriate contacts? My data do not allow me to establish the line of causation here. However, in the states where the policy entrepreneurs established a private business coalition, I do know that initial business group support for school choice was no greater than elsewhere.

6. See, for example, discussions in Olson (1965), Moe (1980), and Sandler (1992).

7. Incidentally, in the following year Baack repealed this provision of the law.

8. See Frank Kermode, ed., *Selected Prose of T. S. Eliot* (London: Faber and Faber, 1975), p. 77.

9. For a useful discussion of the use of such "heresthetics," see Riker (1986), especially chapter 4.

10. "In Oregon, Christian Right Raises Its Sights and Wins." *New York Times*, 18 July 1994, A10.

11. When asked whether he thought he would have obtained the same level of support without using such subthemes, he replied, "I don't think so. I really think that it's important to use those subthemes because who wouldn't be for a world-class education for every kid? You know what I mean? But if you can address how choice, how it's relevant . . . how my prescription to get a world-class education is relevant to these individual audiences, I think I found it useful and helpful."

12. Yes, choice and competition can yield many benefits. But consider the matter further. Because education is "produced" in a social setting, it matters a great deal why people (teachers, students, and parents) have come into that setting, what expectations they hold, and how committed they are to remaining there. Group dynamics can seriously affect outcomes. In contrast, the beneficial outcomes I receive from driving a Volkswagen are not affected at all by whether other customers purchased the car because of the intrinsic qualities it holds or because they sought to escape driving Fords or Chryslers. The benefits I receive from the car are not affected by the group dynamics created by other purchases of the same make or model. In schools that is very different, and this difference matters greatly for school culture. Having reflected on the car production analogy, I have noticed it being used quite frequently, even by apparently rational social scientists. In one of his many presentations given in support of school choice, in 1998 I heard Professor Paul Peterson of Harvard University use this very same car production argument to support his position. This suggests that we should be vigilant in ensuring that *economic logic* does not continue to mystify our understanding of public policy issues where the use of *logic's logic* is appropriate.

13. Limits were subsequently placed on the number of charter schools that could be authorized by state universities in Michigan.

14. Baumgartner and Jones (1993) discuss this issue in some depth.

TEN

Policy Demonstration Projects and School Choice

What policy entrepreneurs would most like to say when advocating policy change, is "I've seen the future and it works."[1] But to convince others of the validity of this claim, they must produce satisfactory supporting evidence. In this chapter I discuss the role that evidence plays when policy entrepreneurs make arguments for the adoption of policy innovations. I do this initially with reference to the evidence used by the policy entrepreneurs identified in my survey of members of state education policy communities. I then discuss the emergence of private voucher programs in cities across the United States during the 1990s, exploring how these local efforts relate to the state-level attempts to secure school choice that I have documented in previous chapters. Through this study of private voucher programs several matters become clear. First, initial efforts by policy entrepreneurs to develop these programs arose out of frustration with state-level policy activities. Recognizing the lack of interest in some state legislatures toward the idea of school choice, policy entrepreneurs decided to channel their energies into creating change at the local level. These efforts perfectly illustrate the entrepreneurial strategy that Frank R. Baumgartner and Bryan D. Jones (1993, 35) refer to as "venue shopping." Second, by offering clear incentives for poor parents and their children to sign up for financial assistance and—by association—join the school choice movement, private voucher programs effectively resolve the collective action problem as explicated by Mancur Olson (1965). Third, the apparent relationship between the creation of these local-level programs and policy activity at the state level suggests that a state-local nexus exists in policy innovation diffusion. Policy innovations such as school choice need not just be seen as flowing horizontally, from state to state. They can also be seen as flowing vertically, from the state level to the local level and vice versa. Finally, the rapidity with which private voucher programs have spread shows how an innovative idea, initially introduced by a particular entrepreneur in a particular place and time, can subsequently take on a life of its own. For the purpose of the broader argument of this book, the evidence presented here highlights the value of working with the concept of the policy entrepreneur. Absent an understanding of the actions of policy entrepreneurs, it is doubtful that we could even perceive coherent relationships among the many efforts now under way to promote school choice, let alone begin to explain those relationships in causal terms.

Policy Entrepreneurs and the Use of Evidence

To promote their ideas for policy innovation and get them onto legislative agendas, policy entrepreneurs often strive to provide high-quality information to decisionmakers. In aspiring to be agents of change, policy entrepreneurs need to both develop new policy ideas and find convincing ways to sell them. Politicians, being risk averse, face incentives to be skeptical of the information provided to them by these entrepreneurs, who themselves face incentives to "talk up" their ideas. To achieve a degree of credibility with politicians, policy entrepreneurs must find ways to demonstrate that their ideas are prudent.[2] All else being equal, the policy entrepreneurs most likely to successfully promote policy change are those who can demonstrate the workability of their ideas and convince politicians that if the ideas are implemented, they will yield greater social benefits than current policy settings. Of course, whether or not the given policy ideas will produce the purported benefits is always an open question. So much will depend upon the details of both the enacting legislation and the politics of implementation.[3]

Drawing attention to actual working examples of the policy innovations they seek to promote can prove extremely helpful for policy entrepreneurs. Frequently, the innovations they choose to discuss will be very different from the innovations that end up being adopted by the politicians in their jurisdictions. Nonetheless, by choosing their cases carefully and determining which elements to make salient in their presentations of the evidence to legislators, policy entrepreneurs can raise their chances of gaining influence in the policymaking process.

The Case of School Choice

The diffusion paths associated with each variant of school choice have been quite distinct. Open-enrollment and charter school initiatives have each swept across the states in somewhat different ways. Private voucher plans appear to have been spreading from city to city in a haphazard fashion. Meanwhile, public voucher plans are so few in number that to speak of a diffusion pattern would be inaccurate. But given all this apparent complexity, can any relationship be discerned in the emergence of these many school choice initiatives across the United States? On the basis of the extant innovation diffusion literature, we might argue that the timing of legislative consideration and adoption of open-enrollment plans and charter schools is a function of, among other things, the number of neighboring states that have considered or adopted the policy and various characteristics of the school system. But this type of explanation neglects to tell us precisely what the mechanism is by which the idea of school choice has come to be on state legislative agendas. In this respect, bringing the role of policy entrepreneurs to the fore can be illuminating.

In my survey of members of the education policy community in each state, I asked how important it was for the school choice policy entrepreneurs to collect evidence from other choice plans to demonstrate the merits of the idea. Collecting and presenting evidence of policy innovations elsewhere can be seen as one way that policy entrepreneurs attempt to improve their ability to convincingly sell their ideas. The respondents could answer on a 5-point scale where 1 meant "not important" and 5 meant "very important." This strategy was reported to be at least moderately important (i.e., to have a score of 3 or more) for 80 percent of the school choice policy entrepreneurs identified in the survey.

Of course, it is relatively easy for anybody to collect at least *some* evidence to help his or her case. Therefore, to test the extensiveness of the search for quality information on these school choice initiatives, I also asked how important it was for the policy entrepreneurs to network with school choice advocates from other states. Making efforts to network with policy entrepreneurs from elsewhere is a strong signal of interest in "borrowing" their ideas and learning from their strategies. Networking with school choice advocates from other states was reported as important for 65 percent of the school choice policy entrepreneurs identified in the survey. But perhaps more significantly, the difference in the importance of networking to the entrepreneurs who achieved state legislative consideration of their idea (3.1) and those who did not (1.7) was considerable ($F = 5$, $d.f. = 1.24$, $p < 0.03$). This evidence suggests that to make a strong and convincing case to state legislators, school choice policy entrepreneurs face strong incentives to collect sound evidence on how similar innovations have been developed elsewhere.

A question that flows from here concerns where exactly the policy entrepreneurs went to gather their evidence. The extant literature on policy innovation diffusion suggests that states simply follow other innovative states,[4] or follow the lead of their innovative neighbors.[5] My survey included an item designed to specifically explore where the state-level school choice policy entrepreneurs got their ideas from. It was worded as follows: "There have been many school choice experiments. Did any of them influence the entrepreneurs in your state?" Specific school choice plans elsewhere were influential on the thinking of 69 percent of the school choice policy entrepreneurs identified in the survey.[6] But what is important for this discussion is that these entrepreneurs reported to have been *more* influenced by three specific *local-level* plans (i.e., Alum Rock, East Harlem, Milwaukee) than by specific *state-level* plans (where Minnesota was most frequently mentioned). In percentage terms, 27 percent of the policy entrepreneurs who were advocating state-level school choice plans were influenced primarily by local-level plans elsewhere, 27 percent were influenced by both local-level and state-level plans elsewhere, and just 15 percent were influenced only by other state-level school choice plans. This evidence shows that policy innovations need not simply be diffused from state to state. Rather, in the case of school choice, to strengthen their appeals to state legislators the policy entrepreneurs identified in the survey frequently used evidence from local-level experiments (instead of evidence concerning legislative actions in other states). So, in a federal system policy innovation diffusion processes can be vertical as well as horizontal. In considering the actions of policy entrepreneurs and the incentives they face in developing plausible arguments for selling innovations to state legislators, at least in the case of school choice, a state-local nexus appears to exist. To further explore this relationship, I next consider the apparently haphazard city-to-city diffusion of private voucher demonstration projects during the 1990s.

The Emergence of Private Voucher Plans

Although the school choice idea has spread rapidly across the United States, some of its most ardent supporters have often characterized the policy outcomes as disappointing. For example, in 1990 John E. Chubb and Terry M. Moe noted that "most of the choice plans that get put into effect (or, for that matter, even gain serious attention) are grafted onto the traditional system and make only marginal changes to it. Choice becomes part of a big compromise among contending political powers" (1990, 208). In the years since that observation was made, many privately funded voucher programs have been started, and more are planned. What connection, if any, exists between these developments and the state-level activities surrounding the school choice idea?

The first privately funded voucher program was established in Indianapolis in the summer of 1991, and students began attending private schools with its assistance in the fall of that year. J. Patrick Rooney, chairman of the Golden Rule Insurance Company, devised and developed the program. This program allows children of low-income parents the opportunity to attend private schools of their choice by providing cash assistance that covers about half of the typical private school tuition costs. Even though Rooney avows that he sought to help the poor children of Indianapolis, he also saw the introduction of this plan as an important political move. In the months before taking this action, a group of corporate CEOs, operating under the name of Commit, had staged a well-publicized but ultimately unsuccessful bid to have Indiana legislators introduce a statewide school choice plan (for details, see chapter 6). The problems Commit ran into seem to have helped stimulate Rooney to develop his private voucher program. Regarding the genesis of his idea, Rooney has said: "When there was discussion in the newspaper . . . about legislation that was trying to be pushed in Indiana, I knew at the time the legislation didn't have a chance, and I said to our President [John M. Whelan of the Golden Rule Insurance Company], 'Why don't we do a privately funded program?'"[7] Rooney saw the development of the Choice Charitable Trust as a way to immediately address problems of social equity through giving people the ability to choose the schools they might attend. Thus, in announcing the project he said: "The wealthy have had choice in education for years. They can send their children to private schools or move to an area with schools to their liking. But low-income families are trapped with no other option." Yet Rooney has also observed this: "Of course . . . if this new competition encourages the public school system to improve, then the Choice program would be a very good investment for everyone."[8]

It is difficult to gauge how much political influence Rooney expected to achieve by setting up the Choice Charitable Trust. Several matters are clear, however. First, the members of the board of directors of the trust were carefully chosen to lay the foundations for a fairly broad-based coalition of school choice supporters. Board members included William Styring III, then vice-president of the Indiana Chamber of Commerce, who had many years of experience as a policy staffer in and around the state legislature, as well as a record of interest in education reform issues. His position in the Chamber of Commerce gave him excellent access to business leaders in the state, many of whom contributed to the Choice Charitable Trust. Carol D'Amico of the Hudson Institute, who had worked closely with the Commit CEOs in Indiana, was also a board member. She could serve to bring expert knowledge to the board and help with broader networking activities. Another strategically chosen board member was Bill Crawford, a black Democratic member of the Indiana General Assembly who represented a poor district in Indianapolis. Aside from bringing insider knowledge of Indiana state politics to the board, Crawford could bring a wealth of insights about the community that would benefit from the trust. Second, in the years since the trust was established, there have been several unsuccessful efforts in the Indiana legislature to adopt school choice laws that would make provision for vouchers to be used at private schools. Although unsuccessful, this legislative activity suggests that school choice was kept alive as an idea among state policymakers, and no doubt the sustained attention given to the trust activities contributed to this. Finally, as evidence of the desire for even broader influence, the Choice Charitable Trust has made a large number of media releases that have gained national attention, and Rooney has frequently spoken at national conferences about the merits of establishing private voucher programs.

Soon after the Choice Charitable Trust began operating in Indianapolis, James Leininger, the CEO of Kinetic Concepts, Inc., a major medical equipment manufacturer in San Antonio, Texas, read about it in an article in the *Wall Street Journal*. Upon doing so, Leininger decided to develop a similar program.[9] Here again, the plan was seen as important for sustaining a broader political agenda concerning school choice. Leininger wanted to create a private model to provide research data that could then be used to persuade legislators in Texas and elsewhere that school choice would improve academic scores and increase parental involvement in schools. With coordination from the Dallas-based Texas Public Policy Institute and the support of several private corporations, including the San Antonio Express News, in April 1992 the Children's Educational Opportunity (CEO) Foundation was launched. Since then, this program has provided tuition scholarships to children of poor families in San Antonio to attend private schools. In 1998, a business group led by Leininger provided the foundation with additional funding of $5 million per year for a decade. The intention behind this support was to give scholarships to any family seeking them in the whole of the 14,000-student Edgeworth School District in San Antonio.

As word spread of the private voucher programs in Indianapolis and San Antonio, staff members at the Texas Public Policy Institute found themselves providing a large amount of information and guidance to others interested in setting up such demonstration projects. To formalize this process, in 1994 the board of the institute created a national entity to lead the private voucher movement, called CEO America.[10] Originally operating out of Dallas, CEO America now operates out of Bentonville, Arkansas. Since its founding, CEO America has been led by Fritz Steiger, who was instrumental in turning James Leininger's ideas for a private voucher program in San Antonio into reality. In a recent statement on its history CEO America proclaimed:

> Two factors were behind the [Texas Public Policy Institute] Board's decision. The most important was the urgency to reach out to more parents of children trapped in failing public schools and giving them the opportunity to choose a better school. The other was rooted in the belief that the programs could be a *vehicle for revolutionary change* [emphasis added by author of this book]. The reason: they would be working models that would show politicians and government officials the clear benefits of school choice. Furthermore, each new program would create a small but vocal constituency of parents and business executives who understood and valued school choice and whose collec-

tive voice could do more to alter public perceptions than could be achieved by even the most massive public relations campaign.[11]

In the years since 1994 CEO America has encouraged the development of over thirty private voucher programs. To do this, the foundation has provided technical advice and financial support to individuals and groups interested in establishing such programs. These initiatives have been deliberately designed to advance broader public policy goals, as the following statement from the foundation makes clear.

> Experience has shown . . . that when confronted by the reality of parental choice, politicians have a hard time saying no to their constituents. Program directors and founders utilize their programs by encouraging parents to testify before committees and lobby their representatives. CEO America helps by identifying, collecting, and distributing these stories to the public in an effort to sway more public opinion in favor of educational choice.

The State-Local Nexus

The evidence presented here suggests that the first private voucher plans emerged because of frustration with the pace of moves toward school choice initiated at the state level. The policy entrepreneurs who initially developed local private voucher plans did so while expressing concern over lack of state legislature interest in the adoption of school choice plans.[12] But more systematic evidence also suggests that the policy entrepreneurs identified in my 1993 survey did a great deal in their states to create a climate of ideas that prompted others to develop privately funded voucher plans. Of twenty-seven demonstration programs in existence by June 1997, eighteen (67 percent) had emerged in states where my survey findings indicate a history of policy entrepreneurs advocating state-level legislative changes to bring about school choice. Further, the majority of those policy entrepreneurs I identified as working to obtain state-level adoption of school choice had, during the course of such work, called for some form of public voucher system.[13] I have traced close connection between the policy entrepreneurs identified through my 1993 survey and the founders of the private voucher programs in at least seven of the twenty states where the private voucher programs are now operating.

Where such personal connections are not apparent, however, it is clear that the work of the policy entrepreneurs identified in my survey helped set the school choice agenda in their respective states.

As those establishing the demonstration projects had hoped, they appear to have spurred further state legislative consideration of school choice plans. For instance, as of June 1997, establishment of fourteen (52 percent) of the local private voucher plans had been followed by state legislative adoption of charter school laws. According to responses from a more recent survey of members of state education policymaking communities conducted in 1997, I found that in the nine states where private voucher programs were in place before charter school laws were adopted, debate over education vouchers was reported to be an important impetus to the adoption of charter school laws in seven (78 percent). In contrast, in the seventeen other states that have adopted charter school laws, debate over education vouchers was reported to be important in only five (29 percent). These differences suggest that those policy entrepreneurs who have established private voucher programs have had an important influence on the nature of the school choice debate that has subsequently occurred in their state legislatures.

This analysis supports the claim that a coherent relationship exists between diverse efforts that are now under way to promote school choice. The analysis also supports the claim that policy entrepreneurs have used local demonstration projects as a way to prove to state legislators that voucher-style approaches to introducing school choice can and do work in their states. Thus, we find more support for the claim that an important nexus exists between state-level and local-level policy innovations. This is something that is not immediately obvious from perusal of the range of school choice plans now in operation. The nature of this nexus becomes clear, however, once we consider the state policymaking contexts, the incentives faced by policy entrepreneurs, and the sort of evidence that policy entrepreneurs find most valuable when proposing policy innovations to legislatures.

Demonstration Projects and Policy Entrepreneurship

The emergence of private voucher programs can tell us a great deal about the ways that creative policy entrepreneurs work to build increasing support for their ideas. In and of themselves, private voucher programs cannot transform public education. But to focus simply upon the local-level effects of the programs would be politically naive. When viewed as part of a broader, concerted strategy designed to make school choice a top agenda item in state legislatures across the country, the willingness of business groups to support these demonstration projects begins to make sense.

Gaining from Shifting Venues

During the 1990s, a considerable number of school choice policy entrepreneurs appear to have concluded that the marginal returns from investing time and energy in local plans will be higher than the returns that could be achieved from continuing to simply talk up ideas to state legislators. By developing these plans in their own states, school choice policy entrepreneurs have positioned themselves to demonstrate clearly to legislators that alternatives to current public school arrangements are workable. This serves to generate evidence about the merits of the approach, and this evidence could, in the future, be used to persuade state legislators to fund public voucher plans. Such an approach may be particularly important when constitutional change is required to bring about the kind of school choice plans that the policy entrepreneurs seek for their states. This observation is supported by policy entrepreneur Paul DeWeese's rationale for seeking the introduction of charter schools in Michigan. That is, DeWeese saw the value in going beyond "just making rational arguments and speeches" and "doing pilot programs or showing people what a choice system might look like, in an incremental kind of way, a nonthreatening kind of way." DeWeese considered that establishing actual, working examples of school choice would be the only way to convince enough people that fundamental policy change was a good idea and worthy of expansion by means of a change in the state constitution.

By working at the local level and using their own resources to support their voucher plans, policy entrepreneurs signal their commitment to school choice. It is one thing to come up with an idea, and even to support it by piecing together evidence from elsewhere of its merits. It is quite another thing to transform that idea into local action and ensure that it works as anticipated. Such action demonstrates to politicians that the policy entrepreneurs are serious in their commitment to the worth of their policy proposals. Also, the local plans help minimize the political risks associated with expanding the innovation, because many of the potential problems will have already been determined. Here we see evidence of how policy entrepreneurs are prepared to lead by example, to "put their money where their mouth is," and to show the merit of their ideas for policy change.

These immediate results of effecting a venue shift have other payoffs as well. In particular, the policy entrepreneurs involved can use these apparent acts of altruism to claim the moral high ground when debating with opponents of institutional reforms in the public school system. This evidence of local-level efforts to assist poor families can be used to suggest that these policy entrepreneurs are as deeply concerned about supporting the aspirations of poor children as educators and administrators in the public school system. The policy entrepreneurs transform themselves from being easy targets for those who would label them as ideologues to being people with a putative track record of concern for the disadvantaged that has been backed up with cash.

An additional benefit of establishing private voucher programs is that policy entrepreneurs see the immediate results of their efforts, which provide help to poor families seeking better educational opportunities for their children. Furthermore, the policy entrepreneurs achieve for themselves and their supporters an important morale booster because they see that their actions are having the effects desired.[14] (This has not been the case for many policy entrepreneurs who have devoted all their energies to arguing for school choice in state capitol buildings.) Along with this, by keeping their programs private these policy entrepreneurs have not had to make compromises, as has always been the case in the development of state-level school choice plans.[15] In fact, these private voucher plans come very close to doing precisely what Milton Friedman (1962) suggested that voucher plans should do.

A final benefit gained from this venue shift is that by developing fully workable, local-level initiatives, policy entrepreneurs suggest that the crucible of educational innovations has shifted from the state capital to the local level. This can serve as a strong goad to state legislators and their staffs to think more about policy innovations. As my discussion of the adoption of charter school laws indicates, this seems to have happened.

Resolving Collective-Action Problems

In establishing private voucher programs, policy entrepreneurs offer selective incentives to families to reveal their dissatisfaction with the public schools their children are currently attending. Clearly Fritz Steiger saw this, which is why the statement from CEO America notes that "each new program would create a small but vocal constituency of parents and business executives . . . whose collective voice could . . . alter public perceptions."[16] Those families that receive scholarships and who partially pay to send their children to private schools constitute new allies for policy entrepreneurs who wish to secure the adoption of broader school choice plans. Even when applicants for a voucher are unsuccessful, they nonetheless signal strong support for the idea that policymakers should be providing education alternatives to the traditional public school system. Thus, savvy policy entrepreneurs can "recruit" both scholarship recipients and nonrecipients into a coalition designed to lobby for the introduction of school choice as a policy innovation.

The efforts of school choice policy entrepreneurs to establish private voucher programs also signal a long-term commitment to securing broader policy change. The private voucher programs in place now are being heralded as representing the future of schooling. For the purposes of maintaining supporters for broader school choice initiatives, these programs provide a vivid representation of the end goal. They also demonstrate that policy entrepreneurs are capable of turning ideas into action, and this can be important for maintaining the commitment of supporters. The policy entrepreneurs who have established these voucher programs have also managed to attract increasing support from high-profile business leaders. To the extent that they continue to do this, they lend strong credibility to their claims that they enjoy the broad support of business. State politicians, ever wary of listening to the wisdom of the corporate community, will no doubt see these emerging coalitions of supporters for school choice as worthy of a serious hearing.

Spurring the Diffusion of School Choice as a Policy Innovation

Overall, the evidence I have presented here and the arguments I have made suggest that the emergence of local-level private voucher plans in the 1990s and the efforts to get state legislative support for school choice, which began in the 1980s, are not independent. Rather, various school choice policy entrepreneurs, either as a result of frustration with the pace of changes at the state level or as part of longer term efforts to win state-level adoption of comprehensive (instead of piecemeal) school choice plans, have turned to developing demonstration projects at the local level. So, the emergence of demonstration projects can be seen as a vital means by which policy entrepreneurs have kept the idea of school choice on the public policy agenda. But this particular strategy also holds considerable risks for those who see it as a springboard for achieving fundamental change of the public education system in their states or in the nation as a whole. First, these plans are expensive: by spring 1999 over $250 million dollars had been spent on them. Given their expense, it is not clear that the funding will continue into the future if these efforts are only to affect the children enrolled in the plans. Second, the efforts are limited. They cannot affect a lot of children, because the amounts of private funding that can be raised and expended are not inexhaustible. Therefore, cynics might see these plans as excellent ways to divert the attention of school choice policy entrepreneurs into something that is meaningful but, ultimately, no threat to the public education system. Finally, those who establish demonstration projects always run the risk that the outcomes might fail to live up to expectations. If demonstration projects have unforeseen problems, they might actually make it harder for policy entrepreneurs to argue for their expansion. To date, whether or not private voucher plans are producing positive results for the students within them remains a hotly debated matter.[17]

Throughout the literature on policy innovation diffusion, various statements can be found that corroborate the importance of particular individuals in the diffusion process. However, scholars working in this tradition have made little effort to model how specific political actors might influence policy innovation and innovation diffusion. The evidence presented in this chapter serves to underscore the important role that motivated individuals can play as conduits for the spread of ideas for policy innovation. The evidence also shows how ideas, once they have achieved sufficient exposure to capture the imagination of others, can come to take on something of a life of their own. It is increasingly difficult to trace back from a given private voucher program to figure out the policy entrepreneur behind it, but that is true of many innovations, be they in the marketplace or in the world of politics. Without the initial actions of the Commit CEOs in Indiana and their failed attempts at securing policy change, it might have taken many more years before people came up with the idea of promoting school choice through private voucher programs.

Summary

Arguments for policy change can be made in a variety of ways. Now and then—with careful reasoning, a fairly accepting audience, and some good luck—policy entrepreneurs can achieve success without too much effort. However, since policy change, by definition, implies upsetting the status quo, it is much more common to find policy entrepreneurs having to work extremely hard to have their ideas taken seriously. In this chapter I have discussed how policy entrepreneurs have come to develop private voucher programs. On first consideration we might wonder what all the fuss is about. After all, such programs allow but a small number of poor families to choose the schools their children will attend. These programs are not ends in themselves, however: they represent an innovative means by which policy entrepreneurs can generate convincing evidence to support their calls for wide-scale introduction of school choice. These programs also serve to keep the media—and hence the public—focused on school choice issues. They also represent a powerful means for policy entrepreneurs to establish cohesive and long-lived coalitions of supporters who, when necessary, can aid them in their efforts to convince state legislators and voters that school choice is an idea whose time has come.

To date, these demonstration projects appear to have kept school choice on the political agenda in many states. But they have not led so far to any state adopting a full-blown voucher program. Such a policy change would essentially signal the end of public schooling as we know it. Increasingly, many scholars and pundits have come to believe that such a scenario is inevitable. Private voucher programs can be credited with contributing to the development of this general climate that supports the creation of broader school choice initiatives. Together with open-enrollment programs and the growing number of charter schools across the country, year by year, private voucher programs are bringing more and more people around to supporting school choice as a policy innovation.

Notes

1. The first use of this statement is attributed to newspaperman Lincoln Steffens, who said it in enthusiastic reference to socialist forms of production. See Lincoln Steffens, *The Letters of Lincoln Steffens* (New York: Harcourt, Brace and Company, 1938). Letter to Marie Howe, 3 April 1919.

2. In the language of game theory, to gain access to politicians and to maintain credibility among them, policy entrepreneurs must send costly signals that distinguish them from other providers of policy advice. For elaboration of this point see Ainsworth (1993).

3. For relevant discussions, see Moe (1990) and Pressman and Wildavsky (1973).

4. See Walker (1969) and Gray (1973).

5. See Berry and Berry (1990, 1992).

6. Sometimes respondents said that no particular school choice plan had been influential, but that books or media stories had alerted them to the school choice idea. For instance, Chubb and Moe's (1990) book, *Politics, Markets, and America's Schools* was sometimes said to have increased interest in the idea among state-level actors.

7. From transcript of tape from CEO America's conference, "Private Voucher Founders Speak Out," Orlando, Fla., 11 March 1995.

8. The Choice Trust press release, 11 May 1992.

9. For more background on the development of the San Antonio program and an analysis of its effects, see Martinez, Godwin, and Kemerer (1995).

10. This information was provided by CEO America.

11. CEO America Web site, http://www.ceoamerica.org.

12. Direct evidence of this linkage is provided in a statement by Senator Richard Posthumus of Michigan. Posthumus was a key player in establishing the Vandenberg Foundation in Michigan that supports the CEO Michigan programs in Detroit and Grand Rapids. He has said that he started this foundation "largely out of the frustration that I ran into as a legislator trying to make Michigan a place where kids could choose the schools that they went to with their parents." Transcript note from "Private Voucher Founders Speak Out," tape of the proceedings of the CEO America Conference, Orlando, Fla., 11 March 1995.

13. That goal, however, has never been realized through state legislative plans, except in the limited case of the Milwaukee plan in Wisconsin, the Cleveland plan in Ohio, and the mechanism for dealing with failing schools in Florida.

14. J. Patrick Rooney said in 1995: "You know, organizations . . . get tapped all the time for money. In terms of all the other things we can do with our money we are getting more bang with our employees out of what we did for these low-income children than anything else we do. . . . There is nothing in the world that we could have done that would create the enthusiasm from our employees as the gift for these low-income children." Transcript of tape from CEO America's conference, "Private Voucher Founders Speak Out," Orlando, Fla., 11 March 1995.

15. Terry Moe (1995, 32) notes: "Thanks to the private voucher movement, there are suddenly a great many voucher systems in operation. These systems, moreover, are based on simple program designs, free of the bureaucratic and political constraints that, in the public sector, have inhibited the operation of choice and made the study of its effects exceedingly difficult and confusing."

16. CEO America Web site, http://www.ceoamerica.org.

17. Paul Peterson has been engaged in a number of studies of these programs, and his research findings have provoked a variety of responses ranging from highly positive to highly negative. See Viadero (1998).

ELEVEN

Policy Entrepreneurs and Policy Change

In the preceding chapters I developed a theory of policy entrepreneurship and then considered how policy entrepreneurs have promoted the idea of school choice in the United States. The term "policy entrepreneur" is increasingly used by scholars interested in explaining instances of policymaking and policy change. Yet the term is often used loosely. Chapters 1 and 2 contained arguments justifying the need for more theorizing about the role that policy entrepreneurs play in prompting policy change. If we are to get beyond using the term policy entrepreneur as a poorly defined figure of speech, then we need to think seriously about the extent to which actors in the policymaking process can be thought of as counterparts to entrepreneurs in the marketplace. With that as the goal, chapters 3 and 4 reviewed the role that entrepreneurs play in the marketplace and the various activities that entrepreneurship entails. Building upon this foundation, chapter 5 presented my theory of policy entrepreneurship, where theory construction is undertaken with explicit reference to what we know about entrepreneurship in the marketplace. The discussion in chapter 5 suggested what we might expect policy entrepreneurs to do in practice. Chapters 6 through 10 presented empirical studies of policy entrepreneurship. I explored the actual behaviors of individuals identified as school choice policy entrepreneurs by knowledgeable participants in state education policy communities. With these theoretical and empirical investigations completed, in this final chapter

I draw out and discuss several matters that, while implicit in the preceding material, deserve more explicit treatment.

This chapter contains four main sections. First, I pick up the core argument of the book, that policy entrepreneurs serve to promote policy innovations that can herald significant policy change. I do this by revisiting the six keys to policy entrepreneurship that I initially introduced in chapter 2 and that I elaborated upon at the end of chapter 5. Here, I reflect upon these elements of policy entrepreneurship in light of material presented in the preceding empirical studies. Coming out of this dialogue of theory and empirical investigation, I next consider the linkages that exist between my understanding of how policy entrepreneurs promote policy change and the explanations of policy change that other scholars have offered. Although my work on policy entrepreneurship makes a unique contribution to our understanding of the policymaking process, it should be treated as a complement to—rather than a substitute for—other approaches. Thus, I take some time to explore the points of convergence and divergence between the theory of policy entrepreneurship and the alternate explanations of policy change originally reviewed in chapter 2. Following this examination of linkages among theories, I discuss the things that remain: Why it is essential that we think about policy entrepreneurs when thinking about policy change. Finally, I draw lessons for the practice of policy entrepreneurship. Much could be said about the implications this study holds for those who, in one way or another, aspire to be policy entrepreneurs. Here, rather than being comprehensive, I distill and discuss several matters with the intention of simply making suggestions and being a little provocative.

Keys to Policy Entrepreneurship Revisited

Whether practiced in the marketplace or in the realm of politics and policymaking, entrepreneurship calls for a range of skills, all of which have decidedly social aspects to them. Theoretical discussions of entrepreneurship serve to draw our attention to these requisite skills. Empirical explorations, while initially guided by theory, provide further insights and suggest both caveats and extensions to our theoretically grounded expectations. In this book I have argued that policy entrepreneurs seek to introduce policy innovations. If adopted by policymakers, these innovations can subsequently generate changes in policy that mark a break with the past. In turn, these changes can lead individuals and groups in society to act in new ways and to establish new habits of thought that reinforce their adjusted behavior.

Securing significant policy change is almost always a difficult task, and for good reason. Current public policy settings permeate and affect our lives in numerous ways. In fact, the reach of government is so long and pervasive that we often become blind to the ways in which it affects us. (Of course, we are not just blind to the effects of public policy. While there is much about contemporary life that is affected in significant ways by market processes, the actions of corporations, and by social norms, typically we do not reflect upon or question these influences.) The benefit we derive from this learned blindness is that it makes it all the easier for us to get through life, conserving our critical faculties for pressing decisions of the moment. Yet, to the extent that we take public policy settings and many other organizational aspects of life for granted, we also risk the possibility of growing complacent, of letting things slide in ways that can be counterproductive. Like other interested and engaged members of society, policy entrepreneurs pay close attention to the ways that government policies affect our lives. They think deeply about policy issues and contemplate how policy settings could be changed in ways that they believe would be socially beneficial. But policy entrepreneurs do more than simply observe and ponder: they take action with the goal of prompting the changes they would like to see. This requires them to go to considerable lengths to persuade others that change is both possible and necessary.

The policy entrepreneurs I have introduced and whose actions I have analyzed have all sought to introduce school choice in the United States. Skeptics—and those who would like to see more radical policy change than has occurred so far—might dismiss the efforts of these policy entrepreneurs as having had limited, if any, effect on public policy. And, yes, the policy entrepreneurs identified in this study have faced considerable difficulties in securing policy change. Many failed in their initial efforts. And those who did achieve the changes they sought often had less grandiose goals to begin with (see chapter 7). Yet none of this negates the relevance of a theory of policy entrepreneurship. After all, recognizing the magnitude of the forces that serve to maintain stability in policy settings, we might wonder why people would ever imagine that they could actually instigate habit-breaking, interest-disrupting change. But people do think they can make a difference. Further, the sort of efforts that go into securing policy change often parallel those of entrepreneurs in the marketplace. We should also note that it is not at all unusual to see entrepreneurs in the marketplace putting enormous amounts of energy into trying to bring innovative products to market, only to see their efforts come to nothing. What are the determinants of success and failure? Whether or not entrepreneurs succeed in their endeavors—be it in the world of the market or the world of politics—is often affected by factors beyond their control. Nonetheless, entrepreneurs *do* have agency. In the empirical studies of earlier chapters, I found that the choices made by the school choice policy entrepreneurs, and the ways that they managed their relationships with others, significantly affected their abilities to influence policymaking.

For the purpose of summarizing a large amount of information, elsewhere in this book I have discussed the activities of policy entrepreneurs using six "keys to policy entrepreneurship." Here I revisit those keys, discussing each with reference to the actions of the school choice policy entrepreneurs.

Creativity and Insight

Policy entrepreneurs must be *creative* and *insightful*, able to see how proposing particular policy innovations can alter the nature of policy debates. The school choice policy entrepreneurs each learned in one way or another about the idea of breaking the one-to-one relationship between residential location and the schools to which families may send their children. They then thought seriously about how they could take this idea and transform it into a compelling proposal for policy change in their respective states. In so doing, the policy entrepreneurs clearly saw themselves as pursuing policy changes that would mark a break with the past. They also recognized that their efforts would place them at odds with many people who benefit from and support the status quo in the delivery of public education. Given this, the policy entrepreneurs often sought to carefully frame education policy issues in their states so that school choice would appear as an appropriate solution to current problems (see chapter 9). But to do this well, policy entrepreneurs must be able to deduce the preoccupations of others and then figure out ways of speaking to them so that their ideas and arguments appear convincing. Policy entrepreneurs cannot take the world as given; they must have the ability to extract relevant information from a range of situations and then find ways of using that information to their advantage. Being able to see that a particular policy idea can be presented as relevant to a given jurisdiction requires a considerable degree of insight. Beyond that, creativity is the necessary ingredient that allows policy entrepreneurs to develop their ideas and present them to others in compelling ways.

Social Perceptiveness

Many people would like to be able to "read" the minds of others and use what they learn for their own gain. Of course, to literally read the minds of others is impossible. Nonetheless, with sufficient insight and the ability to empathize with others, it is possible to develop a high degree of *social perceptiveness.* For policy entrepreneurs this is an invaluable skill. With social perceptiveness, policy entrepreneurs can develop understandings of the ways that other people look upon particular social conditions and, from there, begin to establish how others would most likely react to given proposals for policy change. Probably the only sound way to develop social perceptiveness is to actually spend a lot of time talking with and listening to people from a range of backgrounds. Policy entrepreneurs do this. In the case of the school choice policy entrepreneurs, many found it important to spend time with people from a broad range of backgrounds, learning how they thought about education issues and what changes they would most like to see. It is also instructive to note that some of the policy entrepreneurs who did not secure their hoped-for policy changes were somewhat wrapped up in their own little worlds, detached from many of the people in society who would be affected by their proposals, and apparently uneasy about expanding the range of their social encounters (see chapter 9). Yet entrepreneurs in the marketplace know that keeping in close touch with the customer is vital for honing their social perceptiveness. This is how they learn what others are looking for. And, of course, elected decisionmakers know the importance of keeping in touch with their constituents. To achieve a clear sense of the hopes and desires of others, and to perfect the art of presenting ideas and arguments in ways that others find convincing, policy entrepreneurs must be socially perceptive.

Social and Political Dexterity

Policy entrepreneurs must be *able to mix in a variety of social and political settings*, so that they can readily acquire valuable information and use their contacts to advantage in pursuit of policy change. Among other things, this is how social perceptiveness can be developed and maintained. In this way, policy entrepreneurs can learn what sort of arguments in support of particular policy innovations to make to various people. This is also how policy entrepreneurs can learn about the triumphs and traumas that others have experienced. The school choice policy entrepreneurs were inveterate networkers. Through their networking activities, they learned what others had done to introduce school choice as a policy innovation in their states. The policy entrepreneurs also engaged in large amounts of networking in and around their state governments as they worked to build support for their ideas (see chapter 8). Clever policy entrepreneurs did not simply network with friends and acquaintances who they expected would be "natural allies." Often, having gained a clear sense of the views of their opponents and the ways that they would argue and organize against proposals for school choice, policy entrepreneurs were able to find creative ways to counter those arguments, or neutralize opposition, so as to more readily achieve their policy goals. Being prepared to temporarily suspend belief in your own passionately held ideas and listen carefully to the criticisms that others level upon them takes a considerable amount of patience and maturity. Where many would simply walk away from a fight or surround themselves only with people who confirm what they already think, policy entrepreneurs with social and political dexterity can gain fresh insights from engagement with potential enemies (see chapter 9). After all, learning occurs most rapidly when we find ourselves struggling to succeed. Even when not directly dealing with those who oppose their ideas, policy entrepreneurs can gain from mixing in unfamiliar circles. By working with a range of people who initially perceive themselves as having little in common, policy entrepreneurs can come to develop coalitions of supporters that can aid them in multiple ways as they strive to prompt policy change.

Persuasiveness

Policy entrepreneurs must be *able to argue persuasively*; often this will mean making different arguments to different groups while keeping the overall story consistent. But the last thing that policy entrepreneurs want is to come across as "silver-tongued devils," spinning slick arguments, and having little personal interest in what they are proposing. This suggests that policy entrepreneurs must be able to demonstrate sincere commitment to the policy ideas they are attempting to sell. At the same time, they must be able to strike a delicate balance between being so passionate about these ideas that they lose sight of alternative ways of considering them and being dispassionate enough to bend their ideas to accord with the expectations of everyone they meet. The school choice policy entrepreneurs pursued a range of strategies with the purpose of persuading others of the merit of their ideas.

Some took care to marshal facts and figures about the current condition of education in their states and used this information to then develop arguments explaining why a radical policy like school choice was necessary. Jackie Ducote in Louisiana followed this strategy. She also took great care to document the many efforts she had been involved with to reform the school system from within and the ways that these efforts had been undermined by opponents of change. This became a way that she could establish her credibility as someone with a lot of familiarity with education issues in her state. From there, she could more persuasively argue for school choice as a policy innovation.

Other policy entrepreneurs gathered evidence from working examples of school choice in other states and used this, along with the expert testimony of people from elsewhere, to make the case for school choice (see chapter 6). Yet another strategy used to persuade policymakers involved setting up demonstration projects, often virtually in the backyard of the state capitol. Such efforts demonstrated a great deal of commitment to the school choice idea and could be used to persuade others of both the seriousness of the policy entrepreneurs and of the workability of the ideas they were promoting (see chapter 10).

Strategic Sense

Policy entrepreneurs must be *strategic team builders*, able to determine the type of coalition best able to support their pursuit of policy change. The school choice policy entrepreneurs used a variety of approaches to generate support for school choice as a policy innovation. Clearly, there is not some universally best way that policy entrepreneurs can go about organizing coalitions of supporters for policy change. In Nebraska, state Senator Dennis Baack decided that efforts to build a coalition of supporters outside the legislature could actually be detrimental to his efforts to secure policy change. Therefore, he worked quietly on his proposal for school choice and, only after announcing it, did he begin working carefully to ensure that he would maintain sufficient support that his school choice bill would be adopted. Paul DeWeese in Michigan, who worked outside the legislature, was determined to build a strong coalition of supporters. In so doing, he deliberately labored to establish an organizational form that would directly contradict the arguments of supporters of the status quo who would label advocates of school choice as being racist, elitist, or antigovernment (see chapter 9).

Strategic sense can be important for policy entrepreneurs in many instances. Having a good grasp of when to push hard for policy change and when to either lie low or accept compromises can make the difference between success and failure in the achievement of policy goals. Having a clear view of the end goal and how small, interim steps can take you toward it is critical. Without having thought about such matters, a policy entrepreneur might end up missing opportunities for gain, letting ideals overwhelm the practical value of compromise.

Leadership Qualities

Policy entrepreneurs must be prepared to ***lead by example***, where necessary creating "prefigurative forms" of the policy innovations they seek to introduce. The contrast between the actions of the Commit CEOs and J. Patrick Rooney in Indiana is instructive. Both the Commit CEOs and Rooney served as school choice policy entrepreneurs in Indiana, but they exhibited quite different leadership qualities. The Commit CEOs took the view that they could engage in a top-down strategy of reform, believing that if they could just exert enough pressure on members of the state legislature, then they could rapidly realize their policy goals. While they certainly succeeded in getting the idea of school choice on the policy agenda in Indiana in the early 1990s, the efforts of the Commit CEOs did not lead to any policy change (see chapter 6). J. Patrick Rooney followed a different leadership model. First, he surrounded himself with advisors who could give him many practical insights into education issues in Indiana. Then he launched a private voucher plan in Indianapolis, with the twin goals of demonstrating the workability of a voucher approach to funding education and keeping the spotlight on school choice as a policy idea. While Rooney's efforts are yet to prompt broader policy change mirroring his local-level initiatives, they represent an instance of "leadership by example" (see chapter 10). Furthermore, Rooney's leadership style could be compared with that of an "organic" intellectual, which Antonio Gramsci distinguished from the "ivory tower" notion of the intellectual. In this light, Gramsci (1971, 10) stated: "The mode of being of the new intellectual can no longer consist in eloquence, which is an exterior and momentary mover of feelings and passions, but in active participation in practical life, as constructor, organiser, 'permanent persuader' and not just a simple orator."

The efforts of Rooney in Indiana and school choice policy entrepreneurs elsewhere demonstrate that it is vital for policy entrepreneurs to find ways to transform their ideas into action. In this way, they are able to demonstrate that their visions of the future are *believable*. But to do this successfully, policy entrepreneurs must be able to find ways to "put their money where their mouth is," and thus signal their personal commitment to their arguments and the political movements they attempt to create.

The Keys Revisited

All other things being equal, policy entrepreneurs who exhibit the qualities discussed here are more likely to achieve success than those who do not. However, we should also recognize that policy entrepreneurs are embedded in social contexts and that those contexts change across space and time. Given this, it might happen that a given policy entrepreneur can realize his or her policy goals without necessarily behaving in ways that are consistent with what has been said here. When attempting to assess why any particular policy entrepreneur or group of policy entrepreneurs happened to meet with success or failure, we need to look both at the broader conditions they faced and the individual actions that they engaged in. The keys to policy entrepreneurship represent a starting point for thinking about the things that policy entrepreneurs might do to improve their chances of achieving success. At the same time, the keys suggest a means by which we might diagnose failure. Noting that a failed entrepreneur did not act in accord with our expectations, we might then go on to deduce how particular character flaws or chosen courses of action served to undermine his or her chances of achieving success.

Policy Entrepreneurship and Other Explanations of Policy Change

Throughout this book, I have frequently observed that policy entrepreneurs are embedded social actors and that the effectiveness of their actions will often be influenced by factors beyond their control. Thus, while the actions of policy entrepreneurs have been placed in the spotlight, my intention has never been to suggest that such an effort illuminates all we need to know about the antecedents and the nature of policy change. My argument is that policy entrepreneurs actively promote ideas for policy innovation. In so doing, they can significantly increase the likelihood that policy change will occur. Furthermore, because of the innovative nature of their proposals, the policy changes they prompt can frequently have ongoing consequences. They can create ripple effects in the behaviors and habits of thought of all those who are affected by the policy change. How might we reconcile this portrayal of the efforts and effects of policy entrepreneurs with alternative explanations of policy change? In chapter 2 I introduced and discussed five conceptions of the policymaking process that in their distinctive ways also offer explanations for the emergence of policy change. As I noted in that chapter, policy entrepreneurs often lurk within these conceptions of the policymaking process. However, none of these previous accounts give policy entrepreneurs anything like the sort of exposure they have received here.

Suppose that my account of the efforts made by policy entrepreneurs to secure policy change had been available to other scholars as they were developing their conceptions of the policymaking process. In what ways might this have altered their accounts of the factors that cause policy change? I seek to answer that question here. Admittedly, this thought experiment might strike many as odd. After all, the ideas of those scholars have influenced my own thinking about the actions of policy entrepreneurs. In addition, this open comparing and contrasting of such new work with canonical works in the field of public policy could readily be construed as an act of hubris. But this thought experiment is quite defensible. First, whether we make it explicit or not, all of us are always working within a tradition of ideas and theories that have been offered with the intention of improving our understanding of aspects of society and politics. Thus, thinking about the ideas suggested by others and using them to guide the elaboration of a unique theory constitutes a core feature of the scholarly enterprise. Why not take what you come up with and bring it back to the point in the broader conversation where you started from? Second, making an effort to engage other theories is actually less pretentious than offering up a new theory and arguing—if not explicitly then, by your exclusions, implicitly—that it is better than everything that has come along before. Among political scientists who have developed theories of policymaking and policy change, remarkably little effort has been made to consider how what has been said individually adds to the collective effort of knowledge creation. I do not pretend that my theory of policy entrepreneurship and policy change supersedes other explanations of policy change. In what follows, my interest lies in seeing how what I have to say is strengthened by and, in turn, might strengthen the theories of other scholars whose work I find insightful and inspiring.

Policy Entrepreneurs, Proximate Policymakers, and Incremental Policy Change

Charles E. Lindblom (1968) argued that the policymaking process is dominated by "proximate policymakers"—legislators, political executives, appointed bureaucrats, and some party officials. These proximate policymakers encounter each other both through formal organizational arrangements and through many informal interactions. In the informal realm, a large amount of "mutual adjustment" occurs as those with ideas and proposals attempt to make them as acceptable as possible to others around them. Because of the inevitable divergences that are found in the ways that different people view particular policy issues, and because information problems limit the ability of decisionmakers to perfectly predict the effects of their policy choices, Lindblom suggested that policy change will typically occur in an incremental fashion.

Is there room for policy entrepreneurs in Lindblom's theory? In discussing external pressures that are brought to bear upon proximate policymakers, Lindblom noted that "men who can bring relevant facts and analysis to bear on a political issue can, without holding office or heading an interest group, achieve influence disproportionate to their numbers" (1968, 111). However, Lindblom noted that the effort to gain influence often can be laborious; it is not a suitable vocation for those who are readily dispirited. Lindblom's observations do suggest that there is room in his theory for policy entrepreneurs, but whether those policy entrepreneurs held elected office or they were attempting to gain influence as outsiders, they would most likely have great difficulty persuading others of the merit of their ideas for policy innovation. At a minimum, they would have to be extremely good at networking and at making arguments to a range of people with distinctive viewpoints. Further, any policy changes stemming from their actions would most likely involve incremental steps, rather than dramatic policy shifts.

In light of these considerations, it is useful to recall the actions of the school choice policy entrepreneurs. Those like state Senator Dennis

Baack, Governor Bill Clinton, and Assemblywoman Polly Williams used their positions as proximate policymakers to great advantage (see chapters 2 and 6). These policy entrepreneurs knew how to make arguments to others in persuasive ways, and they knew how to engage in the sort of informal networking and mutual adjustment that could raise their chances of securing their desired policy changes. These individuals took care to limit the scope of the policy changes that they sought to introduce, and this appears to have worked to their advantage. Of course, to be successful as a policy entrepreneur one need not be a proximate policymaker. However, it is clear that pursuing the outsider strategy can only work to advantage if a policy entrepreneur is careful to cultivate close contacts with individuals who are in decisionmaking positions. Joe Nathan and Paul DeWeese managed to secure their desired policy changes, but they engaged in a lot of networking in and around their respective state governments to do so (see chapters 2 and 9).

Sometimes policy entrepreneurs attempt to secure policy change by pursuing an outsider strategy, thus eschewing all the accouterments of business-as-usual politics. In many ways this can be seen as a flawed approach. Just as musicians who have mastered the art of improvisation know the value of a formal music training, so we might say that the policy entrepreneurs most likely to gain by playing an outsider strategy are those who already possess a deep understanding of what it takes to succeed as an insider. An attempt to change public policy through a ballot initiative is likely to succeed only if the policy entrepreneur is prepared to take a lot of time to think about how to word the proposal and how to campaign for it so as to win the support of a majority of voters. Where winning majority support in the polls seems unlikely, and the goal is to pressure the state legislature to take the issue seriously, then the policy entrepreneur has to build contacts with people in and around the seat of power. In the absence of such efforts, it is very unlikely that legislators will consider the idea and work with it in ways that the policy entrepreneur most desires. These observations suggest that the recent efforts by policy entrepreneurs to establish local-level school choice demonstration projects (see chapter 10) could have little broader policy effect unless the policy entrepreneurs augment their local-level work with serious attempts to network, make convincing arguments, and build a coalition of supporters among proximate policymakers.

Overall, we might say that the theory of policy entrepreneurship and policy change provides useful insights into how those seeking to promote policy innovations might operate within the policymaking process, as characterized by Charles Lindblom. My work provides insights into the process by which new ideas and policy proposals get put onto policy agendas. At the same time, Lindblom's work helps us to think more about the nature of policy entrepreneurship and the sort of strategies that are most likely to work for those seeking to promote policy change. His work also provides an important explanation for why policy entrepreneurs with grandiose plans for policy change must often settle for playing a longer game, involving the pursuit of broader change through incremental steps.

Policy Entrepreneurs, Process Streams, and Windows of Opportunity

In John W. Kingdon's (1995) characterization, the policymaking process consists of three independent "process" streams. These are the political stream, the problem stream, and the policy stream. For agenda change to occur, and thus pave the way for policy change, these three streams must be joined. According to Kingdon the joining of these streams occurs rarely, during periods that he terms "windows of opportunity." The joining of the streams themselves is accomplished by the actions of policy entrepreneurs. Thus, for Kingdon, policy entrepreneurs play an integral part in the policymaking process, their persistence and tenacity increasing the chances that their ideas will receive a serious hearing. Viewed alongside Kingdon's work, my study of policy entrepreneurs and policy change is seen to provide additional information about the ways that these individuals have influence in the policymaking process. For the most part, what I have said here does not contradict Kingdon's arguments. However, in reviewing Kingdon's conception of the policymaking process in chapter 2, I questioned the extent to which the three process streams that he identifies are in fact independent. I also suggested that savvy policy entrepreneurs, rather than waiting passively for windows of opportunity to open, might engage in various activities designed to force these windows open, thus providing more opportunities in which to set the stage for the consideration and adoption of policy innovations.

This study of the activities of school choice policy entrepreneurs highlights the importance of the work that they do outside of the immediate policymaking process. For state-level policy entrepreneurs, I found that policy networks extending across the nation could be extremely helpful as conduits and repositories of ideas for policy change and strategies concerning how change can be secured. In addition, the policy entrepreneurs in this study often went to considerable lengths to develop coalitions of supporters, typically consisting of business groups and concerned citizens. Sometimes, these coalitions established political action committees to help finance the elections of politicians sympathetic to the idea of school choice. The more recent efforts of policy entrepreneurs to establish demonstration projects suggest an even greater desire to engage in practical politics with the goal of supporting policy change. Taken all together, these observations suggest that policy entrepreneurs often work beyond the immediate circles of power and that this work can be immensely important for assisting them in securing policy change. Also, policy entrepreneurs often work simultaneously on problem definition, policy design, and politicking. For these individuals, a conception of the policymaking process that contains three independent streams probably seems somewhat artificial and rigid, even though Kingdon's characterization emphasizes the fluid nature of the politics that surrounds agenda setting and policymaking.

To explore these matters further, consider the case of the policy entrepreneurs like J. Patrick Rooney, James Leininger, and Fritz Steiger, who have been active in developing private voucher plans as school choice demonstration projects (see chapter 10). These policy entrepreneurs believe that school choice represents a solution to problems with the public school system. To make this point, they have simultaneously worked at refining their policy solution, defining the policy problem, and building the political support needed to secure broader policy change. Rather than lying in wait for a window of opportunity to open for them, these policy entrepreneurs have been actively working to keep school choice on the policy agenda and thus to increase the likelihood that policy change will occur. These individuals have deliberately sought to join solutions, problems, and politics on a permanent basis.

By contrast, the actions of the Commit CEOs in Indiana appear more suited to analysis using Kingdon's process streams model (see chapter 6). In that case, the delivery of public education in the state had been identified as having problems. The Commit CEOs then attempted to "hook" the idea of school choice as a solution to those problems. The selection of school choice as the solution to the problem was quite deliberate, and, in fact, the whole idea of making broad, systemic change was a topic of debate among business leaders in Indiana. Having joined their solution to the predefined problem, the Commit CEOs attempted to gain influence in the political stream, bringing their package of policy changes to the state legislature for adoption. Yet, ironically, it seems that the compartmentalizing view these policy entrepreneurs had of the policymaking process actually worked against them as they attempted to secure policy change. For budding policy entrepreneurs, seeing the policymaking process as a complex series of interconnected elements, where problem framing and the presentation of solutions is always done with an eye toward the broader political situation, is vital.

For the most part, my theory of policy entrepreneurs and policy change can be seen as lending additional support to Kingdon's conception of the policymaking process. This is hardly surprising, since policy entrepreneurs play a prominent role in Kingdon's discussion. That said, my work offers a more detailed, nuanced portrayal of policy entrepreneurship, and it further elaborates on why policy entrepreneurs engage in particular actions at particular times. In so doing, I acknowledge the importance of thinking about the policymaking process in terms of problem definition, politics, and policy design. Nonetheless, the notion that these activities typically take place in independent "streams" should probably be subjected to more critical scrutiny.

Policy Entrepreneurs, Agency, and Structure

Recent contributions to "the new institutionalism" in the social sciences emphasize the *agency* that individuals have to pursue their particular goals, while acknowledging the ways that institutional arrangements serve to *structure* and limit individual actions. In their effort to "rediscover" institutions, James G. March and Johan P. Olsen (1989) emphasized the importance of informal norms of behavior, such as "the logic of appropriateness" in guiding and constraining individual actions. They also emphasized the limited attention of individual decisionmakers. According to March and Olsen, limited attention and the ability of institutional arrangements to adjust incrementally over time result in long periods of policy stability. However, moments arise when old institutional forms can no longer adjust in desired ways, and this can lead to periods of crisis. During these times new knowledge is generated about alternative approaches to institutional design, and this can prompt abrupt, nonincremental policy change.

March and Olsen's work is useful for helping us understand why policy entrepreneurs must be prepared to spend large amounts of time networking in and around government to promote policy change.

Through such efforts, policy entrepreneurs can learn the preferences of others and establish relationships of trust with various proximate policymakers. For the policy entrepreneurs identified in this study, I found that those who recognized the importance of this sort of networking were the most likely to have their proposals for school choice both considered and adopted by state legislatures (see chapter 8). March and Olsen's work also helps us understand why policy entrepreneurs often devote large amounts of time and energy to building coalitions of supporters and establishing policy demonstration projects, essentially working outside the inner circles of policymaking (see chapters 9 and 10). Such actions signal that policy entrepreneurs are deeply committed to the ideas they are promoting. This, in turn, can serve to mark them out as having ideas worthy of careful consideration.

Our improved knowledge of the actions taken by policy entrepreneurs can usefully inform March and Olsen's institutional perspective. Often in my discussion of policy entrepreneurship, I have emphasized the extent to which particular policy problems are socially constructed. But this perspective serves to emphasize the arbitrariness with which periods of policy stability and policy change occur. In March and Olsen's telling, it is unclear whether the forces that generate, on the one hand, incremental change and, on the other, nonincremental change are inexorable or open to manipulation. My work demonstrates that policy entrepreneurs who are dissatisfied with present policy settings, or who believe they see potential for beneficial policy change, can take a range of efforts that are consciously aimed at forcing the reexamination of the design of institutional structures. Through their efforts to point out the problems associated with current policy settings, policy entrepreneurs can promote the learning process that can eventually lead to the adoption of policy innovations. The policy entrepreneurs identified in this study have attempted to prompt periods of policy crisis in a variety of ways—however, all of the ways involved attempting to alter the discourse surrounding education policy in their states.

These observations suggest that policy entrepreneurs can be thought of as individuals who, through the skills they develop over time, are able to exercise greater levels of agency than other members of policymaking communities. Often, those who are most able to realize success have first spent a great deal of time learning the "rules of the game" with respect to the policymaking process. Knowing these rules—both formal rules and informal norms of behavior—policy entrepreneurs can then seek to use them to their own advantage. For example, successful policy entrepreneurs are able to force proximate policymakers to give serious attention to the problems they identify. This, in turn, can lead to the reevaluation of the merits of present policy settings. For the purpose of this discussion, we see that the concept of the policy entrepreneur can prove helpful for enhancing our understanding of the political and social processes that prompt change in institutional structures.

Policy Entrepreneurs, Policy Images, and Policy Venues

In their explanation of policy change, Frank R. Baumgartner and Bryan D. Jones (1993) argued that stability in any particular policy area is facilitated by both knowledge specialization and the generation of positive policy images. Hence, the system of public education in a state might remain quite stable over time because once the broader institutions of governance are established, significant aspects of policy decisionmaking are delegated to bureaucrats. Furthermore, so long as these bureaucrats can maintain an aura of expertise and keep discourse about public education positive, there is little likelihood of destabilization. For nonincremental policy change to occur, the attention of state legislators has to be drawn to public education. At this point, the policy monopoly presided over by bureaucratic experts could be destroyed, allowing a new institutional structure to emerge in its place. According to Baumgartner and Jones, the stability of a policy monopoly is highly contingent upon its having a positive policy image. Nonetheless, they note that policy images are always vulnerable to manipulation. And it is policy entrepreneurs, through their efforts at problem definition, who often prompt the transformation of positive policy images into negative ones. Thus, for Baumgartner and Jones, the actions of policy entrepreneurs serve as central factors that instigate policy change.

By offering a close analysis of the activities of policy entrepreneurs, my work complements that of Baumgartner and Jones. Note, for example, the observations and the actions of two of the school choice policy entrepreneurs. In speaking of the education establishment in Michigan, Paul DeWeese observed that its members "have always . . . tried to cloak themselves in the kind of mom, apple pie, and the American flag kind of thing." DeWeese was very aware of the deliberate efforts that educationalists make to maintain a positive policy image. He was also highly aware of the ways that they seek to deflect any attempts to tarnish that image: "They accuse people who raise these kinds of things [e.g., school choice] as being racist, or elitist, or underminers of public education." Recognizing the power of the education establishment to maintain a positive policy image and deflect attacks, Paul DeWeese then attempted to construct a countervailing coalition and set of policy arguments. This effort was deliberately planned to call into question the typical claims and deflecting arguments made by supporters of the status quo. If not undermining public education, Paul DeWeese certainly sought to undermine the positive policy images presented by members of the education establishment (see chapter 9).

Consider now the case of Steve Buckstein in Oregon. As a libertarian, Buckstein greatly opposed the idea that government should be involved in the delivery of education. Thus he sought to introduce a voucher-style system of school funding. One means by which Buckstein could have argued for the merits of his version of school choice involved noting the flaws in the present system. But Buckstein was reluctant to pursue this strategy because, in his words, "If you're saying that there are all these problems, who should fix them but experts? And we were certainly not experts." In Buckstein's view, the education establishment in his state had clearly built a sound reputation for itself based upon an aura of expertise. To challenge this establishment, he took the view that he would have to circumvent the usual approaches used to secure policy change. In the words of Baumgartner and Jones, he chose to shift the site for his policy battle to a new venue: the ballot box, rather than the state legislature (see chapter 9). These two stories regarding the actions of school choice policy entrepreneurs underscore the value of thinking about the policymaking process as involving battles over policy images.

My study of the actions of school choice policy entrepreneurs also provide additional evidence on the important role that "venue shopping" can play in efforts to secure policy change. Intimidated or rebuffed in one arena, such as the legislative process, policy entrepreneurs might attempt to pursue policy change elsewhere. Steve Buckstein's ballot initiative in Oregon represents one instance of this. The recent development of private voucher demonstration projects in cities across the United States represents an even more determined effort to change the policy venue in order to pursue policy change (see chapter 10). According to Baumgartner and Jones (1993, 17), once a new policy idea has caught on in one policy venue, an innovation diffusion process often occurs: "Political bandwagons build up power, as politicians and interest-group leaders become active in a new cause as it gains popularity. Ideas diffuse from one policy arena to another, often coming as a surprise to those who had previously operated independently from other arenas."

The rise of school choice in the nation's states conforms to this pattern. However, the theory and empirical analysis presented in this study further illuminate the political activities that support such diffusion processes. In so doing, it offers several caveats to the portrayal and explanation of processes of policy change as presented by Baumgartner and Jones.

The analysis of state legislative consideration and adoption of school choice as a policy idea demonstrates that the process of policy innovation diffusion is by no means inevitable. Rather, it depends to a significant degree upon the ability of policy entrepreneurs to take policy ideas from elsewhere and transform them in ways that make them appealing for local consumption. Without making efforts to develop persuasive arguments, build coalitions of supporters, and network in and around the seat of power, those attempting to promote policy change often meet with failure (see chapters 7–9). Following from these observations, we should also note that—in and of itself—pursuing a venue shift is unlikely to trigger a political bandwagon and, hence, policy innovation diffusion. Much depends upon how policy entrepreneurs make use of this venue shift and the extent to which they maintain open lines of communication back to the venues that originally deflected efforts to secure change. That said, my analysis of the development of local-level private voucher plans demonstrates that venue shopping, when used well, can place policy entrepreneurs in a strong position to challenge currently ascendant policy monopolies and the images they project (see chapter 10).

Policy Entrepreneurs and Advocacy Coalitions

To advance our understanding of the forces promoting policy learning and policy change, and to expose the apparent inadequacies of past theories of policymaking, Paul A. Sabatier (1988) has developed the Advocacy Coalition Framework. According to this framework, the policy world consists of a range of policy subsystems, within which several advocacy coalitions can often be found to coexist. These advocacy coalitions serve to promote subsystem stability and policy learning. The debates occurring within subsystems can promote incremental policy change. More thoroughgoing change is likely to occur as a result of forces outside the immediate policy subsystem. Sabatier argues that these coalitions are long-lived and that they are held together by the shared beliefs of their members. He rejects the view that significant policy change can be instigated by short-term "coalitions of convenience."

Perhaps the major value of the Advocacy Coalition Framework is that it helps us to understand the nature of the broader policy context within which policy change can occur. However, the theory is more limited when it comes to offering powerful explanations of the antecedents of change itself. Sabatier has talked of "shared beliefs" that hold an advocacy coalition together, but it is unclear where these beliefs come from and how they manage to remain stable over time. Furthermore, because advocacy coalitions can be quite extensive, it is not clear how they relate to formal institutional structures. In light of these comments, it seems that the Advocacy Coalition Framework could be improved by being more closely informed by both the work of Baumgartner and Jones and some of the implications of my discussion of policy entrepreneurship and policy change.

Sabatier's definition of advocacy coalitions is broad enough that it includes "people from a variety of positions," some of whom might be proximate policymakers, others of whom might be somewhat disinterested researchers. The difficulty posed by using a broad definition like Sabatier's is that it becomes impossible to determine the boundaries of the coalition. This is problematic because it raises questions about the strength of the "glue" that holds such a group of individuals together. Although such a group of disparate individuals might share some common policy beliefs, it stretches credulity to expect that they could maintain this common bond for long and thus engage in "a nontrivial degree of coordinated activity over time" (1988, 139). My work suggests that there is value to treating such informal interactions among a broad range of individuals and groups as contributions to the development and maintenance of policy networks. In so doing, the notion of the advocacy coalition is preserved for naming groups that really are engaging in cohesive, highly coordinated activities. Thus, I suggest that we think of policy networks as resources for policy entrepreneurs as they develop their ideas for policy innovations. By contrast, coalitions can be thought of as very deliberately structured teams of individuals, established with the goal of pursuing policy change. When policy entrepreneurs in my study developed coalitions they engaged in close, ongoing contact with coalition partners. To this extent, I see coalitions as paralleling the various firm-like arrangements that entrepreneurs in the marketplace establish for the purposes of producing innovative products. Policy networks can be thought of as equivalent to industry-level groups of contacts that individuals can tap into when seeking expert knowledge or skills outside their immediate purview (see chapter 8).

In contrast to Sabatier's contention, my study suggests that short-lived policy coalitions can, in fact, serve as a source of significant policy change. The policy entrepreneurs in this study were quite strategic in the way they made use of coalitions. Where they could secure policy change without resort to coalition building, they did so. However, where necessary, they carefully created coalitions that served them well both in putting pressure on policymakers to change policy and in countering the defensive arguments of members of the traditional education establishment (see chapter 9). Of course, it would make good sense to argue that the education establishment represents a form of advocacy coalition. But in its efforts to maintain the status quo, it is not at all clear how such a coalition promotes anything other than fairly trivial levels of policy learning or policy change. Finally, my work calls into question the merit of assuming that advocacy coalitions must somehow conform to a predefined model. This is equivalent to assuming that all firm-like arrangements established by entrepreneurs in the marketplace must take a particular form. Of course this does not happen. While the recent efforts of school choice policy entrepreneurs to establish demonstration projects may be viewed as a way of improving their ability to supply credible information to state legislators, they may also be viewed as an innovative approach to coalition building. Yet actions of this sort seem quite different from those included under the umbrella of the Advocacy Coalition Framework (see chapter 10).

Using evidence of the activities of the school choice policy entrepreneurs, I have highlighted some ways in which future efforts to refine the Advocacy Coalition Framework might be guided by my findings on policy entrepreneurship. In making these points, my intention is not to be unduly critical of what has proven a quite useful approach to thinking about and explaining aspects of policymaking and policy change.[1] Rather, I suggest that the points made here simply constitute a starting point for more careful thinking about the merits and the limits of Sabatier's contribution.

Summary

The foregoing discussion suggests that there are a number of points of intersection between my theory of policy entrepreneurship and the theories that others have developed of policymaking and policy change. Rather than suggesting that any of these extant theories should be seriously reworked in light of what I have done, this discussion mostly suggests ways that my work and the theories of others are mutually reinforcing. Of course, in focusing upon points of intersection it is easy to lose sight of what it is that makes my theoretical work unique, and how—in its own way—it enhances our understanding of the nature of policy change. To highlight this contribution, I next discuss the ways that this work on policy entrepreneurs and policy change constitutes a new departure, and why I believe it to be very relevant for many scholars of public policy.

Reprise: Policy Entrepreneurs and Policy Change

The concept of the policy entrepreneur and the theory that undergirds it can serve as a powerful tool of analysis when it comes to exploring and understanding instances of policy change. Just as the figure of the entrepreneur is acknowledged as a key actor in explanations of market adjustment and transformation, so the policy entrepreneur should be seen as a prime candidate for inclusion in the stories we tell of the development and diffusion of policy innovations and of policy change. In previous chapters, I have shown how my theory of policy entrepreneurship can illuminate our understanding of a contemporary case of policy innovation and change—the rise of school choice. But this theory and this approach to empirical investigation could be readily applied when thinking about many other cases of policy change.

A Guiding Concept

Political scientists have produced a variety of concepts and theories that help us when thinking about aspects of policymaking and policy change. However, often these contributions have not been well integrated. By placing the figure of the policy entrepreneur at center stage, it becomes easier to see how these contributions can be brought together to provide a coherent explanation of the political behaviors that support policy change. I have shown how policy networks can serve as significant resources for policy entrepreneurs. It is through their location in such networks that policy entrepreneurs can learn about policy ideas and innovations being discussed and developed elsewhere. They can also use networks located in and around decisionmaking bodies to gain insights into the preoccupation of proximate policymakers and the kind of arguments that must be made to persuade them of the merits of considering and adopting particular policy innovations. Policy entrepreneurs also work carefully to think about the presentation of policy problems. Always, problems are presented in strategic ways, with the purpose of winning supporters and improving the chances that decisionmakers will adopt particular proposals for policy change. Thus, we see that problem definition and coalition building, while analytically separable activities, are closely connected in practice. I have also shown how policy demonstration projects, ostensibly designed to generate high-quality evidence to support arguments for policy change, can also double as a means of resolving collective-action problems among coalition partners. For these reasons, it seems appropriate to claim that the concept of the policy entrepreneur can serve a useful purpose in helping us integrate our understanding of the ways in which various political strategies are used to secure policy change.

Admittedly, there will be times when the presence of a policy entrepreneur or group of policy entrepreneurs is not necessary for ensuring the adoption of policy innovations, but starting with the expectation that such individuals might be acting to prompt change can be useful. Thus, I suggest that the figure of the policy entrepreneur be treated as a *guiding concept*. Thinking in terms of policy entrepreneurs, we can come to a more nuanced understanding of the factors causing policy change. This is not to suggest the universal applicability of this theory; just that there will often be times when it will provide a useful starting point for empirical investigation and additional theory construction.

A Concept for Extraordinary Politics

According to Joseph A. Schumpeter (1934), entrepreneurs in the marketplace have little to offer once a new organization has been developed and the production of an innovative product follows a course of business as usual. We might say the same for policy entrepreneurs. In the world of quiet, business-as-usual politics, where incremental policy change is the rule, we should not expect to find individuals acting in the capacity of policy entrepreneurs. The major value of this concept is that it can help us to understand the antecedents of policy innovation and policy change. So, we might call the notion of the policy entrepreneur a concept for ***extraordinary politics***. To say this, of course, is to tightly circumscribe our expectations of the concept's applicability. This, I think, is a good thing. Often in the past, concepts developed for the analysis of business-as-usual politics have been used to explain the adoption of policy innovations and the changes stemming from them. In these circumstances, their explanatory power has been limited. The entrepreneur serves as a ***destabilizing*** figure in the world of the market, engaging in the "creative destruction" that wreaks havoc with the old ways of doing things and ushers in new products, new processes, new behaviors, and new habits of mind. Likewise, we should think of the policy entrepreneur as a figure embodying both creative genius and the ability to lay waste to outmoded governance structures. From here we can come to better analyze instances of significant policy change.

New Times, New Concepts

Over the past two decades, we have observed some significant instances of policy change, both in the United States and elsewhere. Many of these changes have involved either privatization or the reorganizing of traditional areas of government, using market-like incentives to structure the actions of bureaucrats and citizens. Therefore we might speak of an acceleration in the blurring of the boundaries between government and the private sector. Accompanying this change is a tendency for individuals, families, and other social entities to increasingly adopt practices and ways of thinking that were traditionally the preserve of actors in the world of business. In light of these moves toward greater reliance upon markets and individual initiative, it seems reasonable to expect that in the future more people will exhibit the sort of skills that stand as the stock in trade of entrepreneurs. At the same time, we might also expect some of the traditional mediums of citizen engagement in politics, such as public- and private-sector unions, to experience an erosion of both support and influence. Should these changes continue, then it is likely that the figure of the policy entrepreneur will become even more prevalent in politics in the years ahead. Of course party and interest group politics will continue to matter, and various forms of advocacy coalition will continue to go through their life cycles. But the nature of the broader political economy and the changing nature of political communication and networking strategies all suggest a heightening of the conditions under which large numbers of single-issue policy entrepreneurs could emerge and thrive.

Lessons for Practice

Many elements of my discussion in this book, along with the summarizing "keys to policy entrepreneurship," provide insights that could be of practical value to readers who aspire in one way or another to serve as policy entrepreneurs. Here, rather than belabor those aspects of my discussion, I explore several practical implications in a thematic fashion.

Believing in Ideas

In the world of politics ideas matter. Of course interests are also important, but ideas matter in a more fundamental way. It is through the power of ideas that particular individuals and groups come to appreciate where their interests lie. Just as problems and identities are recognized and constituted through the power of language, so we see that interests—far from being immutable—are also subject to redefinition through framing, argumentation, and deliberation. The starting point for policy entrepreneurship is the understanding that there is an arbitrariness to present policy settings and how we have come to interpret and justify them. Having a sound knowledge and deep appreciation of alternative ideas about politics and society is vital for aspiring policy entrepreneurs. The ability to "test" ideas against observed structures and practices in an ongoing way can help nourish a skeptical instinct. From here it becomes easier to imagine alternative ways of organizing the social and political world. Further, an appreciation of the power of ideas can improve the ability of a policy entrepreneur to listen to others and seek to understand why they hold particular views. Believing in ideas does not mean holding tightly to some dogma and relentlessly screening out or ruthlessly criticizing all thoughts, suggestions, or actions that do not conform to it. In fact, such behavior represents the negation both of critical thought and of an awareness of how ideas shape everyday practices. Believing in ideas means being open to alternative ways of thinking about things. This is how scholars in both the humanities and the sciences come to make advances in their knowledge of the world. Through skepticism and an almost playful approach to engaging the world, entrepreneurs in the marketplace come to see possibilities for introducing innovative products and processes. And, through believing in ideas, those drawn to the world of politics can begin developing alternative proposals for the usage and design of public policy.

Learning from Others

Just as believing in ideas can help policy entrepreneurs see possibilities for change, so close engagement with others can provide crucial insights into the ways that others interpret and judge social experiences and public policies. It is often easy to categorize others and imagine that you know what they will say about things without actually taking the time to talk with them. But to do this is to seriously underestimate the value that can come from listening to others and engaging in deliberation about aspects of politics and public policy. Policy entrepreneurs simply cannot achieve their goals unless they can attain an audience for themselves. This does not mean that the person with the biggest megaphone will have the greatest hopes of success. Rather, policy entrepreneurs must be prepared to build their skills as listeners, finding ways to draw others into conversation and thus share their thoughts and concerns. Budding policy entrepreneurs may start out with some particular idea for a policy innovation. Through the process of presenting the idea to others and listening to their reactions, however, it is possible to achieve an awareness of flaws in that original idea and begin thinking about ways to address them. A process of close engagement with others can therefore lead a policy entrepreneur to develop a proposal for policy change that eventually is both more refined and more likely to receive broad acceptance than the idea that he or she began with. Of course, it is impossible to talk to everybody who might have something useful to say about a given proposal for policy change. But, over time, it is likely that a policy entrepreneur will develop an awareness of the people whom it would make most sense to listen to and learn from. Several of the school choice policy entrepreneurs identified in this study gained important insights and support from people who, at first thought, might have seemed unlikely to have been of much help at all. On reflection, perhaps this is not so surprising: entrepreneurs in the marketplace often learn from engaging with people whom they would not interact with in the normal course of things. Similarly, academics often achieve important insights by listening to others and thinking about the ideas of those outside their immediate circles of professional colleagues (see, for example, Krugman 1993).

Maintaining Perspective

In seeking to introduce policy innovations and advance significant policy change, policy entrepreneurs establish ambitious goals. Since current policy settings benefit many people and others grow to accept them—even when they may not be serving them well—efforts to secure change will inevitably meet with at least some resistance. For policy entrepreneurs, this means that maintaining a sense of perspective is crucial. Keeping an eye on the eventual policy goals and having a clear sense of the sequence of steps that must be taken to achieve those goals can prove helpful. Most of the policy entrepreneurs identified in this study had to work very hard to secure the policy changes they desired. They often had to scale back their original plans or make compromises, knowing that eventually they would once again attempt to achieve their initial goals. Some policy entrepreneurs came to see virtue in accepting compromises, realizing that some piecemeal steps toward school choice could help build momentum that later would support attempts at a great leap forward. Nonetheless, in the face of the many real or imagined obstacles that lie in the way of aspiring policy entrepreneurs, now and then the temptation to give up must be strong. At these times, having a group of energetic supporters and being able to readily identify those things that *have* been accomplished can be important for keeping spirits up. This is when having role models and mentors can also be important. Sometimes, it is in these periods of doubt that past mistakes are thrown into clearer relief and new ideas for future strategies can start taking shape. Much about entrepreneurship, be it in the marketplace or in politics, is difficult—and on some occasions giving up might be the best thing to do. Yet many policy entrepreneurs have succeeded in securing policy change against the odds. Reflecting upon what such people managed to accomplish, and how they did it, can be an inspiration. Their accomplishments serve as powerful reminders that individuals with good intentions, well-developed communication skills, and the ability to work closely with a range of others can make big differences to the organization of society. Ultimately, what they achieved mattered far more than where they started from.

Departures

In this book I have established a theoretical basis for the concept of the *policy entrepreneur*. I did this by considering the ways that particular actors in the policymaking process can be thought of as direct counterparts to entrepreneurs in the marketplace. Successful policy entrepreneurs often prompt policy changes that have dynamic effects. That is to say, the changes they bring about trigger further chain reactions. This has begun to happen with the rise of school choice in the United States.

Having closely studied entrepreneurship in theory and practice, I know that the tentative first steps of one individual frequently provide the impetus for others to come forward and initiate truly path-breaking change. But this phenomenon is not confined to the world of the entrepreneur. We see it in many places, including the groves of academe. In this book I have reflected upon discussions of policy entrepreneurship and policy change, and I have taken some first steps in a new direction. These steps contribute to our understanding of policy change and the processes that have supported the rise of school choice. Yet while my work here is done, I know there is much left to understand. An answer is always an invitation to new questions. This should be a cause for excitement rather than despair. Here, then, an end. And also, a site for more departures.

Note

1. With Sandra Vergari, I have combined insights from the Advocacy Coalition Framework and the concept of the policy entrepreneur to analyze the dynamics of education policy reform in Michigan (see Mintrom and Vergari 1996).

APPENDIX: THE SURVEY QUESTIONNAIRE

Survey: State-Level School Choice Policy Entrepreneurs

PLEASE WRITE THE NAME OF YOUR STATE: ______________________

YOUR NAME AND POSITION: ______________________

CONTACT TELEPHONE NUMBER: ______________________

1. BEFORE SCHOOL CHOICE WAS CONSIDERED BY YOUR STATE LEGISLATORS, WHO DO YOU THINK WERE THE MOST IMPORTANT SCHOOL CHOICE POLICY ENTREPRENEURS IN YOUR STATE, AND ABOUT WHAT YEAR DID THEY *FIRST* ADVOCATE SCHOOL CHOICE?

Names of the Most Important School Choice Policy Entrepreneurs	**Year School Choice Policy Was First Advocated**	**Occupation or Business**
a	19___	
b	19___	
c	19___	
d	19___	
e	19___	

NOTE: I care about *proposals* made by the policy entrepreneurs regardless of their success.

2. WERE THERE ANY PARTICULAR EVENTS THAT PRECIPITATED THE PROPOSALS FOR SCHOOL CHOICE?

____

____

3. WHAT WERE THE MOTIVES OF THE POLICY ENTREPRENEURS?

____

____

4. THERE HAVE BEEN MANY SCHOOL CHOICE EXPERIMENTS. DID ANY OF THEM INFLUENCE THE ENTREPRENEURS IN YOUR STATE?

1st ______________________________________

2nd ______________________________________

3rd ______________________________________

5. WHAT PEOPLE OR ORGANIZATIONS WORKING AT THE *NATIONAL* LEVEL INFLUENCED THE POLICY ENTREPRENEURS IN YOUR STATE?

1st ______________________________________

2nd ______________________________________

3rd ______________________________________

6. WHEN THE IDEA OF SCHOOL CHOICE WAS FIRST SUGGESTED IN YOUR STATE, WHAT WERE THE POSITIONS OF THE FOLLOWING INDIVIDUALS AND GROUPS?

(CHECK THE APPROPRIATE CIRCLE ON EACH LINE.)

	Strongly Opposed 1	2	3	4	5 Strongly Supportive	No Clear Position
The State Governor	○	○	○	○	○	○
State Legislators—Upper House	○	○	○	○	○	○
State Legislators—Lower House	○	○	○	○	○	○
The Chief State School Officer	○	○	○	○	○	○
School Superintendents	○	○	○	○	○	○
Public School Boards	○	○	○	○	○	○
Other Bureaucrats: Who?	○	○	○	○	○	○

	Strongly Opposed 1	2	3	4	5 Strongly Supportive	No Clear Position
State Teachers Associations	○	○	○	○	○	○
Private Schools Associations	○	○	○	○	○	○
Private Business Groups	○	○	○	○	○	○
Parents Groups	○	○	○	○	○	○
The News Media	○	○	○	○	○	○
Any Other Important Group or Individual: Who?	○	○	○	○	○	○

7. SPECIFICALLY, *HOW* DID THE POLICY ENTREPRENEURS YOU IDENTIFIED MAKE A DIFFERENCE IN RAISING THE ISSUE OF SCHOOL CHOICE IN YOUR STATE?

(CHECK EACH APPLICABLE CIRCLE AND, IF POSSIBLE, NAME THE RELEVANT ENTREPRENEUR.)

		Which Entrepreneur?
Established a foundation to promote school choice ideas (like the Manhattan Institute's Center for Educational Innovation)	○	
Produced policy advice for legislators in which the implementation of school choice was advocated	○	
Wrote articles for newspapers (like Joe Nathan in Minnesota)	○	
Wrote a book (like Charles Glenn in Massachusetts)	○	
Implemented a local-level choice experiment (as in East Harlem District 4 in New York)	○	
Advocated a *publicly* funded voucher scheme (like Polly Williams in Wisconsin)	○	
Implemented a *privately* funded voucher scheme (like the Golden Rule Insurance Company in Indianapolis)	○	
Other (please specify)	○	

8. FREQUENTLY, POLICY ENTREPRENEURS ATTEMPT TO DEVELOP COALITIONS TO HELP PROMOTE THEIR IDEAS. DID THE SCHOOL CHOICE POLICY ENTREPRENEURS IN YOUR STATE DO ANY OF THE FOLLOWING?

(CHECK EACH APPLICABLE CIRCLE.)

Established a coalition of concerned citizens (like the Georgia Parents for Better Education)	○
Established a private business coalition (like the North Carolina Business Committee for Education)	○
Established a broad-based coalition (like TEACH Michigan, a large, rapidly growing grass-roots coalition of business, government, and minority leaders)	○
Used an established education-related coalition to advocate school choice (what group?)	○
Other (please specify)	○

9. POLITICIANS AND POLICY ADVOCATES USE A VARIETY OF TECHNIQUES TO KEEP THEIR COALITIONS TOGETHER. DID THE POLICY ENTREPRENEURS USE THESE TECHNIQUES?

(CHECK THE APPROPRIATE CIRCLE ON EACH LINE.)

Not Important	1	2	3	4	5	Very Important
Informational devices such as newsletters	○	○	○	○	○	
A stress on public policy goals	○	○	○	○	○	
The ability to make others feel as though they were part of a team that was trying to accomplish an important job for the state	○	○	○	○	○	
Possible professional or personal payoffs from being part of a successful coalition	○	○	○	○	○	
The friendship of individuals in the coalition	○	○	○	○	○	
Benefits from belonging to the group, such as group insurance or travel benefits	○	○	○	○	○	

10. COMPARED WITH INTEREST GROUP LOBBYISTS AND POLICY ADVOCATES IN YOUR STATE, HOW EFFECTIVE WERE THE SCHOOL CHOICE POLICY ENTREPRENEURS YOU HAVE IDENTIFIED IN TERMS OF THE FOLLOWING ACTIVITIES?

(CHECK THE APPROPRIATE CIRCLE ON EACH LINE.)

	Not Effective 1	2	3	4	5 Very Effective
Inspiring and leading like-minded people	○	○	○	○	○
Presenting their message through the media	○	○	○	○	○
Establishing wide support among the general public	○	○	○	○	○
Developing and maintaining good relations with:					
—The State Governor	○	○	○	○	○
—State Legislators	○	○	○	○	○
—The Chief State School Officer	○	○	○	○	○
—School Superintendents	○	○	○	○	○
—Public School Boards	○	○	○	○	○
—State Teachers' Associations	○	○	○	○	○
—Private Schools Associations	○	○	○	○	○
—Private Business Groups	○	○	○	○	○
—Parent Groups	○	○	○	○	○

11. FINALLY, HOW IMPORTANT WERE EACH OF THE FOLLOWING STRATEGIES FOR THE SCHOOL CHOICE POLICY ENTREPRENEURS IN YOUR STATE?

(CHECK THE APPROPRIATE CIRCLE ON EACH LINE.)

	Not Important 1	2	3	4	5 Very Important
Collecting evidence from other choice experiments to demonstrate the merits of the idea	○	○	○	○	○
Finding out the attitudes to school choice of members of the policy elite in your state	○	○	○	○	○
Finding out public opinion on school choice in your state	○	○	○	○	○
Team building among subordinates and colleagues to inspire commitment to change	○	○	○	○	○
Networking with others in and around government and using these contacts to help achieve their policy goals	○	○	○	○	○

	Not Important	1	2	3	4	5	Very Important
Networking with school choice advocates from neighboring states		○	○	○	○	○	
Networking with school choice advocates from other (i.e., nonneighboring) states		○	○	○	○	○	
Using or developing perceptions of crises to increase interest in and support for alternative ways of organizing the school system		○	○	○	○	○	
Framing problems with the state school system to make school choice seem an appealing alternative		○	○	○	○	○	
Presenting the problems with the state school system in a way that led to a realignment of interests into a new coalition supporting school choice		○	○	○	○	○	

ARE THERE ANY OTHER PEOPLE IN YOUR STATE WHOM I SHOULD TALK TO ABOUT THE SCHOOL CHOICE ISSUE? PLEASE WRITE THEIR NAMES, ETC. ON THE BACK OF THIS PAGE.

THANK YOU FOR YOUR TIME AND COOPERATION. PLEASE MAIL BACK THE COMPLETED QUESTIONNAIRE IN THE ENVELOPE PROVIDED.

Bibliography

Ainsworth, Scott. 1993. "Regulating Lobbyists and Interest Group Influence." *Journal of Politics* 55: 41–56.

Akerlof, George A., and Janet L. Yellen. 1985. "Can Small Deviations from Rationality Make Significant Differences to Economic Equilibria?" *American Economic Review* 75: 708–720.

Alchian, Armen A., and Harold Demsetz. 1972. "Production, Information Costs, and Economic Organization." *American Economic Review* 62: 777–795.

Aldrich, Howard, and Catherine Zimmer. 1986. "Entrepreneurship Through Social Networks." In *The Art and Science of Entrepreneurship*. Eds. Donald L. Sexton and Raymond W. Smilor. Cambridge, Mass.: Ballinger.

Allison, Paul D. 1984. *Event History Analysis: Regression for Longitudinal Event Data*. Newbury Park, Calif.: Sage.

Atkinson, Anthony B. 1996. "Political Economy, Old and New." In *A New Handbook of Political Science*. Eds. Robert E. Goodin and Hans-Dieter Klingemann. New York: Oxford University Press.

Bachrach, Peter, and Morton S. Baratz. 1962. "Two Faces of Power." *American Political Science Review* 54: 947–952.

Banerjee, Abhijit V. 1992. "A Simple Model of Herd Behavior." *Quarterly Journal of Economics* 107: 797–817.

Banks, Jeffrey S., and Eric A. Hanushek, eds. 1995. *Modern Political Economy: Old Topics, New Directions*. New York: Cambridge University Press.

Bardach, Eugene. 1972. *The Skill Factor in Politics: Repealing the Mental Commitment Laws in California*. Berkeley: University of California Press.

Barzel, Yoram. 1984. "The Entrepreneur's Reward for Self-Policing." *Economic Inquiry* 25: 103–116.

Barzel, Yoram. 1989. *Economic Analysis of Property Rights*. New York: Cambridge University Press.

Baumgartner, Frank R., and Bryan D. Jones. 1993. *Agendas and Instability in American Politics*. Chicago: University of Chicago Press.

Baumol, William J. 1993. *Entrepreneurship, Management, and the Structure of Payoffs*. Cambridge, Mass.: The MIT Press.

Becker, Gary S. 1976. *The Economic Approach to Human Behavior*. Chicago: University of Chicago Press.

Berliner, David C., and Bruce J. Biddle. 1995. *The Manufactured Crisis: Myths, Fraud and the Attack on America's Public Schools*. Reading, Mass.: Addison-Wesley.

Berry, Frances Stokes. 1994. "Sizing Up State Policy Innovation Research." *Policy Studies Journal* 22: 442–456.

Berry, Frances Stokes, and William D. Berry. 1990. "State Lottery Adoptions as Policy Innovations: An Event History Analysis." *American Political Science Review* 84: 395–415.

Berry, Frances Stokes, and William D. Berry. 1992. "Tax Innovation in the States: Capitalizing on Political Opportunity." *American Journal of Political Science* 36: 715–743.

Bibby, John F., and Thomas M. Holbrook. 1996. "Parties and Elections." In *Politics in the American States: A Comparative Analysis*. Third ed. Eds. Virginia Gray and Herbert Jacob. Washington, D.C.: Congressional Quarterly Press.

Blank, Rolf K., Roger E. Levine, and Lauri Steel. 1996. "After 15 Years: Magnet Schools in Urban Education." In *Who Chooses? Who Loses?: Culture, Institutions, and the Unequal Effects of School Choice*. Eds. Bruce Fuller and Richard F. Elmore with Gary Orfield. New York: Teachers College Press.

Bourdieu, Pierre. 1977. *Outline of a Theory of Practice*. Trans. Richard Nice. New York: Cambridge University Press.

Boyer, Ernest. 1992. *School Choice*. Princeton, N.J.: Carnegie Foundation for the Advancement of Teaching.

Brandl, John. 1989. "An Education Policy Agenda for Legislators." In *Public Schools by Choice*. Ed. Joe Nathan. St. Paul, Minn.: The Institute for Learning and Teaching.

Brandl, John. 1998. *Money and Good Intentions Are Not Enough: Or, Why a Liberal Democrat Thinks States Need Both Competition and Community*. Washington, D.C.: The Brookings Institution.

Bridge, R. Gary, and Julie Blackman. 1978. *A Study of Alternatives in American Education, Volume IV: Family Choice in Education* R-2170/4 NIE. Santa Monica, Calif.: The Rand Corporation.

Cantillon, Richard. (1755) 1931. *Essay on the Nature of Commerce in General*. Ed., trans., and other material, Henry Higgs. London: Macmillan (for the Royal Economic Society).

Capell, Frank J. 1978. *A Study of Alternatives in American Education, Volume VI: Student Outcomes in Alum Rock, 1974–76* R-2170/6 NIE. Santa Monica, Calif.: The Rand Corporation.

Carnegie Foundation for the Advancement of Teaching. 1992. *School Choice.* Princeton, N.J.: The Carnegie Foundation.

Caro, Robert A. 1974. *The Power Broker: Robert Moses and the Fall of New York.* New York: Knopf.

Casson, Mark. 1982. *The Entrepreneur: An Economic Theory.* Totowa, N.J.: Barnes & Noble Books.

Chubb, John E., and Terry M. Moe. 1990. *Politics, Markets, and America's Schools.* Washington, D.C.: The Brookings Institution.

Coase, Ronald H. 1937. "The Nature of the Firm." *Economica* 4: 386–405.

Cobb, Roger W., and Charles W. Elder. 1983. *Participation in American Politics: The Dynamics of Agenda-Building.* Second ed. Boston: Allyn and Bacon.

Cohen, David K., and Eleanor Farrar. 1977. "Power to the Parents?—The Story of Education Vouchers." *The Public Interest* 48: 72–97.

Cookson, Peter W., Jr. 1994. *School Choice: The Struggle for the Soul of American Education.* New Haven, Conn.: Yale University Press.

Coons, John E., and Stephen Sugarman. 1978. *Education by Choice: The Case for Family Control.* Berkeley: University of California Press.

Council of State Governments. 1992. *The Book of the States.* Lexington, Ky.: Council of State Governments.

Cyert, Richard M., and James G. March. 1963. *A Behavioral Theory of the Firm.* Englewood Cliffs, N.J.: Prentice-Hall.

Dahl, Robert A. 1961. *Who Governs?: Democracy and Power in an American City.* New Haven, Conn.: Yale University Press.

Daniels, Timothy H. n.d. "Passing Charter School Legislation in a Change-Resistant State: A Pennsylvania Case Study. Or Cloud-seeding to Make Charter Schools 'Reign' in Pennsylvania." Department of Education, Harrisburg, Penn.

Delaney, Thomas J. 1995. "Participation of Rural Students with Disabilities and Rural Gifted Students in Open Enrollment." *Rural Special Education Quarterly,* 14: 31–35.

Demsetz, Harold. 1991. "The Theory of the Firm Revisited." In *The Nature of the Firm: Origins, Evolution, and Development.* Eds. Oliver E. Williamson and Sidney G. Winter. New York: Oxford University Press.

Derthick, Martha, and Paul J. Quirk. 1985. *The Politics of Deregulation.* Washington, D.C.: The Brookings Institution.

Doig, Jameson W. and Erwin C. Hargrove, eds. 1987. *Leadership and Innovation: A Biographical Perspective on Entrepreneurship in Government.* Baltimore: Johns Hopkins University Press.

Downs, Anthony. 1957. *An Economic Theory of Democracy.* New York: Harper.

Drucker, Peter F. 1986. *Innovation and Entrepreneurship: Practice and Principles*. New York: Harper Business.

Dye, Thomas R. 1966. *Politics, Economics, and the Public: Political Outcomes in the American States*. Chicago: Rand McNally.

Easton, David. 1953. *The Political System: An Inquiry in the State of Political Science*. New York: Alfred A. Knopf.

Education Commission of the States. 1992. "Legislative Activities Involving Open Enrollment (Choice)." Clearing House Notes. Denver, Colo.: Education Commission of the States.

Eggertsson, Thráinn. 1990. *Economic Behavior and Institutions: Principles of Neoinstitutional Economics*. New York: Cambridge University Press.

Ellison, Glenn, and Drew Fudenberg. 1995. "Word-of-Mouth Communication and Social Learning." *Quarterly Journal of Economics* 110: 93–125.

Elmore, Richard F. 1991. "Public School Choice as a Policy Issue." In *Privatization and Its Alternatives*. Ed. William T. Gormley, Jr. Madison: The University of Wisconsin Press.

Elmore, Richard F. and Bruce Fuller. 1996. "Empirical Research on School Choice: What Are the Implications for Policy-Makers?" In *Who Chooses? Who Loses?: Culture, Institutions, and the Unequal Effects of School Choice*. Eds. Bruce Fuller and Richard F. Elmore with Gary Orfield. New York: Teachers College Press.

Evensky, Jerry. 1990. *Economic Ideas and Issues*. Englewood Cliffs, N.J.: Prentice-Hall.

Eyestone, Robert. 1978. *From Social Issues to Public Policy*. New York: John Wiley and Sons.

Fantini, Mario. 1973. *Decentralization: Achieving Reform*. New York: Praeger.

Feigenbaum, Harvey, Jeffrey Henig, and Chris Hamnett. 1999. *Shrinking the State: The Political Underpinnings of Privatization*. New York: Cambridge University Press.

Finnemore, Martha. 1996. *National Interests in International Society*. Ithaca, N.Y.: Cornell University Press.

Fliegel, Seymour. 1990. "Creative Non-Compliance." In *Choice and Control in American Education, Volume 2: The Practice of Choice, Decentralization and School Restructuring*. Eds. William H. Clune and John F. Witte. New York: The Falmer Press.

Fliegel, Seymour with James MacGuire. 1993. *Miracle in East Harlem: The Fight for Choice in Public Education*. New York: Times Books.

Fossey, Richard. 1992. "School Choice Legislation: A Survey of the States." Consortium for Policy Research in Education Occasional Paper. New Brunswick, N.J.: Consortium for Policy Research in Education.

Friedman, Jeffrey, ed. 1996. *The Rational Choice Controversy: Economic Models of Politics Reconsidered*. New Haven, Conn.: Yale University Press.

Friedman, Milton. 1955. "The Role of Government in Education." In *Economics and the Public Interest*. Ed. Robert A. Solo. New Brunswick, N.J.: Rutgers University Press.

Friedman, Milton. 1962. *Capitalism and Freedom*. Chicago: University of Chicago Press.

Fuhrman, Susan H., and Diane Massell. 1992. *Issues and Strategies in Systemic Reform*. New Brunswick, N.J.: Center for Policy Research in Education.

Fuller, Bruce, Richard F. Elmore, and Gary Orfield. 1996. "Policy-Making in the Dark: Illuminating the School Choice Debate." In *Who Chooses? Who Loses?: Culture, Institutions, and the Unequal Effects of School Choice*. Eds. Bruce Fuller and Richard F. Elmore with Gary Orfield. New York: Teachers College Press.

Funkhouser, Janie E., and Kelly W. Colopy. 1994. *Minnesota's Open Enrollment Option: Impacts on School Districts*. Washington, D.C.: U.S. Department of Education/Policy Studies Associates.

Geisel, Jerry. 1997. "J. Patrick Rooney: Promoting MSAs to Give Employees Greater Choice in Health Care." *Business Insurance* 31 (3 November) S94–95.

Gintis, Herbert. 1995. "The Political Economy of School Choice." *Teachers College Record* 96: 492–511.

Glick, Henry R., and Scott P. Hays. 1991. "Innovation and Reinvention in State Policymaking: Theory and the Evolution of Living Will Laws." *Journal of Politics* 53: 835–850.

Goffman, Erving. 1956. *The Presentation of Self in Everyday Life*. Edinburgh: University of Edinburgh Social Science Research Center.

Goffman, Erving. 1974. *Frame Analysis: An Essay on the Organization of Experience*. New York: Harper Row.

Goggin, Malcolm. 1987. *Policy Design and the Politics of Implementation: The Case of Child Health Care in the American States*. Knoxville: University of Tennessee Press.

Gramsci, Antonio. 1934. "The Intellectuals." In *Selections from the Prison Notebooks* (1971). Ed. and trans. by Quintin Hoare and Geoffrey Nowell Smith. New York: International Publishers.

Granovetter, Mark S. 1973. "The Strength of Weak Ties." *American Journal of Sociology* 78: 1360–1380.

Granovetter, Mark S. 1985. "Economic Action and Social Structure: The Problem of Embeddedness." *American Journal of Sociology* 91: 481–510.

Gray, Virginia. 1973. "Innovation in the States: A Diffusion Study." *American Political Science Review* 67: 1174–1185.

Green, David E. 1987. *Shaping Political Consciousness*. Ithaca, N.Y.: Cornell University Press.

Green, Donald P., and Ian Shapiro. 1994. *Pathologies of Rational Choice Theory: A Critique of Applications in Political Science*. New Haven, Conn.: Yale University Press.

Gujarati, Damodar N. 1995. *Basic Econometrics*. Third ed. New York: McGraw-Hill.

Hall, Peter A., and Rosemary C. R. Taylor. 1996. "Political Science and the Three New Institutionalisms." *Political Studies* 44: 936–958.

Hayek, Friedrich A. von. (1946) 1948. "The Meaning of Competition," Stafford Little Lecture, Princeton University, May. Reprinted in *Individualism and Economic Order*. Chicago: University of Chicago Press.

Heckman, James. 1976. "The Common Structure of Statistical Models of Truncation, Sample Selection, and Limited Dependent Variables and a Simple Estimator for Such Models." *Annals of Economic and Social Measurement* 4: 475–492.

Heckman, James. 1979. "Sample Selection Bias as a Specification Error." *Econometrica* 47: 153–161.

Heclo, Hugh. 1978. "Issue Networks and the Executive Establishment." In *The New American Political System*. Ed. Anthony King. Washington, D.C.: The American Enterprise Institute.

Hedge, David M. 1998. *Governance and the Changing American States*. Boulder, Colo.: Westview Press.

Heise, Michael. 1993. "Public Funds, Private Schools, and the Court: Legal Issues and Policy Consequences." *Texas Tech Law Review* 25: 137–150.

Henig, Jeffrey R. 1994. *Rethinking School Choice: Limits of the Market Metaphor*. Princeton, N.J.: Princeton University Press.

Heritage Foundation. 1992, 1993. *School Choice Programs: What's Happening in the States*. Washington, D.C.: Heritage Foundation.

Himmelstein, Jerome L. 1990. *To The Right: The Transformation of American Conservatism*. Berkeley: University of California Press.

Hirsch, Eric D. 1987. *Cultural Literacy: What Every American Needs to Know*. Boston: Houghton Mifflin.

Hirschman, Albert O. 1970. *Exit, Voice, and Loyalty*. Cambridge, Mass.: Harvard University Press.

Horn, Murray J. 1995. *The Political Economy of Public Administration*. New York: Cambridge University Press.

Hosansky, David. 1997. "Phone Banks to E-Mail." *Congressional Quarterly Weekly Report* 55 (29 November): 2942–2943.

Hunter, Floyd. 1953. *Community Power Structure: A Study of Decision Makers*. Chapel Hill: University of North Carolina Press.

Jencks, Christopher. 1966. "Is the Public School Obsolete?" *The Public Interest* 2: 18–27.

Jenkins-Smith, Hank C., and Paul A. Sabatier, eds. 1993. *Policy Change and Learning: An Advocacy Coalition Approach*. Boulder, Colo.: Westview Press.

Jones, Bryan D. 1994. *Reconceiving Decision-Making in Democratic Politics*. Chicago: University of Chicago Press.

Kahneman, Daniel, Paul Slovic, and Amos Tversky, eds. 1982. *Judgment*

Under Uncertainty: Heuristics and Biases. Cambridge: Cambridge University Press.

Kaplin, George R., and Michael D. Usdan. 1992. "The Changing Look of Education's Policy Networks." *Phi Delta Kappan* May: 664–672.

Keck, Margaret E., and Kathryn Sikkink. 1998. *Activists Beyond Borders: Advocacy Networks in International Politics*. Ithaca, N.Y.: Cornell University Press.

Kelman, Steven. 1987. *Making Public Policy: A Hopeful View of American Government*. New York: Basic Books.

Kenis, Patrick, and Volker Schneider. 1991. "Policy Networks and Policy Analysis: Scrutinizing a New Analytical Toolbox." In *Policy Networks: Empirical Evidence and Theoretical Considerations*. Eds. Bernd Marin and Renate Mayntz. Boulder, Colo.: Westview Press.

Kettl, Donald F. 1986. *Leadership at the Fed*. New Haven, Conn.: Yale University Press.

King, Paula J. 1988. "Policy Entrepreneurs: Catalysts in the Policy Innovation Process." Ph.D. diss. University of Minnesota.

Kingdon, John W. (1984) 1995. *Agendas, Alternatives, and Public Policies*. Second ed. Boston: Little, Brown & Company.

Kirkpatrick, David W. 1990. *Choice in Schooling: A Case for Tuition Vouchers*. Chicago: Loyola University Press.

Kirst, Michael W., Gail Meister, and Stephen R. Rowley. 1984. "Policy Issue Networks: Their Influence on State Policymaking." *Policy Studies Journal* 13: 247–263.

Kirzner, Israel M. 1973. "Entrepreneurship and the Equilibrating Process." In *Competition and Entrepreneurship*. Ed. Israel M. Kirzner. Chicago: University of Chicago Press.

Knight, Frank H. 1921. *Risk, Uncertainty and Profit*. Boston: Houghton Mifflin.

Knoke, David. 1990. *Political Networks: The Structural Perspective*. New York: Cambridge University Press.

Kraar, Louis. 1991. "25 Who Help the U.S. Win." *Fortune* 123 (spring): 34–45.

Krehbiel, Keith. 1991. *Information and Legislative Organization*. Ann Arbor: University of Michigan Press.

Kreps, David M. 1990. "Corporate Culture and Economic Theory." In *Perspectives on Positive Political Economy*. Eds. James E. Alt and Kenneth A. Shepsle. New York: Cambridge University Press.

Krugman, Paul. 1993. "How I Work." *The American Economist* 37 (2): 25–31.

Kuhn, Thomas S. 1970. *The Structure of Scientific Revolutions*. Second ed. Chicago: University of Chicago Press.

Lau, Matthew Y. 1994. "The Participation of Students Who Are Identified as Gifted and Talented in Minnesota's Open Enrollment Option." *Journal for the Education of the Gifted* 17: 276–298.

Laumann, Edward O., David Knoke, and Yong-Hak Kim. 1985. "An Organizational Approach to State Policy Formation: A Comparative Study of Energy and Health Domains." *American Sociological Review* 50: 1–19.

Lavoire, Don. 1991. "The Discovery and Interpretation of Profit Opportunities: Culture and the Kirznerian Entrepreneur." In *The Culture of the Entrepreneur*. Ed. Brigitte Berger. San Francisco: Institute for Contemporary Studies.

Lee, Valerie E., and Anthony S. Bryk. 1993. "Science or Policy Argument? A Review of the Quantitative Evidence in Chubb and Moe's *Politics, Markets, and America's Schools*." In *School Choice: Examining the Evidence*. Eds. Edith Rasell and Richard Rothstein. Washington, D.C.: Economic Policy Institute.

Lee, Valerie E., Robert G. Croninger, and Julia B. Smith. 1996. "Equity and Choice in Detroit." In *Who Chooses? Who Loses?: Culture, Institutions, and the Unequal Effects of School Choice*. Eds. Bruce Fuller and Richard F. Elmore with Gary Orfield. New York: Teachers College Press.

Leibenstein, Harvey. 1978. *General X-Efficiency Theory and Economic Development*. New York: Oxford University Press.

Levin, Henry M. 1998. "Educational Vouchers: Effectiveness, Choice, and Costs." *Journal of Policy Analysis and Management* 17: 373–393.

Levin, Martin A., and Mary Bryna Sanger. 1994. *Making Government Work: How Entrepreneurial Executives Turn Bright Ideas into Real Results*. San Francisco: Jossey-Bass.

Libecap, Gary D. 1989. *Contracting for Property Rights*. New York: Cambridge University Press.

Lindblom, Charles E. 1968. *The Policymaking Process*. Englewood Cliffs, N.J.: Prentice-Hall.

Loasby, Bryan J. 1983. "Knowledge, Learning and Enterprise." In *Beyond Positive Economics*. Ed. J. Wiseman. London: Macmillan.

Lowi, Theodore J. 1964. *At the Pleasure of the Mayor: Patronage and Power in New York City, 1898–1958*. New York: Free Press.

Mahajan, Vijay, and Robert A. Peterson. 1985. *Models for Innovation Diffusion*. Newbury Park, Calif.: Sage.

Majone, Giandomenico. 1996. "Public Policy and Administration: Ideas, Interests and Institutions." In *A New Handbook of Political Science*. Ed. Robert E. Goodin and Hans-Dieter Klingemann. New York: Oxford University Press.

March, James G., and Guje Sevón. 1988. "Gossip, Information and Decision-Making." In *Decisions and Organizations*. Ed. James G. March. Oxford: Basil Blackwell.

March, James G., and Johan P. Olsen. 1989. *Rediscovering Institutions: The Organizational Basis of Politics*. New York: Free Press.

Marshall, Alfred. 1890. *Principles of Economics*. London: Macmillan.

Martinez, Valerie, Kenneth Godwin, and Frank R. Kemerer. 1995. "Private

Vouchers in San Antonio: The CEO Program." In *Private Vouchers*. Ed. Terry M. Moe. Stanford, Calif.: The Hoover Institution.

McCracken, Grant. 1988. *The Long Interview*. Newbury Park, Calif.: Sage.

McCraw, Thomas K. 1984. *Prophets of Regulation*. Cambridge, Mass.: Harvard University Press.

McCubbins, Mathew D., and Terry Sullivan, eds. 1987. *Congress: Structure and Policy*. Cambridge: Cambridge University Press.

Meier, Deborah. 1995. *The Power of Their Ideas*. Boston: Beacon Press.

Miller, Gary J. 1992. *Managerial Dilemmas: The Political Economy of Hierarchy*. New York: Cambridge University Press.

Mintrom, Michael, and Sandra Vergari. 1996. "Advocacy Coalitions, Policy Entrepreneurs, and Policy Change." *Policy Studies Journal* 24: 420–435.

Moe, Terry M. 1980. *The Organization of Interests: Incentives and the Internal Dynamics of Political Interest Groups*. Chicago: University of Chicago Press.

Moe, Terry M. 1984. "The New Economics of Organization." *American Journal of Political Science* 28: 739–777.

Moe, Terry M. 1990. "The Politics of Structural Choice: Toward a Theory of Public Bureaucracy." In *Organization Theory: From Chester Barnard to the Present and Beyond*. Ed. Oliver E. Williamson. New York: Oxford University Press.

Moe, Terry M. 1991. "Politics and the Theory of Organization." *Journal of Law, Economics, and Organization* 7 (special issue): 106–129.

Moe, Terry M., ed. 1995. *Private Vouchers*. Stanford, Calif.: The Hoover Institution.

Mohr, Lawrence B. 1969. "Determinants of Innovation in Organizations." *American Political Science Review* 63: 111–126.

Montano, Jessie. 1989. "Choice Comes to Minnesota." In *Public Schools by Choice*. Ed. Joe Nathan. St. Paul, Minn.: The Institute for Learning and Teaching.

Mooney, Christopher Z., and Mei-Hsien Lee. 1995. "Legislating Morality in the American States: The Case of Pre-*Roe* Abortion Regulation Reform." *American Journal of Political Science* 39: 599–627.

Nader, Ralph. 1972. *Unsafe at Any Speed: The Design-in Dangers of the American Automobile*. New York: Grossman.

Nathan, Joe., ed. 1989. *Public Schools by Choice*. St. Paul, Minn.: The Institute for Learning and Teaching.

Nathan, Joe. 1996. *Charter Schools: Creating Hope and Opportunity for American Education*. San Francisco: Jossey-Bass.

Nathan, Joe, and Wayne Jennings. 1990. "Access to Opportunity: Experiences of Minnesota Students in Four Statewide School Choice Programs, 1989–90." Mimeograph. Minneapolis, Minn.: Center for School Change, Hubert H. Humphrey Institute of Public Affairs.

National Commission on Excellence in Education. 1983. *A Nation at Risk*. Washington, D.C.: U.S. Department of Education.

Nelson, Barbara. 1984. *Making an Issue of Child Abuse*. Chicago: University of Chicago Press.

Nelson, Barbara. 1996. "Public Policy and Administration: An Overview." In *A New Handbook of Political Science*. Eds. Robert E. Goodin and Hans-Dieter Klingemann. New York: Oxford University Press.

Nisbett, Richard, and Lee Ross. 1980. *Human Inference: Strategies and Shortcomings of Social Judgment*. Englewood Cliffs, N.J.: Prentice-Hall.

Norquist, John O. 1993. "A Ticket to Better Schools." *Readers Digest* 143: 65–71.

Oliver, Thomas R., and Pamela Paul-Shaheen. 1997. "Translating Ideas into Actions: Entrepreneurial Leadership in State Health Care Reforms." *Journal of Health Politics, Policy, and Law* 22: 721–788.

Olson, Mancur. 1965. *The Logic of Collective Action: Public Goods and the Theory of Groups*. Cambridge, Mass.: Harvard University Press.

Osborne, David, and Peter Plastrik. 1997. *Banishing Bureaucracy: The Five Strategies for Reinventing Government*. New York: Penguin-Putnam.

Ostrom, Elinor. 1965. "Public Entrepreneurship: A Case Study in Ground Water Basin Management." Ph.D. diss. University of California, Los Angeles.

Ostrom, Elinor. 1990. *Governing the Commons: The Evolution of Institutions for Collective Action*. New York: Cambridge University Press.

Peters, Thomas J., and Robert H. Waterman, Jr. 1982. *In Search of Excellence: Lessons from America's Best-run Companies*. New York: Warner Brothers.

Peterson, Mark A. 1993. "Political Influence in the 1990s: From Iron Triangles to Policy Networks." *Journal of Health Politics, Policy and Law* 18: 395–438.

Peterson, Paul E. 1981. *City Limits*. Chicago: University of Chicago Press.

Peterson, Paul E., and Bryan C. Hassel, eds. 1998. *Learning from School Choice*. Washington, D.C.: The Brookings Institution.

Peterson, Paul E., and Chad Noyes. 1997. "School Choice in Milwaukee." *New Schools for a New Century: The Redesign of Urban Education*. Eds. Diane Ravitch and Joseph P. Viteritti. New Haven, Conn.: Yale University Press.

Porter, Michael E. 1980. *Competitive Strategy: Techniques for Analyzing Industries and Competitors*. New York: Free Press.

Pressman, Jeffrey L., and Aaron B. Wildavsky. 1973. *Implementation*. Berkeley: University of California Press.

Quattrone, George A., and Amos Tversky. 1988. "Contrasting Rational and Psychological Analyses of Political Choice." *American Political Science Review* 82: 719–736.

Rash, Wayne. 1997. *Politics on the Nets: Wiring the Political Process*. New York: W. H. Freeman.

Ravitch, Diane. 1996. "Challenging Monopoly: In the Classroom." *Forbes* 158 (21 October): 56.

Ravitch, Diane, and Joseph Viteritti. 1996. "A New Vision for City Schools." *The Public Interest* 122: 3–14.

Raywid, Mary Anne. 1989. "The Mounting Case for Schools of Choice." In *Public Schools by Choice*. Ed. Joe Nathan. St. Paul, Minn.: The Institute for Learning and Teaching.

Raywid, Mary Anne. 1992. "Choice Orientations, Discussions, and Prospects." *Educational Policy* 6: 105–122.

Ricci, David M. 1993. *The Transformation of American Politics: The New Washington and the Rise of Think Tanks*. New Haven, Conn.: Yale University Press.

Riker, William H. 1986. *The Art of Political Manipulation*. New Haven, Conn.: Yale University Press.

Roberts, Nancy C., and Paula J. King. 1996. *Transforming Public Policy: Dynamics of Policy Entrepreneurship and Innovation*. San Francisco: Jossey-Bass.

Rogers, Everett M. (1962) 1995. *Diffusion of Innovations*. Fourth ed. New York: Free Press.

Rosenthal, Alan. 1998. *The Decline of Representative Democracy: Process, Participation, and Power in State Legislatures*. Washington, D.C.: Congressional Quarterly Press.

Rowbotham, Sheila. 1981. *Beyond the Fragments: Feminism and the Making of Socialism*. Boston: Alyson.

Sabatier, Paul A. 1988. "An Advocacy Coalition Framework of Policy Change and the Role of Policy-Oriented Learning Therein." *Policy Sciences* 21: 129–168.

Sabatier, Paul A. 1993. "Policy Change Over a Decade or More." In *Policy Change and Learning: An Advocacy Coalition Approach*. Eds. Paul A. Sabatier and Hank C. Jenkins-Smith. Boulder, Colo.: Westview Press.

Salisbury, Robert. 1969. "An Exchange Theory of Interest Groups." *American Journal of Political Science* 13: 1–32.

Sandler, Todd. 1992. *Collective Action Theory and Applications*. Ann Arbor: University of Michigan Press.

Sassen, Saskia. 1998. *Globalization and Its Discontents: Essays on the New Mobility of People and Money*. New York: New Press.

Savas, E. S. 1987. *Privatization: The Key to Better Government*. Chatham, Mass.: Chatham House.

Saxenian, Annalee. 1994. *Regional Advantage: Culture and Competition in Silicon Valley and Route 128*. Cambridge, Mass.: Harvard University Press.

Say, Jean-Baptiste. 1821. *A Treatise on Political Economy*. London: Longman.

Schattschneider, E. E. 1960. *The Semi-Sovereign People*. Hinsdale, Ill.: The Dryden Press.

Schiller, Wendy J. 1995. "Senators as Policy Entrepreneurs: Using Bill Sponsorship to Shape Legislative Agendas." *American Political Science Review* 39: 186–203.

Schneider, Anne Larason, and Helen Ingram. 1997. *Policy Design for Democracy.* Lawrence: University of Kansas Press.

Schneider, Mark, and Paul Teske with Michael Mintrom. 1995. *Public Entrepreneurs: Agents for Change in American Government.* Princeton, N.J.: Princeton University Press.

Schneider, Mark, Paul Teske, Melissa Marschall, Michael Mintrom, and Christine Roch. 1997. "Institutional Arrangements and the Creation of Social Capital: The Effects of Public School Choice." *American Political Science Review* 91: 82–93.

Schneider, Mark, Paul Teske, Christine Roch, and Melissa Marschall. 1998. "School Choice and Student Performance." Paper presented at the Annual meeting of the Midwest Political Science Association, Chicago. 23–25 April.

Schön, Donald A. 1971. *Beyond the Stable State.* New York: Norton.

Schön, Donald A., and Martin Rein. 1994. *Frame Reflection: Toward the Resolution of Intractable Policy Controversies.* New York: Basic Books.

Schumpeter, Joseph A. 1934. *The Theory of Economic Development: An Inquiry into Profits, Capital, Credit, Interest and the Business Cycle.* Trans. R. Opie. Cambridge, Mass.: Harvard University Press.

Shackle, George L. S. 1955. *Uncertainty in Economics and Other Reflections.* Cambridge: Cambridge University Press.

Shepsle, Kenneth A. 1979. "Institutional Arrangements and Equilibrium in Multidimensional Voting Models." *American Journal of Political Science* 23: 27–60.

Singer, Judith D., and John B. Willett. 1993. "It's About Time: Using Discrete-Time Survival Analysis to Study Duration and the Timing of Events." *Journal of Educational Statistics* 18: 155–195.

Smith, Adam. 1776. *An Inquiry into the Nature and Causes of the Wealth of Nations.* London: W. Strahan and T. Cadell.

Smith, James A. 1991. *The Idea Brokers.* New York: Free Press.

Smith, Kevin B., and Kenneth J. Meier. 1995. *School Choice: Politics, Markets, and Fools.* Armonk, N.Y.: M. E. Sharpe.

Snider, William. 1988. "Parental-Choice Bill Readied in Massachusetts." *Education Week* (7 December).

Steffens, Lincoln. 1938. *The Letters of Lincoln Steffens.* New York: Harcourt, Brace and Company.

Stevenson, Harold W. 1992. *The Learning Gap: Why Our Schools Are Failing and What We Can Learn from Japanese and Chinese Education.* New York: Summit Books.

Stone, Deborah. 1988. *Policy Paradox and Political Reason.* New York: Harper Collins.

Stone, Deborah. 1997. *Policy Paradox: The Art of Political Decision Making*. New York: W. W. Norton.

Swope, Christopher. 1997. "Mr. Smith E-Mails Washington: Constituents On Line." *Congressional Quarterly Weekly Report* 55 (29 November): 2940–2941.

Sunderman, Gail. 1992. "State Variation in Education Reform Initiatives During the 1980s: A Cross State Comparison." Typescript. Department of Education, University of Chicago.

Tenbusch, James P. 1993. "Parent Choice Behavior under Minnesota's Open Enrollment Program." Paper presented at the annual meeting of the American Educational Research Association, Atlanta, April.

Tenbusch, James P., and Michael S. Garet. 1993. "Organizational Change at the Local School Level under Minnesota's Open Enrollment Program." Paper presented at the annual meeting of the American Educational Research Association, Atlanta, April.

Tullock, Gordon. 1981. "Why So Much Stability?" *Public Choice* 37: 189–202.

Tyack, David B. 1974. *The One Best System: A History of American Urban Education*. Cambridge, Mass.: Harvard University Press.

U.S. Bureau of the Census. Annual. *Statistical Abstract of the U.S.* Washington, D.C.: U.S. Government Printing Office.

U.S. Department of Education Center for Choice in Education. 1992. *Issue Brief: Review of State Choice Legislation*. Washington, D.C.: U.S. Department of Education.

Veblen, Thorstein. (1898) 1919. *The Place of Science in Modern Civilization*. New York: Viking Press.

Viadero, Debra. 1998. "A Studied Opinion." *Education Week* 10 (October): 20–21.

Walker, Jack L. 1969. "The Diffusion of Innovations Among the American States." *American Political Science Review* 63: 880–899.

Walker, Jack L. 1981. "The Diffusion of Knowledge, Policy Communities, and Agenda Setting." In *New Strategic Perspectives on Social Policy*. Eds. John E. Tropman, Milan J. Dluhy, and Roger M. Lind. London: Pergamon.

Walras, Léon. (1874) 1954. *Elements of Pure Economics; Or, the Theory of Social Wealth*. Trans. William Jaffe. Homewood, Ill.: R. D. Irwin (for the American Economic Association and the Royal Economic Society).

Weber, Max. 1930. "The Spirit of Capitalism." In *The Protestant Work Ethic and the Spirit of Capitalism*. Trans. T. Parsons. New York: Charles Scribner's Sons, and London: George Allen and Unwin.

Weiler, Daniel. 1978. *A Study of Alternatives in American Education: Summary and Policy Implication* R-2170/7 NIE. Santa Monica, Calif.: The Rand Corporation.

Weisman, Jonathan. 1991. "In Indiana, Business Groups Not Talking as One on Reform." *Education Week*, 18 September.

Weisman, Jonathan. 1997. "Lawmakers Gingerly Step into the Information Age." *Congressional Quarterly Weekly Report* 55 (29 November): 2935–2937.

Weissert, Carol S. 1991. "Policy Entrepreneurs, Policy Opportunists, and Legislative Effectiveness." *American Politics Quarterly* 19: 262–274.

Wells, Amy Stuart. 1993. *A Time to Choose*. New York: Hill and Wang.

Wells, Amy Stuart. 1996. "African-American Students' View of School Choice." In *Who Chooses? Who Loses?: Culture, Institutions, and the Unequal Effects of School Choice*. Eds. Bruce Fuller and Richard F. Elmore with Gary Orfield. New York: Teachers College Press.

White, Lawrence H. 1976. "Entrepreneurship, Imagination and the Question of Equilibration." Unpublished paper, January 14. Reprinted in *Austrian Economics, Volume III*. Ed. Stephen Littlechild. Brookfield, Vt.: Edward Elgar.

Wildavsky, Aaron B. 1979. *Speaking Truth to Power: The Art and Craft of Policy Analysis*. Boston: Little, Brown.

Williamson, Oliver E. 1975. *Markets and Hierarchies, Analysis and Antitrust Implications: A Study in the Economics of Internal Organization*. New York: Free Press.

Williamson, Oliver E. 1985. *The Economic Institutions of Capitalism: Firms, Markets, Relational Contracting*. New York: Free Press.

Wilson, James Q. 1973. *Political Organizations*. New York: Basic Books.

Wilson, James Q., ed. 1980. *The Politics of Regulation*. New York: Basic Books.

Wilson, James Q. 1989a. *American Government: Institutions and Policies*. Fourth ed. Lexington, Mass.: D.C. Heath.

Wilson, James Q. 1989b. *Bureaucracy: What Government Agencies Do and Why They Do It*. New York: Basic Books.

Witte, John F. 1990. "Choice and Control: An Analytical Overview." In *Choice and Control in American Education, Vol. 1: The Theory of Choice and Control in Education*. Eds. William H. Clune and John F. Witte. New York: Falmer Press.

Witte, John F. 1998. "The Milwaukee Voucher Experiment." *Educational Evaluation and Policy Analysis* 20: 229–251.

Witte, John F., and Mark E. Rigdon. 1993. "Educational Choice Reforms: Will They Change American Schools?" *Publius: The Journal of Federalism* 23: 95–114.

Wolf, Charles, Jr. 1979. "A Theory of Non-Market Failures." *Journal of Law and Economics* 22: 107–139.

Wright, Gerald C., Robert S. Erikson, and John P. McIver. 1985. "Measuring State Partisanship and Ideology with Survey Data." *The Journal of Politics* 47: 469–489.

Wright, Peter, Charles D. Pringle, and Mark J. Kroll. 1992. *Strategic Management: Text and Cases*. Boston: Allyn and Bacon.

Yamaguchi, Kazuo. 1991. *Event History Analysis*. Newbury Park, Calif.: Sage.

Yergin, Daniel, and Joseph Stanislaw. 1998. *The Commanding Heights: The Battle Between Government and the Marketplace That Is Remaking the Modern World*. New York: Touchstone.

Young, Ruth D., and Joe D. Francis. 1991. "Entrepreneurship and Innovation in Small Manufacturing Firms." *Social Science Quarterly* 72: 149–163.

Ysseldyke, James E., and Martha L. Thurlow, eds. 1994. *Educational Outcomes for Students with Disabilities*. New York: Haworth Press.

Index